*The Communist Trials
and the American Tradition*
(Revised Edition)

Other books by JOHN SOMERVILLE

Methodology in Social Science: A Critique of Marx and Engels   1938

Soviet Philosophy: A Study of Theory and Practice   1946

The Philosophy of Peace   1949   (Revised)   1954

The Way of Science: Its Growth and Method   1953

The Enjoyment of Study: In School and On Your Own   1954

Selected Essays   1960

The Philosophy of Marxism: An Exposition   1967

Philosophy and Politics Today   1968

The Peace Revolution: Ethos and Social Progress   1975

Philosophy and Ethics of the Nuclear Age   1980

The Crisis: The True Story about How the World Almost Ended
   (A Play in Four Acts)   1987


Editorships

"Soviet Studies in Philosophy," Editor-in-Chief,   1963-1988

"Soviet Marxism and Nuclear War: An International Debate"   1981

Co-editor:

  with Ronald Santoni:

    Social and Political Philosophy—Readings from Plato to Gandhi 1963
    (reprinted 1988, 1991, 1994, 1996)

  with Dale Riepe and David DeGrood:

    Radical Currents in Contemporary Philosophy   1971

  with Howard L. Parsons:

    Dialogues on the Philosophy of Marxism   1974

    Marxism, Revolution, and Peace   1977

# The Communist Trials and the American Tradition

(Revised Edition)

EXPERT TESTIMONY ON FORCE AND
VIOLENCE, AND DEMOCRACY

## John Somerville, PH.D.

Foreword by Denise Lynn

**International Publishers**  **New York**

© 1956 by John Somerville
2nd Enlarged edition, 2000
International Publishers Co., New York
© Rose M. Somerville 2000
Revised Edition © International Publishers 2022

All rights reserved

*Acknowledgements*:

"Law, Logic and Revolution: The Smith Act Decisions" by John Somerville is reprinted from the "Western Political Quarterly," Vol. 14 #4 (December 1961), pp. 839-849 by permission of the University of Utah, copyright holder.

The publisher acknowledges the able and generous assistance of Dr. Rose Maurer Somerville in preparing this enlarged edition. Dr. Howard L. Parsons contributed the Appreciation on p.vi.

The two photos of John Somerville were taken by Helen Shotwell, in Woodstock, N.Y. (1946) and the cover photo in the late 1970s.

Composition by Amnet Contentsource Private Limited

ISBN 10: 0717800296         ISBN 13: 9780717800292

# Contents

|   |   |   |
|---|---|---|
| | FOREWORD | vii |
| 1 | THE TESTIMONY BEGINS<br>*The Declaration of Independence and the Communist* | 15 |
| 2 | THE HEART OF THE ISSUE<br>*The Majority and "The Propitious Moment"* | 36 |
| 3 | THE GOVERNMENT's CASE<br>*"Evidence" of Force and Violence* | 53 |
| 4 | THE PROSECUTION PERSISTS<br>*Cross-examination by Government Counsel* | 74 |
| 5 | THE PROSECUTION FORGETS LOGIC<br>*The Problem of Peaceful Transition* | 106 |
| 6 | RETURN TO THE FACTS<br>*Peaceful Transition in the Teachings of American Communists Today* | 131 |
| 7 | THE CENTRAL ISSUE AGAIN<br>*Importance of the Concept of "Revolutionary Situation"* | 150 |
| 8 | RELATED ISSUES<br>*War, Imperialism, and Revolution* | 167 |
| 9 | THE CONTINUING DANGER<br>*Roots and Perspectives* | 177 |

10  VARIATIONS ON A THEME
        *Two 1956 Trials, Cleveland and Philadelphia*   206

11  THE RIGHT OF REVOLUTION
        *Correspondence with Author of Smith Act
        and Opinion of Mr. Justice Jackson*   223

12  CHAPTER AND VERSE
        *Text and Analysis of Smith Act and Indictments*   240


Index to Text                                           263

APPENDIX                                                265

   *Law, Logic and Revolution: The
   Smith Act Decisions (1961)*

# Foreword

### The Lessons of Anticommunism
### By Denise Lynn

American anticommunism in the middle of the 20th century was so powerful and so ubiquitous that there seemed to be few people willing to stand up for freedom of speech. While communists and those remotely linked to the American Communist Party (CPUSA) were targeted by the growing US surveillance state and legal apparatus, many liberals staked their claims with anticommunism to protect themselves and their interests.

John Somerville, philosopher, teacher, husband, father, chose to make a stand for freedom of speech and association by testifying for those accused of communist subversion. His was a principled stand at a time when principles could lead to marginalization and job loss at best, legal harassment, and imprisonment at worst. His hope was that the rule of law would win the day and that freedom of speech could be preserved.

Somerville believed that anticommunist legal harassment was on its face contrary to the US democratic tradition and in violation of constitutional protections. He was also concerned because those that were targeted were, like him, advocates of peaceful coexistence with the Soviet Union. He watched anxiously as the US military became an outsized behemoth that made large budget demands on the American taxpayer while leaving poverty, disenfranchisement, and underfunded public institutions in its wake. Somerville hoped to convey in his testimony the illogic of anticommunism and in so doing contribute to a larger discourse on peace and democratic freedoms.

### John Somerville

John Somerville Jr. was born in New York City March 13, 1905, to John and Lorie Somerville. John senior had emigrated from

Scotland in 1883 when he was nearly 30 years old. He had taken up work as a hat salesman in a New York department store and in 1898 married Lorie Mulligan, who was 20 years his junior. Lorie Somerville worked as a homemaker. Their first child Hazel was born in 1900, followed by Marjorie four years later. John junior was born only a year after his sister in 1905.[1]

John grew up in Manhattan and attended Columbia University where he would receive a PhD in Philosophy. In February 1929 he married Rose Maurer, the daughter of Austrian immigrants. Maurer studied sociology and the two would embark on a romantic and intellectual relationship. They would have two sons together, Greg and Kent. In the early years of their marriage, John worked as a teacher while Rose was a homemaker. Eventually the two moved to the Soviet Union to study everyday life and Soviet philosophy. They lived in the USSR between 1935 and 1937 and after the family's return to New York, Somerville published a book titled *Soviet Philosophy*. He also began working for Hunter College in New York in 1939. Somerville did several visiting lectureships at prestigious institutions including Cornell, Drake University, University of Michigan, Stanford University, and others. He also lectured at international Universities in places like Canada, Japan, and Czechoslovakia. He left Hunter College in 1967 and moved to San Diego where he worked at the United States International University until retirement in 1972.[2]

Somerville became a renowned scholar of Marxism with an international reputation. Along with his book *Soviet Philosophy*, he also published several other books and articles on Marxism, peace, and social philosophy. In 1949 he published *The Philosophy of Peace*, in 1967 *The Philosophy of Marxism: An Exposition* followed by *The Peace Revolution: Ethos and Social Process* in 1975. In 1962, he and colleagues from the American Philosophical Association (APA) founded the Society for the Philosophical Study of Dialectical

---

[1] New York State Archives; Albany, New York; *State Population Census Schedules, 1905*; Election District: *A.D. 09 E.D. 16*; City: *Manhattan*; County: *New York*; 3; US Census Bureau, "Ancestry.com," *1910 United States Federal Census* [database on-line]. Lehi, UT, USA: Ancestry.com Operations Inc, 2006

[2] Ancestry.com. *New York, New York, U.S., Marriage License Indexes, 1907-2018* [database on-line]. Lehi, UT, USA: Ancestry.com Operations, Inc., 2017; Ancestry.com. *1930 United States Federal Census* [database on-line]. Provo, UT, USA: Ancestry.com Operations Inc, 2002; Howard Parsons, "John Somerville, 1905-1994," *Proceedings and Addresses of the American Philosophical Society*, Vol. 67, 4 (June 1994), 52.

# FOREWORD

Materialism, later renamed the Society for the Philosophical Study of Marxism. He was a well-regarded teacher and a prolific scholar, but he was also an activist for "peace, human decency, and planetary survival."[3]

His anxieties and concern for peace came out of the anticommunist hysteria of the postwar world. Somerville believed that anticommunism led to misunderstanding and a "precarious peace." Atomic weapons made this more terrifying as subsequent nations armed themselves with the deadliest weapons of mass destruction. The United States, the first atomic power, began to pursue an even deadlier hydrogen bomb in 1950. It also interpreted the Soviet Union as an aggressor and itself as committed to peace. But increasingly peace to US officials came at the cost of a heavily militarized society with a civilian economy wedded to military proliferation. Rather than reduce its forces after World War II, the US seemed to be posturing for another world war with a large standing army, an increased military budget, and a hysterical propaganda campaign against the Soviet Union and liberation movements in Asia, Africa, and the Middle East. The American people were told that peace could only be secured at gunpoint, but the US military and policymakers no longer required their consent to wage war. Anticommunism became the weapon the US wielded against decolonizing nations abroad and against its own citizenry.[4]

Somerville was particularly frustrated with the way that hawkish Cold Warriors prevented rational discourse. He wrote that one problem with anticommunism was that the US claimed that nothing communists did was in "good faith" and thus any communist nation, or person, could not be given equal standing in political debates, could not be trusted to tell the truth, and could not be believed when making agreements. This prevented agreements, negotiations, and any understanding that could avoid war. Anticommunists dismissed any negotiation out of hand, and it became they who could not operate in good faith making war and violence inevitable.[5]

---

[3] Parsons, "John Somerville," 53; Ronald Santoni, "John Somerville," *Proceedings and Addresses of the American Philosophical Society*, Vol. 67, 4 (June 1994), 53.

[4] Parsons, "John Somerville," 52.

[5] John Somerville, "Evaluating Exchange Vi: Assumptions Inherent in Free House Approach Questioned," *New York Times*, 31 August 1959, 20.

This interest in Soviet philosophy and dialogue between scholars led Somerville to organize the first conference of American Soviet philosophers in 1963. Unfortunately, with Cold War tensions still high, the State Department refused visas for the Soviets; the conference had to be moved to Mexico City. Somerville was not cowed by anticommunism and gained a reputation for "working relentlessly" against it and to open a dialogue between the Soviet Union and the US. This did mean that he was often "judged controversial" by others, but he "persisted in placing personal integrity and global reconciliation" above the anticommunist hysteria.[6]

Somerville remained committed to peace throughout his life. When he was 70 years old, he wrote a play about the "ethical issues and dangers" in how John F. Kennedy "handled" the Cuban Missile Crisis. Somerville became the "first philosopher" to organize others into the antiwar movement. He helped to found the International Philosophers for the Prevention of Nuclear Omnicide (IPPNO) in 1983 and the Union of Japanese and American Professionals against Nuclear Omnicide. In 1986 he organized IPPNO's first conference in St. Louis, Missouri. Somerville had coined the phrase "omnicide" to describe how war in the nuclear age had become "deceptive" because the use of nuclear weapons could render all life "obsolete." As Somerville said about those who do nothing "against nuclear weapons" they are "casting their vote for omnicide."[7]

Somerville was known as an intellectual less concerned with defining what philosophy is, and more concerned about what philosophers could do for the world. While he earned several prestigious awards, he asked to be remembered not for his scholarship but for his peace work. In 1991, he wrote the APA that he felt it was the duty of philosophers to criticize their government "when their policies threaten human existence." He noted that he felt the APA had failed in that regard. His record was one of an academic devoted to ending the hysterical anticommunism that had prevented intellectual exchange and rational discourse. Somerville died in 1994 in San Diego, at the end of the Cold War era, an era he witnessed in its entire length and breadth. He knew that what the US was committing itself to at the beginning of the Cold War was hostility, violence, and perpetual war. That unfortunately had not changed with

---

[6] Parsons, "John Somerville," 52; Santoni, "John Somerville," 53.
[7] Parsons, "John Somerville," 52-53; Santoni, "John Somerville," 53-54.

FOREWORD

the end of the Cold War, and he knew that in a world with atomic weaponry, war and conflict could be apocalyptic.[8]

## The Smith Act

One way Somerville spoke out for peace was in his defense of those accused of violent sedition. In 1954 and 1956 he provided expert "non-communist" testimony in three trials in Pennsylvania and Ohio. The defendants had been charged under the Smith Act. The act, also known as the Alien Registration Act of 1940, was a "peacetime antisedition law" sponsored by Congressman Howard Smith from Virginia. It was passed in June of that year and represented a "dramatic shift" in how free speech was legally defined. The act aimed to "prohibit certain subversive activities" by making it illegal to interfere with the morale of the armed forces at a time when many Americans were preparing for US intervention in the European war. It also made it illegal to advocate or belong to an organization that advocated the overthrow of the US government and prevented the printing and distribution of material that advocated the overthrow of the US government. It also allowed for the removal of printed material from a suspected person or their home. If found in violation, a convicted person could face a $10,000 fine and up to ten years in prison; and if found in violation again after conviction that person was no longer eligible to work in the United States.[9]

As with most other anti-radical laws, it was aimed, in part, at immigration control. American officials, often baffled by the idea that conditions in the US could radicalize citizens, targeted immigrants as importers and purveyors of radical ideology. The Smith Act allowed for the easy deportation of immigrants in violation of its provisions. It also required alien finger printing and registration. This association between sedition and immigration goes beyond suspicion of immigrants, it was part of how US policymakers constructed an idealized citizenry through exclusion. Antisedition laws name and target immigrants and are frequently deployed against Black Americans whose citizenship was (is) often seen as contingent.

---

[8] Parsons, "John Somerville," 53.
[9] Alien Registration (Smith) Act, 18 U.S. C. §2.385 (1940); Donna Haverty-Stacke, "Punishment of Mere Political Advocacy: The FBI, Teamster Local 544, and the Origins of the 1941 Smith Act Cases," *Journal of American History*, Vol. 100, 1 (June 2013): 71; Parsons, "John Sommerville," 52.

This is true in terms of actual claims to being American, but also regarding the exercise of citizenship rights. Anticommunism, therefore, assumed that foreign ideas were imported into the United States and used against vulnerable Americans. These radical ideas undermined the belief in US democracy and allegedly inflamed an otherwise temperate population. This foreignness meant that anticommunists never had to confront the reality of conditions in the country, rather, they could dismiss radical claims for equality and justice as part of a foreign plot to usurp American democracy.

Anticommunism has also been used to limit labor organization and has been deployed by the federal government in league with capitalist interests. While free market ideology has been used to reign in any regulation against business practices, heavy handed government interference is used to police and restrict labor organizing. Donna Havery-Stacke argues that the first use of the Smith Act was to ensure that labor organization did not hinder war preparation. Franklin Roosevelt increased the surveillance power of the Federal Bureau of Investigation in 1939 centralizing intelligence gathering in that agency, a boon to FBI director J. Edgar Hoover. The Smith Act increased the FBI's "statutory authority," and it would first be deployed against Minneapolis Teamsters, many of whose members were also Trotskyites that had consistently opposed World War II. The act therefore meant the state served as law enforcement to allow for the smooth operation of capitalist interests.[10]

The case against the Teamsters would lay the foundation for the later use of the Smith Act. However, it also reveals what Samuel White has described as "popular anticommunism." While intelligence and legislative agencies used anticommunism to silence labor and civil rights demands, many Americans were also eager to silence their radical neighbors. The Minneapolis Teamsters case was helped by unionists who wanted to get rid of the Trotskyites in their midst. Samuel White describes the case of a local Indiana CIO union whose members wanted to silence the radicals in the organization. To do that they collaborated with a House committee to oust the members. As Ellen Schrecker argues, mainstream unions like the American Federation of Labor (AFL) worked with federal agencies to expel radicals in their ranks, only to find

---

[10] Haverty-Stacke, "Punishment of Mere Political Advocacy," 71.

FOREWORD

later that anticommunism allowed businesses to undermine labor organizing by constructing *all* labor demands as radical and foreign influenced.[11]

Anticommunism operated on the federal, state, and local level to limit the free expression of speech for radicals. The Smith Act became an effective tool in undermining social justice demands and promoting popular anticommunism. It was used against radicals who were critical of US Cold War policy and instead promoted peace, specifically peace between the United States and the Soviet Union. These radical activists came to believe that anticommunism manifested war and violence aimed at the already exploited and oppressed, particularly in the United States and in newly decolonizing states. Somerville, a committed peace activist agreed and feared that Cold War policy would lead to global devastation and destruction. He felt it was his duty to testify when the fate of the US hung "in the balance."[12]

J. Edgar Hoover focused his attention and the mechanisms of anticommunism, the Smith Act specifically, on the CPUSA in 1948. There were over fifty members of its National Committee, all of whom Hoover wanted to arrest. He hoped that taking down the leadership would lead to the Party's collapse. Instead, prosecutors focused first on the top visible leaders of the Party, much to Hoover's dismay. In June, an indictment was issued that claimed the CPUSA had been in violation of the Smith Act since 1945; in July, 12 of the Party's leaders were arrested – Ben Davis, Eugene Dennis, William Foster, John Gates, Gil Green, Gus Hall, Irving Potash, Jack Stachel, Robert Thompson, John Williamson, Henry Winston, and Carl Wittner. Foster would not be tried with the other 11 due to illness. The trial began in January 1949 and lasted until October.[13]

---

[11] Samuel White, "Popular Anticommunism and the UE in Evansville, IN" in *American Labor and the Cold War: Grassroots Politics and Postwar Political Culture*, eds., Robert Cherny, William Issel, Kiernan Walsh Taylor (New Brunswick: Rutgers University Press, 2004), 142-143; Ellen Schrecker, "Labor and the Cold War: The Legacy of McCarthyism," in *American Labor and the Cold War: Grassroots Politics and Postwar Political Culture*, eds., Robert Cherny, William Issel, Kiernan Walsh Taylor (New Brunswick: Rutgers University Press, 2004), 7-8; Haverty-Stacke, "Punishment of Mere Political Advocacy," 72.

[12] John Somerville, *The Communist Trials and the American Tradition: Expert Testimony on Force and Violence, and Democracy* (New York: International Publishers, 1956, Reprinted 2000), 15.

[13] Ted Morgan, *Reds: McCarthyism in America* (New York: Random House, 2004), 314; Ellen Schrecker, *Many are the Crimes: McCarthyism in America* (Princeton: Princeton University Press, 1998), 196.

The 11 men were all convicted. Historian Ellen Schrecker argues that the convictions "removed ...many restraints" that the government was using in its surveillance and harassment of the Party and its members and allowed the FBI and legislative and legal bodies to use "whatever politically repressive measures" they wanted to use. The conviction led to the arrest of more CPUSA leaders and members and by 1951, when the Supreme Court upheld the convictions in its *Dennis v. United States* decision, the government was further empowered in its anticommunist repression. By the 1950s, Schrecker argues that communists "had few rights that any official body had to respect" and its members could barely lead "a normal life."[14]

Lawyers defending those charged under the act faced an uphill legal battle. When Somerville testified, he was "forbidden" to "introduce any reference" to the Declaration of Independence. Limited in his testimony, in 1956, he articulated his ideas in the book *The Communist Trials and the American Tradition*, reprinted here. In it he described how he became involved. At a speaking engagement in Philadelphia, he was approached by a young communist and his lawyer. They explained that nine CPUSA leaders of the Pennsylvania chapter had been arrested and charged under the Smith Act. Because they were communists, the government charged that they were involved in a conspiracy to "teach and advocate" for the violent overthrow of the US government. They asked if he, someone not involved with the CPUSA, could provide expert testimony on communism and its "teachings on the use of force and violence." The act never targeted or named communism or communists specifically and instead focused on anyone involved in anti-US conspiracies. Somerville, then had to testify whether communists "teach the duty, necessity, desirability or propriety of overthrowing or destroying any government in the United States." In other words, he was tasked with explaining why being a communist did not infer violent intentions against the government.[15]

Somerville found the Smith Act indictments troubling for many reasons; one of which was that to prove the communists intended to

---

[14] Schrecker, *Many are the Crimes,* 190; Russell Porter, "11 Communists convicted of plot," *New York Times,* 15 October 1949, 1; Erick McDuffie, "Black and Red: Black Liberation, the Cold War, and the Horne Thesis," *Journal of African American History*, Vol. 96, 2 (Spring 2011): 236.

[15] Parsons, "John Somerville," 52; Somerville, *The Communist Trials and the American Tradition,* 16.

violently overthrow the US government, the courts used the writings of Marx, Lenin, and Stalin. This was the evidence used for each of the defendants. In a normal criminal case when an individual is on trial, the prosecution is meant to present evidence to prove that person's guilt. Instead, with the Smith Act trials, each person who was in the CPUSA was presumably guilty because they advocated Marxist-Leninist literature and that literature, according to the government, advocated future violent action. Somerville noted that the same could be said about the Declaration of Independence because it noted that if a tyrant ascends to leadership, then the people have the right to overthrow said tyrant. Did the US tradition, therefore, violate the Smith Act?

Somerville argued that the communist corpus does include the "pre-conditions" of revolution but does not include "unconditional advocacy" of violent revolt. The prosecution in the cases Somerville testified in, used specific quotations rather than the full text, and primarily from Lenin and Stalin. He noted that in any reference to violence, the prosecution assumed that it was an "indication of criminal intent." For anyone unfamiliar with Marxism, which Somerville argued included all juries, lawyers, and judges, there seemed to be an "acceptance of indiscriminate violence." But this did not make the writings unique in the larger political literature. He noted that you could find descriptions of violence in the writings of John Locke, Thomas Jefferson, and Abraham Lincoln, and no one presumed that those who subscribed to capitalism or democracy had violent intent. That belief was reserved strictly for Marxists. By using this rationale, the state had little difficulty prosecuting communists under the Smith Act.[16]

Somerville noted that while justice is supposed to be blind, "she is not supposed to be blind to the facts" or to the "elementary principles of logic." He feared that justice was supposed to be blind to larger prejudices and anti-factual distortions "born of ignorance" but that during the Cold War, anticommunism had swept rationality aside. Somerville argued that the state had to concern itself with how the majority felt and not a small minority of people; thus, if violent revolution required resistance to an unstable government, then the fear of a violent overthrow was rational. The CPUSA and

---

[16] John Somerville, "Law, Logic, and Revolution: The Smith Act Decisions," *Western Political Quarterly*, Vol. 14, 4 (December 1961): 842; Somerville, *The Communist Trials and the American Tradition*, 53-52.

its leadership did not present that threat, even if the organization and its members did advocate violence, it was a small organization. Somerville introduced the words of CPUSA leader William Foster as evidence; Foster noted that a minority could not succeed in a coup, they would need an "overwhelming majority." Somerville concluded that no one familiar with communist doctrine could "entertain the idea" that it does not discuss the necessity of a majority, a word frequently used in the literature. The government's case against the communists was based on prejudice, misunderstanding, and distorted language. The fact was that anticommunism based in the assumption that a foreign-inspired revolution was on the horizon was equally guilty of failed logic, prejudice, and distortion.[17]

In the first Pennsylvania case the defendants were charged with "conspiring" to advocate the overthrow of the government; in the second Pennsylvania case the defendant was charged under the "membership clause" of the Smith Act. This meant that instead of being charged with conspiracy, the defendant was being charged with being a member of a group that advocated the violent overthrow of the government. For Somerville this was a paradox because all the people charged with conspiracy could just as well have been charged with membership as they were all visible members of the Party. The "overt acts" that they were accused of were carrying out the usual responsibilities of a Party member or leader like attending meetings. Whether charged with conspiracy or membership, the evidence was the same. Membership carried a harsher penalty after a 1948 clause to the Smith Act reduced the conspiracy penalty to five years in prison. Somerville suspected that the earlier defendants were not charged with the harsher penalty of membership because "conspiracy" sounds more insidious to an American audience, thus suggesting that the trials were for propaganda purposes. Charging conspiracy was for public benefit rather than concern about an actual crime.[18]

The first Philadelphia trial involved nine CPUSA leaders. The trial lasted 71 days, the longest in the federal Eastern District of Pennsylvania at that point. In August 1954 all nine were found guilty of conspiracy; 81 people, including the Philadelphia nine, had been found guilty under the Smith Act by then. The first convictions in the Smith Act trial in 1949 made it increasingly difficult for

---

[17] Somerville, *The Communist Trials and the American Tradition*, 145, 151.
[18] Somerville, *The Communist Trials and the American Tradition*, 200.

FOREWORD

defendants to secure proper representation as attorneys willing to stand up to the government became scarce or overworked. Hundreds of communists had been arrested, were tried, awaiting trial, or imprisoned by the second wave of trials in 1954. But the government kept up its momentum and a third wave of trials occurred in 1956. That year, Somerville testified in Philadelphia and in Cleveland. The Cleveland trial took place in January and lasted 14 weeks. The ten defendants were charged with conspiracy, four were acquitted and six were convicted. The six convicted were all leaders of the Ohio CPUSA.[19]

A month after the first Philadelphia trial in 1954, the government tried a new tactic. Claude Lightfoot became the first communist to be charged under the membership clause, his trial started in September 1954. Lightfoot was also the first to be tried alone as the others had been tried in groups. He had a long history in the Party and had become the Chicago branch educational director. During World War II, he served two years in Europe and was honorably discharged. He helped to reconstitute the Party in Chicago after the war and when the leadership was indicted, he became an alternate on the national board making him a leading Party member. Lightfoot was found guilty, sentenced to five years and a $10,000 fine. The charges would eventually be dropped on a technicality, but the successful conviction on the harsher membership clause in 1955 empowered further indictments. In March 1956, Somerville testified in the case of Dr. Albert Emanuel Blumberg in Philadelphia, charged under the membership clause. Like Lightfoot, Blumberg was tried alone; he was also found guilty.[20]

In 1957, the Supreme Court reversed some of the Smith Act convictions in the *Yates v. United States* decision. It created a higher standard for conviction under the Smith Act and required staying "closer to the constitutional demands" of the US. The *Yates* decision required proving whether speech was "calculated to incite action" at the moment spoken, or in the future. Any language that expressed "belief," but was not meant as an incitement would not count. Somerville found the decision surprising not only because it

---

[19] *United States v. Blumberg*, 207 F. Supp. 28 (E.D. Pa. 1962); *United States v. Brandt*, 256 F. 2d 79 (6th Cir 1958)
[20] Peter Edson, "New Phase of War on Reds," *The Plain Speaker*, 23 September 1954, 12; "9 Philadelphians Convicted as Reds," *New York Times*, 14 August 1954, 5; *United States v. Blumberg*, 207 F. Supp. 28 (E.D. Pa. 1962).

reversed the government's earlier eager attempts to silence communists, but also because it tried to continue to justify its decision in 1951. *Yates* avoided the "teaching of revolutions problem," which is to say, how to decide if speech is invoking revolutionary action. The 1951 *Dennis* decision claimed that advocating violent action at some unknown, unspecified time in the future was enough for conviction. In 1957, the court decided that it was not proven the defendants were inciting a future "violent overthrow" of the government. This baffled Somerville who argued that were the defendants convicted with different evidence, then the conclusion in *Yates* might have made sense, but the communists were all convicted using the "published teachings of Marxism-Leninism." It was logically unsound and a rational leap to suggest that the cases were somehow distinct, the defendants had to be "either all guilty together or all not guilty together." By the time of the decision, many of those accused had already served their prison sentences, had been deported, or had their lives otherwise disrupted. The Philadelphia and Ohio groups had their convictions reversed based on *Yates*.[21]

In 1961, the Supreme Court handed down the *Noto v. United States* decision which reversed a conviction on the membership clause; the court decided that there was not enough evidence to suggest the Party promoted violent insurrection. Blumberg's conviction was reversed based on *Noto*. The only person to be successfully prosecuted after the *Yates* decision was the former communist Junius Scales. Scales, who left the CPUSA in 1957, was prosecuted in 1961, and sentenced to six years in prison for advocating the use of violence. Scales openly encouraged violence and held martial arts classes. His conviction was upheld by the Supreme Court, though President Kennedy would commute his sentence on Christmas Eve 1962.[22]

## Lessons of Anticommunism

There is no question that the legacy of the Cold War remains salient in the United States today. Intelligence agencies learned that the American attention span is limited regarding surveillance, police power, and the harassment of those demanding social justice. The government realized it could suppress aspirations for justice and

---

[21] Somerville, "Law, Logic, and Revolution," 839-840.
[22] Somerville, "Law, Logic, and Revolution," 840-841.

wage war abroad without the consent of its citizens. The United States today is more militarized, increasingly intent on penalizing everyday behavior, and still invested in anticommunism. Somerville sought to demonstrate the illogic and antidemocratic nature of anticommunist thinking and its expression in the courtroom and while today some look back at the period called McCarthyism with disdain, we remain in the grasp of hysterical antiradicalism and anticommunism.

Somerville shared with the Smith Act defendants concern about the growing militarism of the United States government. At the advent of the Cold War, the United States postured itself as the leader of the free world in contrast to Soviet communism. In its attempts to become the voice of democracy, the United States became one of the greatest enemies of democracy in the world and used its financial and military superiority to quash liberation aspirations in the United States and abroad. In an age of atomic weaponry, Somerville warned that mass destruction could result from another global conflagration. While the United States has not used atomic weapons against others since 1945, it has reigned down destruction in several theaters of conflict since then, most obviously in Korea, Vietnam, Afghanistan, and Iraq; but also surreptitiously and sometimes by proxy across Latin America, Asia, the Middle East, and Africa.

In 2021, at a time when the country is ostensibly at peace, the United States has the largest military budget in world history. Meanwhile, the American taxpayer, who is funding the military-industrial complex is faced with a non-existent public health infrastructure, limited social welfare programs, regular cuts to public services including education and mental health, and an increasingly policed society. This was the nightmare that the Smith Act defendants warned against, the fear that the military would preempt all other priorities.[23]

Anticommunism deserves much of the blame. Anticommunists argued for military proliferation to prevent communist infiltration; in the meantime, defense contractors' wealth and influence grew creating the perfect marriage between the civilian and military economy. As Michael Brenes has argued a "Cold War coalition" brought together military and civilian interests who recreated the

---

[23] Alexandra Jaffe, "Biden authorizes &768.2 billion in defense spending; a 5 percent increase," PBS, 28 December 2021, Accessed 21 February 2022, https://www.pbs.org/newshour/politics/biden-authorizes-768-2-billion-in-defense-spending-a-5-increase.

American political system in their favor. Military spending became a way for politicians to create jobs when no conflict existed; the outflow of money into the military-industrial complex has become so ubiquitous that politicians have found it impossible to turn off the spending lest they risk increased unemployment. War has become America's business.[24]

The United States also maintains hundreds of bases overseas as an expression of "white, male, Christian superiority." As David Vine has argued, this makes violence easily deployable and a simpler solution than doing the work of diplomacy. The United States, therefore, has become devoted to a state of permanent war, something radical activists within the CPUSA warned against. The Cold War, which as Vine argues, was not very cold at all since it led to over ten million deaths, led to a period of austerity for social needs and prosperity for the military-industrial complex.[25]

One of the most dangerous legacies of anticommunism is its ingrained anti-Blackness and xenophobia. Anticommunism was used to force consensus on Americans by defining who did and did not fit into the body politic. Those who demanded dignity and respect were considered a radical fringe and were dismissed as part of an alleged communist plot. As Gerald Horne has argued, there were concessions made to the civil rights movement, including conservative demands for integration, but calls for economic justice were seen as communist. These concessions were to demonstrate progress to white America while silencing further demands from Black Americans. Meanwhile, immigrants remained outsiders bringing with them radical ideas and encouraging discontent in the US. Still today, immigrants must confirm they are not communists on naturalization forms.[26]

The communists Somerville defended warned that the United States was far more prone and vulnerable to fascism than it was communism. Historians have argued that American fascists eagerly targeted social justice and labor activists in the era of the Great Depression, while after World War II, anticommunist legislation was passed that criminalized political dissent. Populist fascism

---

[24] Michael Brenes, *For Might and Right: Cold War Defense Spending and the Remaking of American Democracy* (Amherst: University of Massachusetts Press, 2020).

[25] David Vine, *The United States of War: A Global History of America's Endless Conflicts, From Columbus to the Islamic State* (Oakland: University of California Press, 2020), 168.

[26] Gerald Horne, *Black Liberation/Red Scare: Ben Davis and the Communist Party* (New York: International Publishers, 2021): 13.

continued into the postwar years as anticommunism encouraged limiting free speech, this was aimed specifically at the peace movement, the most popular expression of which was Henry Wallace's 1948 presidential campaign on the Progressive Party ticket. This campaign faced populist fascism across the country. For example, Wallace was denied airtime and speaking locations. On at least two occasions, he and his organizers faced violent mobs who believed anticommunist propaganda that Wallace's anti-racist and anti-militarist campaign was in league with an imagined communist conspiracy.[27]

In Evansville, Indiana, Wallace's organizers were met with a violent mob who injured two of his campaign staffers and a local supporter. The group had a hard time even getting a location for the talk and had to concede to demands that prohibited Paul Robeson, the famous Black entertainer of the time, from speaking and performing. That same year, Evansville had a House Committee travel to town to hold hearings on the local CIO branch to expel suspected communists from its ranks. The local college, under pressure from the businessmen on its Board of Trustees, fired a professor who attended the Wallace talk, and the Evansville city council tried to pass a law making it illegal for communists to live in the city. This kind of populist fascist reaction to progressive organizing was not geographically limited; Wallace's group faced violence in Red Hook, Brooklyn as well, and were accused of being communist by local newspapers, veteran's groups, and politicians across the country.[28]

Anticommunist hysteria informed conspiratorial thinking throughout the 20th century convincing some Americans that the United States was under an imminent threat of violence. It led American policy makers to pursue unconstitutional legislation and harassment; but it also led some Americans to look askance at their neighbors. Others became willing to use violence against their fellow Americans. Paul Robeson, barred from performing in Evansville and other locations, faced violent mobs in August 1949 when he went to perform at a fundraiser in Peekskill, New York. Robeson

---

[27] Joseph Fronczak, "The Fascists Game: Transnational Political Transmission and the Genesis of the U.S. Modern Right," *Journal of American History* (December 2018): 563-565, 586.

[28] White, "Popular Anticommunism and the UE in Evansville, IN," 142-143; Randy Mills, "The Real Violence of Evansville:' The Firing of Professor George F. Parker," *Indiana Magazine of History* XCIV (June 2003): 130, 133.

was forced to flee to safety while people in the crowd were injured. The group tried to reschedule, and the mobs returned. These mobs believed that Robeson was a Soviet agent trying to usher in a Soviet America. They were also motivated by racism as they greeted Robeson and the others at Peekskill with a hand gesture that meant "hey n---r." As Charisse Burden-Stelly argues, anticommunism works in tandem with anti-Blackness as civil rights demands are dismissed as communist and Black radicals were "virtually flagellated" when compared to their fellow white radicals.[29]

In the American imagination, anticommunism does not require communists. As Burden-Stelly writes, anticommunism is about anyone "challenging some aspect of the status quo," who are then "red-baited as communist." Anticommunism is "a durable mode of governance" that operates as a defense mechanism for racial capitalism. Racial capitalism is a "racially hierarchical political economy constituting war and militarism, imperialist accumulation, expropriation by domination, and labor superexploitation." Anticommunism allows for the criminalization of "racial and political others" who threaten the white supremacist racial and economic order. It also serves to prevent alliances between Black America or other racialized groups and white workers. White workers become invested in anticommunism to preserve white supremacy, though it continues their own economic disenfranchisement and exploitation. Anticommunism also motivates everyday Americans to violate the constitutional rights of others.[30]

Populist reaction continued throughout the 20th century; violence against the civil right movement of the 1950s and 1960s is another example. While federal officials monitored civil rights activists and local law enforcement disciplined individuals organizing for their rights, people in local communities acted out against antiracist campaigns. Americans often focus on these acts as outliers or unique individuals acting on their own impulses, but the violence against

---

[29] Gerald Horne, *Paul Robeson: The Artist as Revolutionary* (New York: Pluto Press, 2015), 121-124; Charisse Burden-Stelly, "Constructing Deportable Subjectivity: Antiforeignness, Antiradicalism, and Antiblackness during the McCarthist Structure of Feeling," *Souls*, Vol. 19, 3 (July-September 2017): 342-343,

[30] Charisse Burden-Stelly, "Modern U.S. Racial Capitalism: Some Theoretical Insights," *Monthly Review*, 1 July 2020, https://monthlyreview.org/2020/07/01/modern-u-s-racial-capitalism/; Charisse Burden-Stelly, "Anti-Communism, Anti-Blackness, and imperialism," *MR Online*, 23 November 2021, https://mronline.org/2021/11/23/anti-communism-anti-blackness-and-imperialism/.

these activists is part of a long tradition of populist fascism in which white America uses violence to discipline others. One example is the Selma-to-Montgomery march for voting rights. Police violence encapsulated in Bloody Sunday in March 1965 demonstrates how the state shut down Black Freedom Struggles. But the white supremacists that murdered two white allies of the march, Viola Liuzzo and James Reeb, illustrate the use of violence by non-state actors to police their fellow Americans. More recently, the murder of Joseph Rosenbaum and Anthony Huber and the injuring of Gaige Grosskreutz at a Black Lives Matter protest in 2020 and the exoneration of the shooter, Kyle Rittenhouse, demonstrate that white supremacist violence remains a potent tool of control.

The Trump presidency led many people to worry that fascism was on the rise again, but others have argued that for some Americans, fascism has always operated within the United States. As Alberto Toscano argues, racial fascism is a "distinctly American" form of fascism that has marginalized racialized groups from the body politic. Trumpism is therefore not an aberration but a continuation of American tradition. Bill Mullen and Christopher Vials have argued similarly that "white supremacist democracy" has deployed different mechanisms to ensure white rule and economic domination. Anticommunism works in tandem with racial fascism as mechanisms of discipline to eliminate those that challenge the status quo, prop up the white racial order, and normalize poverty and want as a natural part of a capitalist system.[31]

Trump authoritarianism, therefore, is an expression of long traditions of racial capitalism, anticommunism, and fascism in the United States. Its most visible expression was the January 6th insurrection when Trump followers, many of whom were white, wealthy, or small-scale capitalists, violently stormed the Capitol, murdered one police officer, trampled to death a fellow Trump supporter, and led to the suicide deaths of other police in the days that followed. In contrast to heavy handed police violence against Black Americans, only one insurrectionist was killed by law enforcement that day. Trump, who regularly deploys anticommunism, fed the false narratives of election tampering directly fueling the violence, yet he

---

[31] Alberto Toscano, "The Long Shadow of Racial Fascism," Boston Review, October 28, 2020 (Accessed October 8, 2021, https://bostonreview.net/race-politics/alberto-toscano-long-shadow-racial-fascism); Bill V. Mullen and Christopher Vials, eds., The U.S. Anti-Fascism Reader (London: Verso, 2020), 7.

and his fellow top officials have faced no repercussions. Rather than a national reckoning with the false narratives that fueled the violence, and a confrontation with the privileges of white supremacy that led the largely white rioters to believe in their rights to overturn an election, states have used it to pass even more restrictive voting legislation aimed specifically at Black Americans. In 2021, 19 states passed over 34 laws limiting access to voting. Meanwhile states have used gerrymandering to dilute Black, Latinx, Asian American, and Indigenous voting power. Anticommunism operates along with authoritarian police, government officials, and populist fascism to delimit the rights of those demanding social justice. January 6 was not an aberration; it was another example of white racial terrorism motivated by the fear of democratic pluralism.[32]

John Somerville witnessed the illogical lengths anticommunists went to silence those who sought peace and justice. He tried to demonstrate that anticommunist arguments about using "force and violence" to overthrow the US government were fallacies. He argued that if we as a nation took this seriously then our own founding documents that also suggested the use force and violence, were in violation of the same laws used against communists. Therefore, every teacher, law enforcement official, politician, and others, could be arrested and charged with the same crime. Since this was not the case, then the Smith Act defendants were innocent as well. But the point, as Somerville well knew, was not to prevent some future revolution, it was to silence a group of people and to make communism illegal.

There are many lessons to be taken from the Cold War prosecutions, but one important one to remember is that the government learned that it could silence and oppress its own citizens, make war abroad in our name without our permission, and make claims to democracy while some obediently agreed and participated in the disciplining of their fellow citizens. Somerville's defense of the Smith Act defendants was a testament to what brave people could do in the face of oppression.

---

[32] "Voting Laws Roundup: 2021," Brennan Center for Justice, 21 December 2021, https://www.brennancenter.org/our-work/research-reports/voting-laws-roundup-december-2021.

*The Communist Trials
and the American Tradition*
(Revised Edition)

To the spirit that moved Voltaire when he wrote

*I do not agree with a word that you say*

*but I will defend to the death*

*your right to say it.*

*John Somerville, 1946*

# John Patrick MacPherson Somerville (1905-1994)

John Somerville wrote articles bearing on the philosophy of Marxism for the *Encyclopedia Americana, The Dictionary of Philosophy, Encyclopedia Slavonica, Colliers Encyclopedia,* and many scholarly journals including *American Slavic and East European Review, Philosophical Review, Philosophy of Science, Philosophy and Phenomenological Research, Journal of Philosophy* and others.

He contributed chapters, prefaces or introductions to 26 books in the years 1942-1982. He was the author of some 60 articles on philosophical subjects published in scholarly journals. He also wrote over 30 book reviews that were accepted by a variety of academic periodicals. From 1935-1986 he presented papers at 20 international conferences in the USA, Mexico, Canada, Western Europe, Bulgaria, Israel and Japan.

Honors and Awards include:
1980 Honorary Degree, Doctor of Humane Letters, Denison University
1981 Peace Essay Prize, Institute for World Order
1981 Gandhi Peace Award, Promoting Enduring Peace
1987 Peace Award, The Bertrand Russell Society
1987 United Nations Peace Messenger Award

John Somerville fulfilled visiting lectureships at the Catholic University of America, Cornell, Drake, University of Michigan, State University of New York, University of Oregon, University of the Pacific, University of Pennsylvania, Pennsylvania State University, University of South Carolina, and Stanford University. He was also a visiting lecturer at universities abroad in Belgrade, Bucharest, Hiroshima, Moscow, Prague, Sofia, Tbilisi, Western Ontario and Yerevan.

His papers have been placed with the Herbert Hoover Institution and Library on War, Revolution and Peace at Stanford University.

## IN APPRECIATION

JOHN SOMERVILLE (1905-1994) earned three degrees in philosophy from Columbia University, his Ph.D. in 1938. In 1935-37 he and his wife, Rose Maurer Somerville, a sociologist, lived in the USSR and studied Soviet philosophy, both theory and practice. The project laid down the direction of his life and career: the analysis and evaluation of philosophical concepts in their application to the solution of social problems both national and international. The product of this study was Soviet Philosophy (1946), "the first Western book on Soviet philosophy from an examination of original sources."

From 1939 to 1967 at Hunter College (CUNY), John Somerville advanced from Instructor to Professor Emeritus. He was founding editor of a translation quarterly, "Soviet Studies in Philosophy" and Chief Editor from 1962-1988. He taught at the U.S. International University from 1967-1972.

John Somerville situated his thought and action in the tradition of Socrates, Spinoza, Marx, Comte, Bertrand Russell, and other philosophers whose schisms with social convention put them in trouble with received opinion, cautious institutions, and established law. Their pre-eminent care was not "What is philosophy?" but "What is going on in the world of human society and what can be done about it?" They sought "the relationship of philosophical theory to social and political practice."

Forbidden at the Philadelphia trials to introduce any reference to the Declaration of Independence, he clarified the principles of democracy and revolution, and exposed the government's distorted interpretation of Marxist philosophy on these questions.

His growing anxiety over the precarious peace led him in 1962 to join others in the founding of the Society for the Philosophical Study of Dialectical Materialism (later, the Society for the Philosophical Study of Marxism). Through his enterprise, the first binational conference of American and Soviet philosophers was convened at the XIII World Congress of Philosophy in August 1963 in Mexico City. At the XVII World Congress of Philosophy in Montreal in 1983, he took the lead in forming the International Philosophers for the Prevention of Nuclear Omnicide (IPPNO), organizing its first conference in 1986 in St. Louis. Highlighting his own term—omnicide—he argued that war in the nuclear context had become a deceptive and obsolete word, because now all life on the planet could be irreversibly exterminated by nuclear exchanges.

Besides the record of his thought and deeds, he has left us the memory of his person—composed, passionate, cheerful, militant, independent, gentle—a philosopher of peace in a world where human endeavor and peace need each other to survive and thrive.

# *Dramatis Personae (I)*

IN THE UNITED STATES DISTRICT COURT
FOR THE EASTERN DISTRICT OF PENNSYLVANIA

UNITED STATES OF AMERICA
    *vs.*
JOSEPH KUZMA
ROBERT KLONSKY
JOSEPH ROBERTS
BENJAMIN WEISS                  CRIMINAL ACTION 17418
DAVID DAVIS
THOMAS NABRIED
IRVIN KATZ
WALTER LOWENFELS
SHERMAN MARION LABOVITZ

Philadelphia, Pa., July 21, 1954

Before HON. J. CULLEN GANEY, J., and a Jury

*Appearances:*

W. WILSON WHITE, United States Attorney
THOMAS J. MITCHELL, BERNARD V. MCCUSTY and JAMES A. CRONIN,
    Special Assistant Attorneys General For the Plaintiff

THOMAS C. MCBRIDE
JOSEPH S. LORD, 3rd           FOR
WILLIAM J. WOOLSTON       *Robert Klonsky*
JOHN R. CARROLL             *Joseph Roberts*
JOSEPH N. DU BARRY, 4th    *Benjamin Weiss*
CHARLES C. HILEMAN, III    *Thomas Nabried*
BENJAMIN H. READ          *Irvin Katz*
HENRY W. SAWYER, 3rd      *Sherman Marion Labovitz,*
EDMUND B. SPAETH, Jr.                Defendants
ROBERT W. SAYRE
JOSEPH S. LORD, 3rd, for *Walter Lowenfels,* Defendant
DAVID COHEN, *for David Davis,* Defendant
JOSEPH KUZMA, *pro se,* Defendant

# *Dramatis Personae (II)*

IN THE DISTRICT COURT OF THE UNITED STATES
NORTHERN DISTRICT OF OHIO
Eastern Division

UNITED STATES OF AMERICA
*vs.*

JOSEPH BRANDT
GEORGE WATT
MARTIN CHANCEY
ANTHONY KRCHMAREK
ROBERT ALFRED CAMPBELL
JOSEPH MICHAEL DOUGHER
ELVADORE CLAUDE GREENFIELD
FRIEDA ZUCKER KATZ
DAVID KATZ
FRANK HASHMALL
LUCILLE BETHENCOURT

CRIMINAL ACTION
NO. 21076

Cleveland, Ohio, January 25, 1956

Before Hon. CHARLES J. MCNAMEE, J., and a Jury.

*Appearances:*

SUMNER CANARY, United States Attorney
BERNARD V. McCUSTY, Special Assistant Attorney General For the Plaintiff

| | FOR | |
|---|---|---|
| GEORGE FARR, Jr. | | *Martin Chancey* |
| RALPH RUDD and YETTA LAND | | *David Katz and Frieda Katz* |
| MARTIN A. McCORMACK | | *Joseph Brandt and George Watt* |
| WARREN BRIGGS and HYMEN SCHLESINGER | | *Joseph Michael Dougher* |
| ANTHONY KRCHMAREK | | *Pro se* |
| ROBERT ALFRED CAMPBELL | | *Pro se* |
| WILLIAM J. McDERMOTT | | *Elvadore Claude Greenfield* |
| WILLIAM A. GARDNER | | *Frank Hashmall* |
| FRED MANDEL | | *Lucille Bethencourt* |
| | | Defendants |

# Dramatis Personae (III)

IN THE UNITED STATES DISTRICT COURT
FOR THE EASTERN DISTRICT OF PENNSYLVANIA

UNITED STATES OF AMERICA
*vs.*
DR. ALBERT EMANUEL BLUMBERG

CRIMINAL ACTION 17963

Philadelphia, Pa., March 8, 1956

Before HON. C. WILLIAM KRAFT, JR., J., and a Jury

*Present:*

DAVID H. HARRIS, ESQ., Special Deputy Attorney General
and
JOSEPH T. EDDINS, ESQ., Special Deputy Attorney General, representing the United States Government.

MICHAEL VON MOSCHZISKER, ESQ., representing the defendant.

# 1  The Testimony Begins

## The Declaration of Independence and the Communist

This is not a book about personalities. The issues I am going to write of cannot possibly be settled by reference to personalities. It is a book about ideas and facts. Yet these ideas and facts are so bound up with the living experience of individual human beings like you and me that the only way they can be properly explained is to show how they operate in the lives of actual persons.

Perhaps this is all to the good; but it is the sort of thing that makes professional scholars somewhat uncomfortable. We do not usually feel called upon to explain serious ideas in any personal frame of reference whatever, let alone to take the witness stand in a trial. But if these matters are to be explained at all—and they must be, since our fate as a nation hangs in the balance—probably it can be done only by utilizing some elements usually associated with a novel or play rather than with a work of logical analysis. Yet I can assure the reader that, however much he might be tempted at certain points to think he is reading fiction, it is very real fact. I only hope I can do the situation some approximate degree of justice.

It all began after I had spoken to an annual meeting of teachers in the city of Philadelphia on the subject of civil liberties. Two youngish men asked if they could talk with me for a few minutes. I said certainly, and we sat down in a hotel lounge. I was rather startled when one explained he was a lawyer and that the other was his client, a leader of the Communist Party of Pennsylvania, who was then on trial for conspiring to teach the overthrow of the government of the United States by force and violence.

Perhaps I should not have been startled. Among my published works are two books and several articles, based on many years of research here and abroad, in connection with UNESCO and other scholarly projects, analyzing the ideas and doctrines of various social movements, including Communism. Their question was, would I, as a scholar who had never been connected with the Communist Party, come before the court and give expert testimony on the principles of Communism, particularly its teachings on the use of force and violence. I told them I would have to think it over and asked them to give me the facts of the case, which I had not heard about until that time.

They explained that nine leaders of the Communist Party of Pennsylvania had been arrested under the federal law known as the Smith Act. The charge against them was that because of their beliefs as Communists they were in a conspiracy to teach and advocate that the government be overthrown by force and violence.

Here was the familiar pattern, which in fact has since been brought into even sharper focus by the passage of legislation more stringent than the Smith Act itself. Trial after trial, legislative act after legislative act has centered on the same issue—the claim that to be a member of the Communist Party, to accept and follow its teachings, puts the individual in the position of a criminal conspirator, committed to the overthrow of the government by force. By the time the trial had begun in which the two men talking to me were involved, more than seventy Communist leaders had been convicted under the Smith Act, and the act itself had survived its first test of constitutionality in the Supreme Court.

It is necessary to understand that the Smith Act does not mention the Communist Party by name. It simply says that it shall be a criminal offense for anyone to "teach the duty, necessity, desirability or propriety of overthrowing or destroying any government in the United States by force and violence." The whole point, then, is whether Communists do or do not fall into that category of persons.

However, it is not only a matter of court trials and convictions. Through the whole fabric of our lives today runs the disturbing thread of this endlessly ramified issue. Teachers are dismissed, lawyers are disbarred, clergymen are unfrocked, actors are denied contracts, scientists are denied clearance, citizens are denied passports, employees are discharged, workers are beaten up by fellow-workers, union officials are forced to resign, students are suspended, housewives are prevented from holding office in parent-teachers' associations, a mother is denied custody of her own children (as in the Jean Field case)—and all these things are done on the alleged ground that Communism is necessarily a criminal conspiracy. In many such instances they are not done on the basis of any alleged Communist *membership* but merely on the basis of alleged Communist *sympathies,* whatever that may mean.

People in practically every walk of life are subject to "investigation," often followed by unfavorable publicity damaging to reputation and career. Individuals are penalized because of the political beliefs of relatives. Books are removed from library shelves. Printed matter from abroad which is deemed subversive by the postal authorities is subject to nondelivery (without notice to the addressee). Motion pictures are withdrawn from circulation. The production of an ancient Greek play is abandoned. Community leaders pronounce the story of Robin Hood dangerously subversive. UNESCO is attacked as a threat to national sovereignty.

In the course of, and as a result of, such happenings a new and increasing group of specialists is arising, known as "investigative personnel." Investigating committees are spreading from federal to state and local governments, and from government agencies to all sorts of private organizations. The informer is becoming a national institution. Students fear to join student clubs. Teachers fear to deal with controversial subjects. Practically everyone fears to have anything to do with any one of hundreds of organizations (all legal-otherwise they would be disbanded by the police) placed on lists promulgated from time to time by government bodies in such increasing numbers that the citizen is prey to the additional fear that he may not be abreast of the latest list—and all this is only part of the story.

Why are such things happening among us, things so alien to the traditional spirit of American life, so strange in the face of our present claim to be the model leader of the "free world," so dangerous to the survival of one after another of our personal freedoms without which we cannot help but feel a decent human life is impossible? Beyond the shadow of a doubt, the answer to that question goes back to the same idea which is at the bottom of the court trials and jail sentences, that same idea the pressure of which had brought the lawyer and the Communist to make their request of me in Philadelphia.

Put in the bluntest possible terms, Communism, one of the most radical social movements in opposition to the capitalist *status quo,* is claimed to be a criminal conspiracy committed to the violent overthrow of our government. That is the root idea. We are not at the moment discussing whether it is a true or a false idea. We shall come to that presently. Nor are we discussing motives. But it is perfectly clear how this idea has given rise to waves of mounting devastation in our national life.

The mental process involved in these waves is something like this: Since Communism, by the nature of its doctrine, is a criminal conspiracy every member of or believer in the movement is dangerous. Therefore, every member should be found out; every believer should be identified so that all decent people may be put on their guard. Furthermore, it is clearly dangerous to the local community, or a threat to national security, or both, to allow members of or believers in this movement to hold positions where they can exercise intellectual or moral influence on others, or where they have charge of any important matters.

All these members and believers are thus regarded as so many potential traitors, since certain foreign countries are already Communist. So it is imperative to find out who are the possible members and believers. In order to find this out, those who are suspected must be investigated. And of course the more "radical" a person's ideas, behavior, associations, friends, or relatives may be, or may be thought to be, the more he will be suspected.

And so the hunt goes on, extending in ever widening circles throughout the country and into every aspect of the public and private lives of the citizens. Fear, panic, and hysteria are the sort of things which fit Shakespeare's saying: appetite doth grow by what it feeds on; so that with each passing month more and more opinions, activities, books, periodicals, associations, organizations, words, and expressions previously deemed acceptable may become ground for suspicion and hence for investigation, with all the damaging publicity which follows in consequence.

First it is only things that are outright Communist which fall under the ban. Then anything radical. Then anything liberal. First it is only what the individual himself does and thinks that is held against him. Then what his relatives do and think is also held against him. Then what his friends and acquaintances do and think. First it is only what he is now doing and thinking that is considered. Then it becomes a matter of what he was doing and thinking five years ago, ten years ago, twenty years ago. Finally it is thought necessary to go back to his school days, lest any possible ground for suspicion be overlooked.

One of the moral ironies of this situation lies in the fact that, in so many cases, "liberal" groups sought to protect themselves by joining in and contributing to the waves of popular suspicion directed against those further to the "left" than they happened to be themselves. But this pattern of conduct has not succeeded in a single case in warding off die devastating blows of those very waves, the impact of which when they presently struck the "liberals" was all the more powerful and indiscriminate because of the added force given to them by those very "liberals" themselves.

Thus, some of the most damaging accusations against the extreme left were contributed by individuals and groups who presented themselves under a new label, apparently thought capable of passing the test of respectability—"the non-Communist left." But it was speedily brought home to all such hopefuls that it was not just this or that kind of leftism that was under suspicion but leftism in general. In fact, the very term liberal became no longer safe, making it unlikely anyone could gain advantage from such a possible invention as the label "non-left liberal."

The logic is inescapable: If leftism is really in the nature of a dangerous disease, then the liberal, though he may not as yet be outwardly affected, may well be a carrier or host who ought to be guarded against almost as much as the victim with pronounced symptoms. Equally unfruitful were the efforts of some romantic souls to salvage respectability for some kind of "leftism" by attempting to transform the terminology and make out a case that Communism was not really of the "left" but should be recognized as a form of "rightism."

The term conservative is about the only one that sounds really safe when the trend toward total conformity becomes more and more pronounced. But it must be noted that this kind of conformism is not toward a *fixed* standard but toward a standard which is itself steadily shifting to the "right." Now what lies on the extreme "right" is, of course, fascism in its many forms.

The peoples of Europe are far more alert to the dangers of this situation than we are, having suffered the consequences of fascism and nazism at much closer range and at incomparably greater cost than we did. Hence, when they see the steady drift of our domestic situation, together with the steady drift of our foreign policy in a similar direction (for the point need hardly be labored that these two aspects of our national life are connected with each other), it is not too much to say that they stand aghast at the possible outcome.

In many west European countries there have long been Communist movements of greater or lesser degrees of influence. Communist candidates have often been elected to local and regional as well as national offices and Communists have often been on the government payroll in other capacities, openly and legally, of course. One finds Communist teachers, Communist scientists, Communist artists, even, on occasion, Communist clergymen.

Although there is no evidence that a majority of the people of any west European country prefer Communism, it is a fact that Communist Party candidates have sometimes gained a very considerable proportion of the total vote in national elections in important countries of that region, such as France and Italy. In other words, European people generally accept the fact that Communism is one of the social faiths of the modern world, which can be expected to play a certain part in the national life along with many other political creeds and movements.

Moreover, in reflecting upon this matter it must always be taken into account that on the average Europeans know far more than we do about the theory and practice of Communism. Not only do Europeans read far more extensively and study far more intensively the classic doctrines of Communism than do their opposite numbers in our country, but they are and always have been far closer to the actual practices of Communist governments and large Communist parties than we have been.

In fact, precisely what multiplies the anxieties of Europeans when they contemplate present trends in our domestic and foreign policies is their own painfully vivid experience of the last few decades. They remember that whenever a government of marked power began to make the theme of anti-Communism more and more the central focus of all its policies, when repressive measures against the left began to pile up one after the other, when laws to restrict, to censor, and then to penalize with jail sentence began to multiply, when the activity and influence of secret police and the military began to increase sharply, when the public institutions—education, the arts, science, trade unions, bar associations, the churches, press, radio, screen, and the like—began more and more to accept and act upon the idea that they must get rid of the radicals and purge themselves of any taint of leftism, when the government began to construct large concentration centers where those thought politically dangerous could be held in an "emergency" (many American citizens do not seem to realize that a program of such construction has been authorized by the federal government), when things of this kind began to happen in increasing volume Europeans saw, time and again, that the country in question soon became saddled with an outright fascist or nazi regime, whether the people of the country had intended such a result or not.

This was the story of Fascist Italy and of Nazi Germany. "You must tolerate us," said such regimes to their peoples. "Nay, you must welcome us, because we are going to free you from the Communist menace. Harsh measures will of course be necessary, but are we not agreed that the menace must be completely stamped out?" Apparently, the people of those countries reached a point where they so agreed, or at least where they were afraid to say that they did not agree. And they paid a price which neither they nor their immediate neighbors are likely to forget for a long time.

To speak candidly, it is highly improbable that when many Europeans are moved to weigh the possible consequences of our present lines of policy they are thinking primarily of the sufferings which the American people might be bringing down on their own American heads. What they are thinking of primarily is war, and the impact of war on themselves.

In this regard, two facts have been very painfully graven on the tablets of their memory: (1) Once an outright fascist regime has been fastened on a country it cannot be gotten rid of until it loses a war. (2) That sort of regime, far from being afraid of war, becomes a cult of war, placing more and more reliance upon, and taking more and more pride in, the development of military power, so that wars are precipitated where they might otherwise have been avoided.

Europeans have far more experience than we do of the literal meaning of falling bombs. When they put that recent past experience together with the present realities of atomic, hydrogen, and other super weapons, the depth and gravity of their feelings can scarcely be exaggerated. Everything is at stake.

All these considerations were in the background of my reflections as I thought over the request put to me that day in Philadelphia. My mind went back over my own studies, researches, and writings dealing with these issues for more than a quarter of a century. For example, I had been sent by Columbia University in 1935 through its grants known as the Cutting Fellowships to pursue intensive research for a year in Soviet Russia (access was not difficult in those days) in order to find out what had been done in that country in the development of the doctrines on which its whole system was based.

I had learned the Russian language first, in order to do my work independently and at first hand. While I was abroad Columbia reappointed me to the grant for a second year, to make the study as thorough as possible and to gather the maximum of materials. I was thus one of the last American scholars to leave Russia before the tensions of the war situation set in (1938-'39) and it became virtually impossible for any independent researcher to make extensive observations in that country.

After thorough analysis of my data and materials, which took several years, I had published a book, *Soviet Philosophy: A Study of Theory and Practice,* embodying the main results of the project. It has since been translated into a number of languages and has been widely used in colleges, universities, and research centers. I had subsequently been called upon by a number of universities—Columbia, Cornell, Stanford, Michigan, and others—to give lectures and institute courses bearing on the analysis of Soviet Communist doctrines. I had been asked by various scholarly, scientific, and religious bodies, such as American Philosophical Association, International Congress of Philosophy, Society for Religious Culture, American Friends Service Committee, and American Association for the Advancement of Science, to present papers before them dealing with my researches in the field of these same doctrines.

I had been asked by UNESCO and the International Federation of Philosophic Societies to prepare analyses of aspects of that field in connection with several of the international research projects of UNESCO, subsequently published by that organization in its symposium volumes. At the invitation of standard encyclopedias and dictionaries, such as Encyclopedia Americana, Collier's Encyclopedia, and The Dictionary of Philosophy, I contributed detailed entries and definitions explaining many of the basic doctrines and concepts of that same field. At the invitation of scholarly journals such as

*American Slavic and East European Review, Journal of Philosophy, Philosophical Review, Philosophy and Phenomenological Research,* and *Philosophy of Science,* I reviewed books and wrote articles dealing with the same subject.

Let me frankly state that I go into such detail, first, because I want the reader to know from the start that what I have to say about these issues and problems is not said lightly or irresponsibly, but only after prolonged study and experience; and second, because I want the reader to be aware of the reasons which made it impossible for me, in good conscience, to refuse to take the witness stand.

The point can be summed up briefly. It appeared and appears very clear to me that if ever there comes a time in this country when the citizen who possesses special knowledge relating to some public issue is afraid to come forward and place it at the disposal of a judge and twelve jurors in a courtroom, justice will be dead and the moral meaning of this country will have vanished.

The question of the actual content of Communist doctrine has clearly become one of tremendous importance. Whatever I or anyone else may know about that matter certainly ought to be passed on to others and utilized. It would be difficult to believe that anyone acting responsibly and in good faith could counsel me to do otherwise.

It was thus I found myself on July 21,1954, in Philadelphia in the United States District Court; on Jan. 25, 1956, in the same kind of court in Cleveland, and again on Feb. 27, 1956, in Philadelphia, raising my right hand and swearing to tell the truth, the whole truth, and nothing but the truth, so help me God, and stating under oath, of course, that I had never been a member of the Communist Party. The basic issues in these three cases, as in all the Smith Act cases in which Communists were prosecuted, proved to be the same. While the story is here told chiefly in terms of what happened at the first Philadelphia trial, the argumentation in the courtrooms proceeded along the same general lines. The full text of each indictment appears in our chapters. In the first Philadelphia case there were nine defendants; in Cleveland eleven were charged; in the second Philadelphia case a single defendant was tried.

The question central to the whole business was always this: Do the doctrines of the Communist movement include the teaching that the government of the United States must be overthrown by force and violence? Put in other words, if an individual accepts the doctrines of this movement and becomes a member of the Communist Party, is that individual by virtue of that acceptance and membership necessarily taking part in, or in any way conspiring to form, an organization that teaches violent overthrow of our government? Or, contrariwise, is it possible for an individual to be a loyal member or a leading officer of the Communist Party, accepting in good faith the doctrines and discipline of the Communist movement, and still not be helping to form or carry on an organization that teaches that our government must be overthrown by force and violence?

However one words the issue, it comes back to this fundamental point: What is the position taken in the actual doctrines of the Communist movement on the question of overthrow of government by force and violence? The effort to answer that question leads, of course, to detailed scrutiny of Communist doctrine. It is scarcely necessary to point out that everyone concerned agreed that this doctrine, often referred to as Marxism-Leninism, was to be found primarily in the basic writings of Marx, Engels, Lenin, and Stalin. Of significance also are the writings of national leaders of the movement, such as William Z. Foster, and other outstanding figures in the Communist Party of the United States and of other countries.

It is good logic, good morality, and good law that the burden of proof is on the prosecution, that is, on the side making an accusation. In this case, therefore, the government side, which was accusing the defendants and had ordered them arrested and brought to trial, had to select and bring before the judge and jurors those passages in the writings of Communist authorities which, in the prosecution's view, constituted advocacy of forcible and violent overthrow of our government.

I could be sure, therefore, that any portions of the basic Communist writings which in any way tended to lend support to the government's case would be brought out and emphasized. In fact, this had already been done in all the preceding trials, so that one could gain a detailed idea of exactly what it was the government felt was the basis of its case.

My own procedure was as follows: I took each one of these passages and went back to the original work to examine its content and context, in order to analyze its exact meaning and place in this school of thought. What these passages were and my analysis of them will be dealt with shortly. What I especially wanted to do, since it was clearly at the heart of the whole matter, was, from a survey of the total body of basic Communist doctrine, to sum up in positive terms the overall attitude taken on the question of forcible overthrow of government.

In the course of the various researches I had been called upon to undertake through the years I had naturally gone over every piece of writing of any doctrinal importance in the works of the major authorities, most of them a good many times. What had to be done now was in the nature of a sifting out and boiling down. After a good deal of close work of that kind I was finally able to put the central point within the compass of a few pages. Following is the text of this summary exactly as I had prepared it for presentation to the court.

### The Issue of Force and Violence

What is the relationship of the principles of Marxian Communism, as expounded in the works of Marx, Engels, Lenin, and Stalin, to the question of overthrow of government by force and violence—in particular, the forceful overthrow, under present conditions, of our own government? Let us try to throw clear and sober light on this matter.

Any school of thought which takes a stand of any kind on violent revolution, overthrow of government by force, is necessarily faced with two separate questions: First, is forceful overthrow of government ever justified, under any circumstances at all? Second, if so, under what circumstances?

The Marxist-Leninist social philosophy, technically called historical materialism, which lies at the basis of the American Communist Party, clearly shares the practically universal belief of modem schools of political theory in the right of revolution itself—that is, when there is no peaceful way in which the needs and demands of the majority of people can be met. Thus we find the exponents of this philosophy, Marxism-Leninism, answering the question— do people have the right to rebel at all?—in the same way as the founders of the modem democratic tradition in general. The same principle is asserted in either case. Indeed, it is the general judgment of scholars that Marx and Engels derived this principle in part from earlier thinkers like John Locke, Thomas Jefferson, and others.

A special word should be said about the concept of the majority in this attitude toward revolution. Some doctrines of revolution reject the idea that any attention should be paid to numbers, to the question of majority and minority. This is not the case with Marx, Engels, Lenin, or Stalin. These writers evidently conceived of valid revolution in terms of a mass, of having majority support. In their view, any revolution which in its nature was not a response to the felt needs of the majority could not be really successful and should never be undertaken. Marx himself used the term *putschist,* from the German word *putsch* (insurrection), to designate believers in indiscriminate or constant attempts at revolution, and emphatically rejected their doctrines.

Lenin, and Stalin after him, emphasized again and again that revolution by force was justified only when two conditions were simultaneously present:

a. when the existing government was unwilling or unable to carry out the will of the majority in vital matters, and

b. where so drastic a step as forcible revolution had the support of the majority and represented the will of the majority.

These two conditions amount to saying that revolution is justified only where the government represents some kind of a tyranny which will not carry out the will of the people peacefully, and where the majority are ready to support revolutionary action against such a government. But there must be *majority* support

Thus, Lenin stated bluntly in 1917: "We are not Blanquists; we are not in favor of seizure of power by a minority."[1] This was characteristic of Lenin's and Stalin's repeated rejection of the doctrine of indiscriminate force and violence, associated with the Frenchman Blanqui, also associated with various Russian and West European anarchist groups.

Lenin took the trouble to cite actual examples of revolutions which in his judgment did not fulfill these conditions and hence were not to be regarded as acceptable. "If," he wrote, "we take for examples the revolutions of the twentieth century, we shall, of course, have to recognize both Portuguese and Turkish revolutions as bourgeois. Neither is a 'people's' revolution, inasmuch as the mass of the people, the enormous majority, does not make its appearance actively,

---

[1] Edward Hallett Carr, *The Bolshevik Revolution,* Vol. I, p. 18. Macmillan, New York. Cited from Lenin: *Sochineniya (Collected Works),* Vol. XX. p. 96. Russian. Also Lenin: *Selected Works,* Vol. VI, p. 29, "A Dual Power." English.

independently, with its own economic and political demands in either the one or the other."[2]

Thus Lenin stated it both negatively and positively: He is not in favor of revolution by a minority. A revolution, to be valid, must represent the will of the mass of the people, the "enormous majority," in his words. Subsequent spokesmen like Stalin follow Lenin's position.

Indeed, before Lenin and Stalin, both Marx and Engels had pointed out clearly that wherever there were legal and peaceful means which would permit the will of the majority to be actually carried out in practice there would be no need of a violent revolution. In 1872 Marx cited England and the United States as countries "in which the workers may hope to secure their ends by peaceful means."[3] In 1874 Marx further cited Holland as a country in which, at that time, conditions were such that if the mass of the people desired a radical change in the social system that change might be peacefully carried into practice. Engels echoed this position in 1886 in his preface to the first English translation of Marx's *Capital*.

Lenin and Stalin later maintained that conditions had altered in those particular countries so that in their judgment it could no longer be said that the governments would peacefully accede to the wishes of the people if the majority really wanted Communism. However, neither Lenin, Stalin, nor any other leader of the movement in the United States or any other country has ever denied or rejected the principle which Marx and Engels laid down—that wherever conditions are such that there are legal and peaceful means for the majority to gain its will no forcible revolution should be entered upon. This is, of course, the plainest common sense. No leader of any mass movement would want to risk his own life and that of his followers in bloody revolution if he thought he could gain success by peaceful means.

As we have said, these four leaders of this movement—Marx, Engels, Lenin, Stalin—maintain that revolution by force is justified only when the existing government is unwilling or unable to carry out the wishes of the majority and when the revolutionary step has

---

[2] V. I. Lenin, *Collected Works,* Vol. XXI, bk. II, p. 180. International Publishers, New York. *State and Revolution,* Little Lenin Library, p. 34.

[3] Stekloff, G. M., *History of the First International,* p. 240. International Publishers, New York.

the support of the majority. In their essence these conditions are basic to what all democratic political science recognizes as the "right of revolution."

For purposes of clarification by comparison, consider our own American Declaration of Independence, which is our very birth certificate as a nation. This Declaration exactly expresses a principle central to Marxism-Leninism when it states that one of the "self-evident" truths is that "whenever any form of government becomes destructive of these ends [life, liberty, pursuit of happiness], it is the right of the people to alter or abolish it." Another passage of the Declaration is an even better expression of this principle: "But when a long train of abuses and usurpations, pursuing invariably the same object, evinces a design to reduce them [the people] under absolute despotism, it is their right, it is their duty to throw off such government, and to provide new guards for their future security."

To understand the attitude of Marxism-Leninism we must carefully note and emphasize that this principle, which advocates belief in the right of revolution under *certain* circumstances, is a very different thing from advocating revolution itself under *any* circumstances. That difference is clear and compelling. It is the difference between believing that I have a right to do something under certain unusual conditions and the belief that I have a right to do that thing irrespective of conditions. For example, most people believe that they have a right to strike or even kill another human being under certain circumstances, such as self-defense, but they do not believe they have a right to strike or kill others irrespective of circumstances.

It is quite clear that it would be highly illogical and would convey a totally false impression to say of such people, believers in the right of self-defense, that they are advocating force and violence against others. What they are advocating is the right to use force and violence under certain conditions. When we neglect the existence of the qualifying circumstances we commit what is known in formal logic as the converse fallacy of accident.

In exactly the same fashion it would create a totally false impression about the followers of Marx, Engels, Lenin, and Stalin (or the followers of Jefferson) for anyone to say of them, without qualification, that they advocate the violent overthrow of the government. The most we can say, if we are to speak in the light of serious and thorough examination, is this: If they are true to their own principles they would advocate such an action only under highly unusual conditions of tyrannical oppression wherein the majority were being denied the peaceable fulfillment of their inherent and inalienable rights—that is, conditions wherein any believer in the Declaration of Independence would be logically bound to advocate the same thing.

Put in other words, it is clear that a consistent belief in or adherence to the Communist Party philosophy we are examining would not *necessitate* advocacy of any attempt to overthrow the government by force. A given individual might conceivably be a sincere adherent to that philosophy his life long and yet never be faced with any set of circumstances which in the light of his cherished beliefs would call for any such action. That is, he might obtain what he desired by peaceful and orderly processes of legislation, as Marx pointed out, or, failing that, he might never be faced with a situation in which he had confidence in the support of the majority. In either of these cases, if he followed the basic teachings of this philosophy he would never take part in violent revolution.

If it is possible to adhere to the Marxian or Communist philosophy without ever taking part in any actual attempt to overthrow government by force and without advocating that any specific or concrete attempt be initiated to that end in a given capitalist country like the United States, then it is logically required to conclude that this philosophy is not one that makes necessary an attempt at, or advocacy of, violent overthrow of any government in the United States.

Such was the statement as I prepared it for presentation to the court. There is no doubt whatever in my mind that anyone using reason and having a knowledge of the facts as a whole will come to the same conclusion that I did. There is nothing really difficult about it as a problem in logic. You have a certain body of writings. Those writings take a certain position on violent overthrow of government. That position turns out to be essentially the same as the one taken by the founding fathers in the Declaration of Independence, which is certainly the keystone of our whole structure of sovereignty. Are we, then, going to put United States citizens in jail for believing the principle laid down by the signers on July 4, 1776? Are we not all supposed to believe in that principle?

Logically, there are only two possible alternatives at the bottom of this whole aspect of the matter. Either we say that there are no conditions under which revolution is right and proper or we say that there are certain conditions under which it is right and proper. We can not say the first, because that would involve a repudiation of the Declaration of Independence—an impossible attempt to cancel the validity of our only birth certificate as a nation. If we say the second, which is all that remains, it is clear that we cannot consistently throw Communists into jail for saying the same thing. I believe that the analysis which I had prepared, relatively brief as it was, expressed the logical substance of the matter.

Unfortunately, however, the jury never heard the statement as I had prepared it. No sooner did I try to refer to the Declaration of Independence than the following situation, as reported in the official record of the trial, came about. (All portions of the court record reproduced in this work are taken from the first Philadelphia trial unless otherwise noted.)

> The Witness: For purposes of clarification by comparison, consider our own American Declaration of Independence.
> Government Counsel: I object ...
> The Court: Strike that out.
> Defense Counsel: Will Your Honor hear me? I think that is basic to the principle if it can be demonstrated that quotation from the Declaration of Independence is similar to the position taken in the classics [of Marxism].
> The Court: No, he has been asked as to the totality of Marxism. I think he can do it without bringing in the Declaration of Independence.
> Defense Counsel: Well, even if he can, is it impermissible, sir? The Court: Yes, I think he ought to answer your question. Defense Counsel: Well, I think he is, sir.
> The Court: Well, I don't in that regard. I think we will leave that out.

Thus any reference to the Declaration of Independence was forbidden. I was unable to quote to the jury the two passages from that document contained in my analysis. I was unable to explain to the jury that the principle expressed in those passages is the same principle contained in the doctrine of Marxism-Leninism in regard to the specific question of what conditions, if any, make it right and proper to advocate revolution. I had to omit that entire portion of my analysis, the very portion which connected the discussion with something the jurors were familiar with, something they could have understood from their own past reading and thinking. Moreover, it was a portion which contained an undeniable historical fact of central significance and unquestionable relevancy to the root issue of the trial-forcible overthrow of government.

I wish to emphasize at this point that I am not criticizing either the judge or government counsel as individuals, in their capacity of jurist or lawyer. Throughout the four days of my appearance in court, I must say, I was treated with consistent personal courtesy. Whether their hands were tied by legal technicalities so that they had no alternative but to take the position they took I must leave to legal experts. But the fact remains that in a trial focusing on the question of revolution, held in a United States court in the very city where the Declaration of Independence was signed, an expert witness was prevented from stating to the jury that his researches led to the conclusion that a central doctrine taught by the accused was the same as that found in the Declaration.

This is clearly an absurd situation. If there is something in the law which at present makes such a situation unavoidable, surely some changes or adjustments in the law can be made in the interest of common sense. One can explain something to a group of persons only by relating it to what they already know, by comparing it to something with which they are already acquainted. If an expert witness is prevented from doing that he is being prevented from doing what he was called in to do.

This same pattern of frustration was repeated when I came to that portion of my analysis where I tried to point out that the Communist attitude toward the right of revolution is exactly the same as the attitude of the general public toward the right of self-defense. That is, it is regarded as a right that can be exercised only under certain exceptional conditions. Now this is not only a fact, and an important fact. It is the kind of fact which helps the average person, who is not a technical scholar, to understand a concept that might otherwise be difficult or impossible to understand. But instead of hearing something that might have clarified a basic idea, what the jurors actually heard was this:

> The Witness: To understand the attitude of Marxism-Leninism we must carefully note and emphasize that the principle of revolution here espoused, which advocates belief in the right of

revolution under certain circumstances, is a very different thing from advocating revolution itself under any circumstances. That difference is clear and compelling.

    Government Counsel: I move to strike this part out as argument.

    The Court: I think that is right. I don't think he can say whether it is clear and compelling at all. He can give us an answer, but that is for the jury....

    The Witness: It is the difference between believing that I have the right to do something under certain unusual conditions and the belief that I have the right to do that thing irrespective of conditions. For example, most people believe they have the right to Strike-

    Government Counsel: I object to this part—the examples, Your Honor.

    The Witness: I am drawing a comparison between this and the right of self-defense—

    Government Counsel: The right to strike.

    The Witness:—to illustrate the meaning of the doctrine.

    The Court: No, I am going to sustain the objection there....

    Defense Counsel: When you started to read "the right to strike" did you mean the right to go on strike applicable to labor unions, or the right to strike another person?

    The Witness: I was talking about the right to self-defense.

    Government Counsel: That is stricken.

    Defense Counsel: It is stricken because you did not even let him complete it, and nobody understood what he was about to say.

So the better part of another page was taken out of my already sadly crippled analysis, from the sentence beginning "For example, most people believe that they have a right to strike or even kill another human being under certain circumstances," through the sentence ending "... any believer in the Declaration of Independence would be logically bound to advocate the same thing." Yet, if anyone is really trying to understand the position of this school of thought in the framework of American conditions today it is just the doctrinal situation pointed to in that passage which must be confronted.

    That is, everyone knows there is such a thing as the right of self-defense. But no one would think of throwing into jail a believer in the right of self-defense on the ground that such a believer is teaching and advocating the killing of human beings. Everyone would recognize that such a believer is not teaching and advocating the killing of human beings in general, indiscriminately, irrespective of circumstances. He is teaching and advocating that a given human being may legitimately be killed under certain highly exceptional conditions—when that human being attempts to murder another person.

Now, what were the Communist defendants charged with? They were charged, not only in this trial but in all the trials of record, with conspiring to advocate the violent overthrow of the government. It is certainly clear that to put the charge in this way, without qualification, is exactly the same as to charge believers in the right of selfdefense with teaching and advocating the killing of human beings, without qualification, For no Communist doctrine can be found which teaches and advocates the right of revolution irrespective of circumstances.

The doctrines of this movement, as we have seen, teach and advocate that revolution is justified only under certain highly exceptional conditions: when the government in power is unable and unwilling to carry out the will of the majority and there is majority support for the revolutionary action. Are these conditions acceptable to Americans generally? They must be, for, as we have seen (but as the jurors may not have seen since they were prevented from hearing an explanation of it at the time), these conditions are the same as those laid down in our American Declaration of Independence. If we cannot penalize believers in the right of self-defense, since they advocate killing only under certain acceptable conditions, then we also cannot penalize Communist believers in the right of revolution, since they advocate revolution only under certain acceptable conditions.

In the principles of formal logic, as I pointed out, there is a name for the kind of fallacy that would be committed if we tried to apply penalties in either of these cases—the converse fallacy of accident. Since I have been teaching it to logic classes long enough to be dealing with the children of my first students I cannot be expected to overlook it now. The defining characteristic of this fallacy is that it asserts that what is true in some special case must be true as a general rule.

Thus a person would be committing this fallacy if he said: "Dr. Jones used a knife on Mr. Smith in the operating room yesterday. Therefore Dr. Jones may be expected to use a knife on anyone he meets." Such a person would be trying to say that what is in actuality true only for special circumstances must be true for all circumstances. Relative to any general rule the special case is termed an accident. (Here the general rule is that Dr. Jones does not plunge a knife into those he meets. The surgical operation is exceptional.)

The mistake thus consists in trying to take the exception as if it were the rule. It is called *converse* fallacy of accident because the direct or simple fallacy of accident is considered to occur when the opposite procedure is followed, that is, when the attempt is made to take the rule as if it were the exception or as if there were no exception. Thus a person would be committing the direct fallacy of accident if he said: "Since those who use knives on others are guilty of a crime Dr. Jones, who used a knife on Mr. Smith in the operating room yesterday, is guilty of a crime." (The rule that people should not use knives on others is valid in general, but there are justifiable exceptions.)

The fallacy that is committed in the kind of trial we are discussing is of the converse form, since the implicit claim is that because Communists believe in revolution under certain special circumstances they must believe in revolution under any circumstances or they must at present be in a conspiracy to bring about a revolution. But there is no basis for such a conclusion.

In this connection it is important to emphasize that the Communists were presumed to be in this conspiracy to overthrow the government by force because they accepted the doctrine of Marxism-Leninism.

That was always the evidence against them. No claim was ever made that there was any evidence of their intent to overthrow the government apart from their acceptance of the teachings found in the works of Marxism-Leninism.

No claim was ever made that they possessed or tried to obtain physical instrumentalities—bombs, guns, lethal weapons of any kind. No claim was ever made that any insurrectionary plans of any tactical or military nature had been drawn or even discussed. Had such claims been made, the essence of the case would have been wholly different. What was actually produced in court by the prosecution was a superabundance of one kind of "evidence": passages from the books which teach the doctrines of Marxism-Leninism. In other words, the prosecution was not saying these defendants are guilty of criminal conspiracy because they are going to act *in violation* of their own professed doctrines and teachings. Such a contention would have called for physical evidence. The prosecution was maintaining throughout that the defendants were guilty because, acting *in accordance* with their own professed doctrines and teachings, they must be in a present conspiracy to use force and violence to overthrow our government.

What are the passages which contain these doctrines and teachings, as adduced by the prosecution? That is what the government's entire case rests upon, and is what we must now examine.

# 2  The Heart of the Issue

## The Majority and "The Propitious Moment"

Just before I took the stand the prosecution had produced what it obviously considered its most telling bit of evidence among all the quotations gathered from the teachings of Marxism. This passage seemed to suggest a readiness, at least on that occasion, to have entered into revolution without the support of the majority. It was a portion of text quoted by Stalin from Lenin in Stalin's work, *Problems of Leninism*. It read as follows.

" 'In order to win the majority of the population to its side,' Lenin continues, 'the proletariat must first of all overthrow the bourgeoisie and seize state power and, secondly, it must introduce Soviet rule, smash to pieces the old state apparatus, and thus at one blow undermine the rule, authority and influence of the bourgeoisie and of the petty-bourgeois compromisers in the ranks of the non-proletarian toiling masses. Thirdly, the proletariat must *completely and finally destroy* the influence of the bourgeoisie and of the petty-bourgeois compromisers among the *majority* of the non-proletarian toiling masses by the *revolutionary* satisfaction of *their* economic needs *at the expense of the exploiters."* (P. 641. Lenin: *Collected Works,* Vol. XXIV, Russian edition.)"[1]

It is of course true that when one is trying to determine the position of a certain school of thought on a certain issue one must be guided by the direction taken in the overwhelming preponderance

---

[1] Stalin, Joseph: *Problems of Leninism,* p. 21. International Publishers, New York, 1934. Emphasis in original.

of instances rather than in one or two isolated exceptions. Even so it is very interesting to see if the seeming exception is a real one. In this case the reader must first understand the somewhat technical vocabulary in use in this kind of literature.

"Bourgeoisie" means, in general, the capitalist class. "Proletariat" is, of course, the working class—in its strict sense, the industrial working class, not including farm workers nor clerical and office help. These latter groups in low-income occupations are referred to as "non-proletarian toiling masses."

Capitalists in general are regarded as "exploiters" because it is considered that in hiring wage workers to produce things which are then sold at a profit the capitalist employers never return to the workers the full value of what the workers have produced. As Communists and many Socialists see it, the profit which goes to the owner of capital for no other reason than that he is the owner of capital is an unnecessary drain, and creates injustice on a large scale.

Now one may disagree to one's heart's content with the necessity or desirability of defining such terms in such ways or with the implications of these definitions, once they are set up as definitions. But the fact remains that that is the way the terms are defined in this school of thought and, as long as freedom of thought exists, any school can argue for its definitions in the market place of ideas. It is certainly not the correctness or incorrectness of doctrine which is in question here or which was in question at the trial. That is an altogether different issue. The only points in question are the *meaning* of the doctrine and whether teaching that meaning necessarily involves a *criminal* act.

What, then, does the passage mean? Whenever a single excerpt taken out of a certain context seems to mean something contrary to the normal expectation or the general rule there is only one thing to do. It is necessary to go back and examine the original context from which this excerpt was taken and see whether the material preceding and following it throws any further light on its meaning.

Stalin had given as the source of the quotation Vol. XXIV, page 641, of the original Russian edition of Lenin's *Collected Works* without, however, citing the title of the particular article or book from which he had quoted. The reader will bear in mind that not all the writings of Lenin have been translated into English so that I had as yet no way of knowing whether this particular work as a whole, whatever it was, had ever been translated. The best thing, then, was to go back to the Russian original, but no one knew whether that could be obtained in the brief interval that was at our disposal. Fortunately, however, a copy of the volume was located in the nick of time and I was able to take it on the stand and translate the sentences directly preceding the quotation, which indeed threw new light on the meaning of the passage.

What I found was that the portion Stalin had quoted came from an article written by Lenin in 1919 under the title "The Elections to the Constituent Assembly, and the Dictatorship of the Proletariat." And what was of cardinal importance was the fact that the passage quoted was directly preceded in the original by these sentences: "Here is the dialectic which the traitors, blockheads and pedants of the Second International could never understand. The proletariat cannot triumph without winning to its side a majority of the population; but to limit and restrict this winning to the attainment of a majority of votes in elections held under the rulership of the bourgeoisie is either impenetrable stupidity or a sheer deception practiced on the workers."

In other words, when taken as a whole this passage, far from indicating any desire on Lenin's part to repudiate the majority principle, actually emphasizes that principle by stating bluntly: "The proletariat cannot triumph without winning to its side a majority of the population...." But Lenin obviously had two further points in mind, both related to the thought thus expressed by him.

One was that the business of "winning to its side a majority of the population" goes much further than just having the support or consent of that majority for a certain step, whether such support be indicated by elections or in some other way. In other words, the "support" of the majority, in the sense of approval and consent, is, in this school of thought, a thoroughly understood *precondition* to any forcible insurrectionary step, as we shall demonstrate by further quotation in a moment. But Lenin, in the passage quoted by Stalin, is talking about something much more complex than the consent and approval of the majority for the initial insurrectionary step. He is talking about what the proletariat must do "in order to win the majority of the population to its side," that is, to make them full-fledged participants in the unfolding events, fully convinced advocates of the Communist cause. We shall return to this aspect of the matter presently.

## THE MAJORITY AND "THE PROPITIOUS MOMENT" 39

The second point Lenin had in mind in the context quoted was that there are certainly times and places where the ordinary processes of elections are not possible and other measures are of necessity used. Both these points are further clarified in this particular article of Lenin and in his other works. For example, within the article here under discussion Lenin says:

> "It is essential that the party of the revolutionary proletariat should participate in bourgeois parliamentarism for the purpose of educating the masses by means of elections and the struggle of parties within parliament. But to confine the class struggle to the parliamentary struggle, or to regard the latter as the supreme and decisive form of struggle, to which all other forms of struggle are subordinate, is in practice to desert the proletariat for the bourgeoisie."

This passage will be found in English translation on page 482 of Volume VI of Lenin's *Selected Works*. Having located the article in the original Russian, I was later able to find it by chronological reference among the extant translations. The text, printed in its entirety, occupies pages 463 to 485 of Volume VI of the English edition, and is dated Dec. 29, 1919. On the next day that I took the stand I read the passage just quoted, and also another very much to the same point from page 293 of the same volume in the English edition:

> "If a revolutionary party has not a majority among the front ranks of the revolutionary classes and in the country generally, there can be no question of insurrection."

That is the kind of statement one finds again and again as one goes over these teachings. Indeed, it is further emphasized that majority support by itself is not enough. There must be other objective conditions present in addition, as we noted previously, before this doctrine would sanction any attempt at forcible revolution. Lenin makes a classic and detailed statement of these conditions in his work entitled *The War and the Second International*. His words in this connection merit careful analysis. I quoted them in full from the International Publishers edition (Little Lenin Library), 1932, page 13:

> "For a Marxist there is no doubt that a revolution is impossible without a revolutionary situation; furthermore, we know that not every revolutionary situation leads to revolution."

Let us interrupt this passage for a moment to observe that it is obvious from this very first sentence that we now have in hand something of tremendous importance to the whole issue of forcible revolution, forcible overthrow of government. That is, Lenin is here making the definite commitment that there must be what he calk a "revolutionary situation" before there can be any possibility of revolution in the Marxist view. In fact, he even goes so far as to say that the revolutionary situation might be present on certain occasions without actually resulting in a revolution. But even though there might sometimes be a revolutionary situation without a revolution he insists that for a Marxist there could be no such thing as a revolution without a revolutionary situation. A very great deal, therefore, hinges on Lenin's definition of just what kind of situation that is. Let us now continue with the quotation, for, in the very next sentence, that is the question Lenin undertakes to answer:

> "What are, generally speaking, the characteristics of a revolutionary situation? We can hardly be mistaken when we indicate the following three outstanding signs: (1) it is impossible for the ruling classes to maintain their power unchanged; for there is a crisis 'higher up,' taking one form or another; there is a crisis in the policy of the ruling class; as a result, there appears a crack through which the dissatisfaction and the revolt of the oppressed classes burst forth. If a revolution is to take place, it is usually insufficient that 'one does not wish way below,' but it is necessary that 'one is incapable up above,' to continue in the old way; (2) the wants and sufferings of the oppressed classes become more acute than usual; (3) in consequence of the above causes, there is a considerable increase in the activity of the masses who in 'peace time' allow themselves to be robbed without protest, but in stormy times are drawn both by the circumstances of the crisis and *by the 'higher-ups' themselves* into independent historic action.
>
> "Without these objective changes, which are independent not only of the will of separate groups and parties but even of separate classes, a revolution, as a rule, is impossible. The co-existence of all these objective changes is called a revolutionary situation." (Italics in original.)

In other words, in Lenin's view it is far from being true that an insurrection brings about the breakdown of the present order. He is clearly saying the exact opposite: only a major breakdown of the

## THE MAJORITY AND "THE PROPITIOUS MOMENT" 41

existing order brings about the possibility of any successful insurrection. This thought must have seemed to him of cardinal importance, for he expresses it in three different ways in the one passage. That is, he says that before there can be any attempt at overthrow of government things must first have reached a point where "it is impossible for the ruling class to maintain their power ..." where "there is a crisis 'higher up'...," where " 'one is incapable up above,' to continue in the old way...."

Clearly, he has in view here the thesis, of basic significance to every Marxist, that capitalism is the kind of system which cannot solve problems like large-scale unemployment, colonialism, and economic exploitation, and that the condition of the masses is bound to grow so bad that orderly processes of social life and government will break down. When disordered conditions come about, whether from these or other causes—such conditions as were prevalent for example in our revolution of 1776, or the French revolution of 1789, or the revolutions of 1848 in western Europe or that of 1917 in Russia—it is understood that normal electoral procedures have become physically impossible.

Moreover, Lenin gives the most explicit emphasis to the fact that the prior breakdown he has in mind, the kind of changes that must come about before any forcible overthrow of the existing government can be thought of, must be of such scope and scale as to be beyond the will of any political group, Communist or non-Communist, or even of any economic class as a whole, proletarian or nonproletarian. His thesis about the root causes of a fundamental social breakdown may be right or wrong as an economic and sociological explanation. But there can be no doubt about the fact that it is a fundamental social breakdown that he has in mind as a vast, objective precondition to any valid revolution. (As we shall see later on, he even adds certain "subjective conditions" that must also be present—mainly a dedicated political leadership.)

In other words, when Lenin said what was quoted by Stalin, "In order to win the majority of the population to its side, the proletariat must first of all overthrow the bourgeoisie and seize state power ...," it was understood by him and by Stalin that such an action was unthinkable unless a gigantic social breakdown had already occurred, a breakdown which made normal electoral procedures impossible. In such a situation some group always tries to take control. (This is, of course, exactly what had happened in their own country in 1917 and what Lenin, writing in 1919, had primarily in mind.)

As we have seen, a further aspect of what was understood by him and by Stalin was that there must be convincing objective evidence of majority support for the revolutionary step. It needs to be emphasized that in circumstances of that kind there is an important difference between having the support of a majority for a revolutionary step and winning the majority to one's side in active participation. A majority, of course, can support a certain decision merely in the sense of giving its consent in one way or another. But it might then stand aside to see how the thing will work out, without taking an active part in the carrying out of the decision, in all the efforts, struggles, and conflicts that may be involved in the carrying out of the decision.

It was naturally these aspects of the matter that were mainly in the minds of Lenin and Stalin when they referred to winning the majority of the population to the side of the proletariat in the actual course of the revolution in its various steps and phases, as the wording of the passage shows—first, seizure of state power, then setting up of Soviet organs, then establishing new economic forms. They were obviously thinking of active cooperation extending over a considerable period. But they never abandoned or repudiated their principle that there must be majority support, and objective evidence of majority support, for the taking of the initial revolutionary step.

What is equally important, no Communist authority has ever maintained that there was any revolutionary situation in the United States, that is, any situation which would justify the taking of the initial insurrectionary step. As soon as I had finished reading the lengthy quotation from Lenin defining and analyzing the revolutionary situation I was questioned about the relation of that doctrine to the United States movement in the following way:

> Defense Counsel: Now, Doctor, according to the teaching and advocacy of the Communist Party of the United States, is there any advocacy or teaching on their part that there is any revolutionary situation in the United States of America?
>
> The Witness: No, there is not....
>
> Defense Counsel: Do you know of any writing or any Communist writer in America who has said that the conditions of such a revolutionary situation exist in America?
>
> The Witness: Certainly not.

It is interesting, in the light of this situation, to reflect upon the wording found repeatedly in some of the most important court decisions rendered up to the present time in this type of case. For example, as reported in *The New York Times* of Oct. 15, 1954,

> "The United States Court of Appeals yesterday upheld the 1953 conviction of thirteen secondary Communist leaders on charges of conspiracy to teach and advocate overthrow of the Government by force and violence.... The court found that the jury ... had ample evidence for its verdict that the defendants intended violent overthrow of the Government 'at the first propitious moment.'"

This phraseology had also been used several years earlier by the Court of Appeals, as noted by the late Chief Justice of the Supreme Court, Mr. Vinson, when he handed down the latter court's decision on June 4, 1951, regarding certain aspects of the original (Dennis) case against the top Communist leaders. Chief Justice Vinson then remarked:

> "That court [the Court of Appeals] held that the record in this case amply supports the necessary finding of the jury that petitioners, the leaders of the Communist Party in this country, were unwilling to work within our framework of democracy, but intended to initiate a violent revolution whenever the propitious occasion appeared." (P. 3.)

Further on in the course of the same opinion Chief Justice Vinson showed his evident agreement with that conception when, in discussing the meaning of "clear and present danger," he gave detailed expression to his ideas as follows:

> "Obviously, the words cannot mean that before the Government may act, it must wait until the *putsch* is about to be executed, the plans have been laid and the signal is awaited. If Government is aware that a group aiming at its overthrow is attempting to indoctrinate its members and to commit them to a course whereby they will strike when the leaders feel the circumstances permit, action by the Government is required.... In the instant case the trial judge charged the jury that they could not convict unless they found that petitioners intended to overthrow the Government 'as speedily as circumstances would permit.' This does not mean, and could not properly mean, that they would not strike until there

was certainty of success. What was meant was that the revolutionists would strike when they thought the time was ripe." (P. 15)

The obvious trouble with this whole line of reasoning is that it does not go far enough. It suddenly and arbitrarily stops, so that the heart of the matter is never reached or considered. It tries to draw a conclusion without taking into account a whole body of major evidence. It says that Communist doctrine teaches and advocates that revolutions should be undertaken "whenever the propitious occasion appeared," "at the first propitious moment," "as speedily as circumstances would permit," "when they thought the time was ripe." Now, having gone that far in the analysis of Communist doctrine is it not logically mandatory to raise immediately the further questions: Does that doctrine take a position on what the propitious occasion, the first propitious moment, is? Does it take a position on the kind of circumstances that would permit revolution? Does it take a position on just what time would be ripe for revolution? We have seen that it does.

Its teachings point out in great detail, over and over, that the propitious moment, the fitting circumstance, the right time is when the existing government will not carry out the will of the majority and has reached a point of breakdown where it is no longer capable of functioning normally, and where there is majority support for the revolutionary step. As we have seen, this doctrine repeatedly takes the emphatic position that all these conditions must exist simultaneously before any Marxist can sanction any attempt at violent overthrow of government.

One who wishes to proceed logically will realize that we are now faced with the following alternatives: either we take into account these aspects of Communist doctrine concerning the preconditions of valid revolution or we do not. Suppose we try to refuse to take them into account at all; what would we be doing then? We would be arbitrarily selecting certain statements of Communist doctrine, closing our eyes to the qualifications attached to them. Then, basing ourselves on those statements alone, as if the other statements which qualify them did not exist, we would conclude that certain people should be thrown in jail. If such a method of using statements is to be permitted, who could not be thrown in jail?

But suppose one were to conceive of a sort of refinement of this method, wherein the modifying statements were not ignored

## THE MAJORITY AND "THE PROPITIOUS MOMENT" 45

outright but were simply not regarded as made in good faith. In that case, why should any of the doctrinal statements be regarded as made in good faith? If the claim that a certain group should be thrown in jail is based on the alleged content of its doctrine, all aspects of the doctrine must be taken into account. We cannot base our judgment on some part of the doctrine that sounds damaging by itself and then simply rule out as insincere another part of the doctrine which might render the first part acceptable. Again, if we could do that there is little doubt that we could throw in jail practically anybody who believed in any political or social doctrine.

This point is all the more important when the reader reflects that no evidence of intent to overthrow the government was ever alleged against any of the accused in any of these trials besides the alleged evidence in the content of their teachings. The situation would be altogether different if the prosecuting authorities had found physical evidence to support the charges—caches of guns or bombs, plans of military action, and the like—something that would demonstrate readiness to enter into insurrection against a government still willing and able to carry out the will of the majority.

Then it might be argued with some semblance of reason that those sections of published doctrine which stated that no revolution was valid save where the government was unwilling and unable to carry out the will of the majority were published in bad faith and should be discounted as insincere. But there is no such supporting physical evidence. In all these trials the prosecuting authorities came into court not with caches of guns or bombs to show the jury but with stacks of books. There is not a single exhibit of military plans but there is quotation after quotation from the teachings of Marx, Engels, Lenin, and Stalin.

Sometimes this strange attempt to regard one part of the doctrine as published in good faith while discounting another part as allegedly published in bad faith seems to be based on the premise that Communists are clever and habitual liars whose words simply cannot be trusted. Here we are confronted again by the question raised a moment ago: If they are habitual liars how could any part of their doctrine be taken as in good faith and used in court? If they are habitual liars judgment should be based on their actions alone; their doctrine should be left out of account altogether.

But the only "actions" that were adduced were the "actions" of spreading the doctrine! The "reasoning" implicit in this strange approach would actually be of this character: The word of a Communist cannot be believed. Why not? Because he is a criminal conspirator. How do you know he is a criminal conspirator? Because he himself in his own doctrine says he is going to overthrow the government. That is, his word cannot be believed but we know he is going to overthrow the government because we have his word for it.

This type of fallacy is ordinarily so obvious that logic texts scarcely bother to analyze it. It is a case where the premises not only fail to prove the conclusion but, if accepted, would positively disprove the conclusion.

In the light of these considerations it is impossible to find cogency in Chief Justice Vinson's remarks when he says:

> "Obviously, the words ['clear and present danger'] cannot mean that before the Government may act, it must wait until the *putsch* is about to be executed, the plans have been laid and the signal is awaited. If Government is aware that a group aiming at its overthrow is attempting to indoctrinate its members and to commit them to a course whereby they will strike when the leaders feel the circumstances permit, action by the Government is required."

Focus attention for a moment on Mr. Vinson's thought: "If Government is aware that a group aiming at its overthrow ..." But what government is meant? As we have seen, no evidence was ever brought forward to show that this group aimed at the violent overthrow of any government that ever existed in the United States, either in the past or at the present time; they have made no such attempt in the whole course of their history in this country. The most anyone could say, as we have seen, is that this group aims at the violent overthrow of a *possible future* government in the United States *if* that possible future government shows itself unwilling and unable to carry out the will of the majority.

But is not that what we all aim to do if and when such sorry circumstances should arise? It is impossible to see how that could be an instance of "clear and present danger." In fact, it is impossible to see how it can be regarded as a "danger" at all, unless we are willing to repudiate the principles on which our very sovereignty as a nation was based, as set forth in our Declaration of Independence.

For those principles clearly state that whenever any government shows itself to be of such a character that it is unwilling and unable to carry out the will of the majority of people it is not only our right but our duty to overthrow it and set up a new government. If this teaching constitutes a conspiracy it is a conspiracy involving every teacher who instills in her pupils respect for the principles of the Declaration and every public official or citizen who praises what the founding fathers did in 1776 on the original Fourth of July.

The alternative is to give a blank check to all future governments in the United States for all time, which is a patent absurdity. But this is where Mr. Vinson's reasoning leads, though it is highly unlikely he intended such a result. It might even be regarded as a sort of insult to his memory were one to suggest that he would not have been ready to do what our founding fathers did if similar circumstances had developed. There are, unfortunately, many possible ways a tyrannical government might arise in the course of time in any country in the world, including our own.

An existing government, in allowing the teaching of the doctrine that it is the right and duty of the people to overthrow any government unable and unwilling to carry out the will of the majority, is lending no more encouragement to its own overthrow than an individual allowing the right of self-defense is lending encouragement to his own injury or death. Such an individual says, in effect: If at any future time I should become so abnormal or psychotic that I approach an innocent person with intent to kill, I grant that person a right to kill me if that be necessary to protect his own life. In the same fashion a government says, in effect: If in the future any persons occupying these offices of authority become so tyrannical or corrupt as to be unwilling or unable to carry out the will of the majority of people, the majority have the right to remove the government made up of such persons, by force if necessary.

For example, there is no doubt that Chief Justice Vinson himself, as a lawyer and jurist, fully acknowledged and sanctioned the right of self-defense. Now suppose he were sitting in judgment on a person accused by a neighbor of teaching the doctrine that it is right and proper to kill people under certain circumstances, to wit, when, armed with a deadly weapon, they advance upon an innocent victim with intent to kill.

Suppose further that no evidence is found that the accused person, or anyone who accepts the doctrine the accused teaches, is actually working out any concrete plans to kill anyone or preparing weapons, but the nervous neighbor who brought him into court argues as follows: I feel this man constitutes a sort of threat to my life. He might consider that I am one who ought to be killed. Must I wait until he has laid plans and is about to take action along such a line? I want him put in jail now. After all, he might be quite mistaken in his judgment as to what time is ripe, as to the actual circumstances, the propitious moment. He might just imagine that I am advancing upon him with a deadly weapon and with intent to kill, whereas such might not be the case. I am and always have been a law-abiding person. Why should I have to live with this constant threat next door?

There is no doubt Chief Justice Vinson would have felt it necessary to point out to such a complainant that, in the first place, he, the complainant, as he is now behaving, is not threatened by the defendant's doctrine. He would be threatened by it only were he, the complainant, to advance upon an innocent person with intent to kill. But at such a point he *should* be threatened by it, for he has no right to advance upon an innocent person with intent to kill.

In the second place, the complainant himself would have to resort to this doctrine, in self-protection, were he attacked by some mad or criminal individual with murderous intent. As for the possibility that any person acting on this doctrine might misinterpret circumstances, such a possibility is of course one that we must accept in relation to all the rights of an individual. But we cannot abolish rights because mistakes might be made in their application.

When people assert that they have a right to break the windows of a train in order to escape in an accident, to drive through a red light if a building is toppling into the highway, to disregard "No Trespassing" signs in order to save life in a forest fire, and to do thousands of other ordinarily impermissible things (even to take life) when some drastic emergency arises, we cannot put them in jail on the ground they might possibly be mistaken in the future as to when such an emergency has actually arisen. We must wait until there is some evidence that they *are* making a mistake, or *have* made a mistake, or *are about to* make a mistake in action, in interpreting the actual circumstances in one of these matters, before we can legitimately arrest them and place them in jail. Otherwise, we are simply arresting people now because they might later make mistakes in the exercise of their rights. On that basis we would all have to be arrested.

## THE MAJORITY AND "THE PROPITIOUS MOMENT" 49

These are surely the considerations Justice Vinson would have had to point out to any individual who tried to have his neighbor jailed because that neighbor advocated the doctrine of the right to kill in self-defense. Why not, then, point them out to a government which is trying to put a party in jail for advocating the right of revolution? Why not point out to such a government that, in the first place, as it is now functioning it is not threatened by this party's doctrine? It would be threatened by that doctrine only were it to change into so corrupt a regime that it became unable and unwilling to carry out the majority will.

But at such a point it should be threatened, for no government has a right to go on ruling contrary to the wishes of the majority. In the second place, the very officials of the present government, being men of energy and courage, would probably be among the readiest to apply the right of revolution if they became convinced that persons occupying the seats of highest authority had become so tyrannical that they were no longer willing and able to carry out the majority will. (See Chap. 11, correspondence with the author of the Smith Act.)

As for the possibility that any group acting on this doctrine might misinterpret circumstances, such a possibility is, of course, one that we must accept in relation to all the rights possessed by groups. Here again, we cannot abolish the rights of groups because mistakes might be made in their application. We should not put people in jail now because they might possibly make a mistake about emergency circumstances in the future. Yet the conclusion is inescapable that that is precisely what we are doing when we say that a particular government cannot wait until plans have been laid. If the government will not wait for some physical evidence that *its* physical overthrow is intended, how can it claim there is a "clear and present danger" of physical violence against *itself?* A refusal to wait for evidence is a refusal of justice.

It would seem that such a government has become so extremely fearful for its own safety that it wants to go the length of prohibiting any talk of overthrow of government under any circumstances whatsoever. Yet it is perfectly clear that, were any actual emergency to arise, such attempted prohibitions would lose all practical effectiveness. This was the truth expressed in the seventeenth century by John Locke, certainly one of the greatest contributors to the development of the Anglo-Saxon democratic tradition. Locke was considering this very fear that recognition of the right of revolution would unduly encourage violent overthrow of government, when he wrote in his classic work, *Two Treatises of Civil Government:*

> "But it will be said that this hypothesis lays a ferment for frequent rebellion. To which I answer:
>
> "First: no more than any other hypothesis. For when the people are made miserable, and find themselves exposed to the ill usage of arbitrary power, cry up their governors as much as you will for sons of Jupiter, let them be sacred and divine, descended or authorized from Heaven; give them out for whom or what you please, the same will happen. The people generally ill treated, and contrary to right, will be ready upon any occasion to ease themselves of a burden that sits heavy upon them. They will wish and seek for the opportunity, which in the change, weakness and accidents of human affairs, seldom delays long to offer itself. He must have lived but a little while in the world, who has not seen examples of this in his time; and he must have read very little who cannot produce examples of it in all sorts of governments in the world.
>
> "Secondly: I answer, such revolutions happen not upon every little mismanagement in public affairs. Great mistakes in the ruling part, many wrong and inconvenient laws, and all the slips of human frailty will be borne by the people without mutiny or murmur. But if a long train of abuses, prevarications and artifices, all tending the same way, make the design visible to the people, and they cannot but feel what they lie under, and see whither they are going, it is not to be wondered at that they should then rouse themselves, and endeavor to put the rule in such hands which may secure to them the ends for which government was at first erected...."

The reader will not fail to notice the similarity which this reasoning, expressed by Locke in 1690, bears to that expressed by Thomas Jefferson in 1776. Indeed, not only is the reasoning the same but the very phrasing is in part identical, as in the sentence beginning, "But if a long train of abuses...." It is a historical fact that Locke, the great philosopher of the British revolution of the seventeenth century, was a teacher for Jefferson, the great philosopher of the American revolution of the eighteenth century. And it is also a historical fact that Marx and Engels, in their doctrine of revolution, were influenced by both Locke and Jefferson.

## THE MAJORITY AND "THE PROPITIOUS MOMENT"

As we have seen, Marx and Engels and their followers, Lenin and Stalin, emphasize essentially the same conditions and restrictions as do Locke and Jefferson: the government must have reached a point where it is an oppression or tyranny, unwilling or unable to carry out the will of the people. There must be deep-seated resentment among the masses of the people, not merely some minor grievances. The people must wait for weakness and breakdown of the existing government before they can take revolutionary steps to set up a better one. This is the gist of Lenin's thought when he speaks of those "way below" not wishing to go on in the old way and those "up above" becoming "incapable" of carrying on the old order, and when "the wants and sufferings of the oppressed classes become more acute than usual."

Abraham Lincoln expressed the same concept on more than one occasion. For example, in a speech in the House of Representatives on Jan. 12, 1848, he said:

> "Any people anywhere being inclined and having the power have the right to rise up and shake off the existing government, and form a new one that suits them better. This is a most valuable, a most sacred right—a right which we hope and believe is to liberate the world."

Again, in no less a document than his first Inaugural Address, on March 4, 1861, Lincoln said:

> "This country, with its institutions, belongs to the people who inhabit it. Whenever they shall grow weary of the existing government, they can exercise their constitutional right of amending it, or their revolutionary right to dismember or overthrow it."[2]

Thus it is impossible to understand how the position taken in the majority opinion of the Supreme Court in the Dennis case, as we have seen it set forth by Chief Justice Vinson, can be logically reconciled with the position taken by Locke, Jefferson, and Lincoln. If there is a right of revolution under certain circumstances, and the existence of that very right was the precondition to the sovereignty of our own government, how could we justify jail sentences for people on the ground that they teach belief in that right? Can we look

---

[2] For statements of this kind from numerous American authorities, see Chap. 11: Opinion of Mr. Justice Jackson.

upon the right of revolution as something that somehow ceased to exist after 1776? But how could such a restriction be justified? It would fly in the face of common sense, for it would be tantamount to declaring that no government could possibly become a tyranny again.

The reader will bear in mind a very important distinction which applies to our entire discussion. That is, no one could blame any government for arresting any individuals found plotting the violent overthrow of that government. Such a situation would be a very different thing from putting in jail persons who teach the doctrine that it is necessary to overthrow government under certain circumstances but against whom no evidence is even claimed that they are seeking violent overthrow of the present government under the present circumstances. It is clearly the latter situation we are dealing with in these trials. The accused were never charged with calling for any specific revolution anywhere or at any time, nor were they even charged with attempting to make any physical preparations for any specific revolution anywhere or at any time. What they were charged with was teaching a doctrine of revolution.

We said a while back in our discussion that, in examining this charge, we had these alternatives: We could either take into account the whole of that doctrine of revolution or we could try to base our judgment on only a part of it, as if the other part did not exist. We have seen that the latter alternative involves obvious moral and logical contradictions. And we have also seen that the only remaining alternative leads to a conclusion very clear on the moral and logical level: If we persist in putting people in jail for teaching that particular doctrine of revolution, we are repudiating our own philosophy and we are embarked upon the impossible attempt to cancel, by due process of law, our only birth certificate.

# 3  The Government's Case

## "Evidence" of Force and Violence

The heart of the government's case, in this trial as in all the trials of this type, turned out to be a series of quotations from the "classics of Marxism"—mainly, in fact, from the writings of Lenin and Stalin. It fell to me, as I have said, to examine these passages, each in the light of its context, to determine what relation they might have to the idea of violent overthrow of our government. The first of these excerpts was the one reported upon in the preceding chapter. After finishing with that, the questioning in court proceeded as follows:

Defense Counsel: Doctor, the prosecution has offered certain excerpts in evidence, one from Stalin's *Foundations of Leninism*.... Will you read that excerpt and then I will ask you a question on it?

The Witness: "In other words, the law of violent proletarian revolution, the law of the smashing of the bourgeois state machine as a preliminary condition for such a revolution, is an inevitable law of the revolutionary movement in the imperialist countries of the world....

"Therefore, Lenin is right in saying: 'the proletarian revolution is impossible without the forcible destruction of the bourgeois state machine and the substitution for it of *a new one*....' *(Selected Works,* Vol. VII, p. 124.)" *(Foundations of Leninism,* p. 56. Emphasis in original.)

Defense Counsel: The first question, Doctor, is: According to the Communist Party of the United States, what relation, if any, does the existence of a revolutionary situation have to that excerpt?

Government Counsel: Objected to.

The Court: Objection overruled.

The Witness: According to the teaching of the Communist Party of the United States the doctrine of the revolutionary situation which we referred to has a direct bearing upon the understanding of this passage, because it is accepted by die Communist Party of the United States that none of the events associated with a violent revolution, violent proletarian revolution, would or should take place except when a revolutionary situation is present.

Therefore, the events referred to in this passage—the smashing of the bourgeois state machine, the forcible destruction, and so on—would, in the understanding of the Communist Party of the United States, only apply or take place when there is first a revolutionary situation, and that revolutionary situation involves the breakdown of the existing forms of government to the extent where normal electoral procedure is not possible, and where there is majority support for the revolutionary step.

As the reader will see, this same situation emerged again and again in the excerpts presented in evidence by the government. That is, it seemed to be presumed by the government that any reference to force and violence was in itself illicit and an indication of criminal intent. Indeed, such passages, read out in isolation from their context, have a portentous and conspiratorial sound, and to those not familiar with Marxism generally (a group including, in our country at any rate, practically all juries and most judges and lawyers), seem to suggest an acceptance of indiscriminate violence.

But the whole point is, under what conditions is this violence conceived of? Anyone who reflects will realize that any system of social philosophy that deals with basic issues concerning the state and government is bound to talk about revolution, insurrection, force and violence. If it did not, it would simply not be confronting the problems of the real world, since there have been so many very important revolutions in history, in our own cultural tradition (the British revolution of the seventeenth century and the American revolution of the eighteenth century, for example) and in the tradition of every culture. It is too much to expect either that revolutions will simply be ignored or that they will simply be condemned in blanket fashion.

## "EVIDENCE" OF FORCE AND VIOLENCE

Thus, if one reads the works of figures like John Locke, Thomas Jefferson, Abraham Lincoln, one can find plenty of discussion of forcible overthrow of government. In fact, Jefferson went so far as to say, in referring to the armed insurrection known as Shays' Rebellion which took place in Massachusetts in 1786:

> "God forbid we should ever be twenty years without such a rebellion. The people cannot be all, and always, well informed. The part which is wrong will be discontented, in proportion to the importance of the facts they misconceive. If they remain quiet under such misconceptions, it is a lethargy, the forerunner of death to the public liberty.... And what country can preserve its liberties, if its rulers are not warned from time to time, that this people preserve the spirit of resistance? Let them take arms. The remedy is to set them right as to facts, pardon and pacify them. What signify a few lives lost in a century or two? The tree of liberty must be refreshed from time to time, with the blood of patriots and tyrants. It is its natural manure."

These words were written by Jefferson in 1787 in one of his letters to William S. Smith. As he saw it, those who took up arms against the state in Shays' Rebellion acted largely on a misconception of the facts and of the real intentions of the government. Even so, he reasons, it is better that they should have rebelled, since if they had not done so when they *thought* they were being tyrannized over it would have meant that they would have done nothing even if they were *actually* being tyrannized over. And that would have meant that the spirit of liberty had died among them.

It is with these considerations in view that he says, "God forbid we should ever be twenty years without such a rebellion." This thought, however, goes far beyond the doctrine expressed in the classics of Marxism. As the reader can judge for himself in the light of our examination, the Marxian doctrine would justify revolution only where the actual facts demonstrate that the existing government is unwilling to carry out the majority will and where that government has already broken down to the point where it is no longer able to carry out its normal functions. The conclusion is inescapable that Marx would have regarded this "timetable" thesis of Jefferson as an example of *putschism,* that is, of a belief in excessive or indiscriminate insurrection, and therefore as something to be rejected because it went too far.

The conclusion is also inescapable that under the interpretation so far given to the Smith Act by the Supreme Court Thomas Jefferson could be jailed more quickly than the Communist defendants. No Communist doctrine could be found (and none was ever alleged by the prosecution) setting an actual time limit within which a revolution should occur in this country. Yet that is exactly the thought expressed in this portion of Jefferson's writings. Have we then reached the point where we are being asked to regard thoughts expressed by our greatest American political philosopher as dangerous, disloyal, un-American, and criminal?

When Jefferson formulated the question "What signify a few lives lost in a century or two?" he had in mind, of course, an implied comparison. That is, what signify a *few* lives lost in the struggle against tyranny, or what was considered to be tyranny, as compared with the *many* lives destroyed by the perpetuation of tyranny where the people are unable to summon enough courage and strength to throw it off? He expressed something of this same idea when, in 1793, referring to the French revolution, he wrote in a letter to William Short:

> "In the struggle which was necessary, many guilty persons fell without the forms of trial, and with them, some innocent. These I deplore as much as anybody, and shall deplore some of them to the day of my death. But I deplore them as I should have done had they fallen in battle. It was necessary to use the arm of the people, a machine not quite so blind as balls and bombs, but blind to a certain degree. A few of their cordial friends met at their hands the fate of enemies. But time and truth will rescue and embalm their memories, while their posterity will be enjoying that very liberty for which they would never have hesitated to offer up their lives. The liberty of the whole earth was dependent on the issue of the contest, and was ever such a prize won with so little innocent blood?"

Thus, argues Jefferson, even though people are bound to make mistakes in revolutions, mistakes which cost some innocent lives, that situation is preferable to the attempt to deprive them of the instrumentality of revolution in general. Two reasons evidently led him to this conclusion. One was that many more lives are sacrificed under a tyranny like the *ancien regime* in France than during a revolution. The other was that to forbid revolution as such was to run the risk of offering a perpetual lease on life to a tyrannical government. These are but a few of the passages discussing violent revolution which could be cited (but apparently not in court!) from the writings of a founding father of our own tradition. Passages bearing on the same subject, though with differing opinions, could be quoted from the writings of ancient thinkers like Plato and Aristotle and a whole host of schools and movements both before and after them.

Were this to be done, the lay reader might easily be given the impression that the Jeffersonian, and many another, school of thought was so preoccupied with the theme of force and violence that it scarcely dealt with anything else. This would be just as untrue of Jefferson as of Marx, Engels, Lenin, and Stalin. Anyone who actually read twenty or thirty volumes of Marxian "classics" would find only a small portion of them concerned with the question of violent insurrection. He would find detailed discussions of economics, political theory, sociology, ontology, methodology, ethics, history, philology, literature, and esthetics, among other things.

However, it is difficult to see how the average member of a jury would be in any position to appreciate this sort of fact. In view of the procedures followed in these trials, such a member is much more likely to gain the simple impression that the doctrine of Marxism-Leninism is all about force and violence and, on that very basis, is naturally to be regarded with suspicion.

Questioning continued in the following manner:

Defense Counsel: Turn to the second quotation, Doctor, Government's Exhibit 15, pages 19 and 20, Stalin's *Problems of Leninism*—
The Witness: Shall I read the passage?
Defense Counsel: Yes.
The Witness: It begins on page 19.
"Can such a radical transformation of the old bourgeois system of society be achieved without a violent revolution, without the dictatorship of the proletariat? Obviously not. To think that such a revolution can be carried out peacefully within the framework of bourgeois democracy, which is adapted to the domination of the bourgeoisie, means one of two things. It means either madness, and the loss of normal human understanding, or else an open and gross repudiation of the proletarian revolution."

Defense Counsel: What connection, if any, does that have with the view of the Communist Party of the United States as to the necessity of a revolutionary situation?...

The Witness: It has a direct relationship. That is to say, the teaching of the Communist Party of the United States in respect to the principle of a revolutionary situation has a direct bearing upon the meaning of this passage because the teaching of the Communist Party of the United States follows the doctrine of Lenin that none of these things would take place except in the presence of a revolutionary situation.

The violence referred to in this passage, the impossibility of carrying out peacefully within the framework of bourgeois democracy, and so on—these statements in the passage have reference to what happens in the course of a violent revolution. But it is of course understood and known to those writers and those who follow the principles of the Communist Party in the United States that this passage must be taken in connection with the other passages which state clearly that there are preconditions to any of these things taking place, and that those preconditions involve an absolute necessity of a certain kind of situation in which there is sufficient breakdown of the normal processes of government to make adequate electoral processes impossible, and in which there is majority support for the revolutionary step.

Defense Counsel: Page 9 of Government's Exhibit No. 16, *The History of the Communist Party of the Soviet Union,* had a passage read in evidence. I hand you Government's Exhibit 16 and direct your attention to page 9, the language beginning with the words, "Marx and Engels taught ..."

The Witness: Yes, I see. I quote:

"Marx and Engels taught that it was impossible to get rid of the power of capital and to convert capitalist property into public property by peaceful means, and that the working class could achieve this only by revolutionary violence against the bourgeoisie, by a *proletarian revolution,* by establishing its own political rule—the dictatorship of the proletariat—which must crush the resistance of the exploiters and create a new, classless Communist society." (Italics in original.)

Defense Counsel: Does the Communist Party of the United States advocate beginning to do any of the things stated there?

Government Counsel: Objected to. He doesn't know what they advocate, sir.

The Court: Objection overruled.

# "EVIDENCE" OF FORCE AND VIOLENCE

The reader will notice that the prosecution, in raising objections to my testimony, tried to take the rather odd line that since I was not myself a Communist I could not know what the doctrines of Communism were. This strange thesis, which would have had the novel effect of rendering objective scholarship superfluous in an examination of doctrines, was rejected by the court and these objections were consistently overruled.

> The Witness: The Communist Party of the United States does not advocate the doing of any things mentioned in this paragraph as such.
> Defense Counsel: What is the position of the Communist Party of the United States in respect of that quotation?
> Government Counsel: Objected to.
> The Court: Overruled.
> The Witness: The teaching of the Communist Party of the United States is that these things will happen only in a revolutionary situation, that is, in a situation in which there is already sufficient breakdown of all normal processes in government operation to make impossible the holding of normal or adequate electoral procedures; and also in which there is majority support for the revolutionary step contemplated.
> Defense Counsel: Does the Communist Party of the United States, in connection with the violence mentioned in that paragraph, teach whence such violence will come?
> The Witness: Yes, it does.
> Defense Counsel: What does it teach in respect of that?
> Government Counsel: That is objected to.
> The Court: Objection overruled.
> The Witness: The teaching of the Communist Party of the United States is that this violence comes from the resistance of the minority who are opposed to some radical change which represents the will of the majority, and that that resistance is what precipitates the violence.
> Defense Counsel: Now, I ask you to return to Stalin's *Foundations of Leninism,* which is Government Exhibit No. 7, and go to pages 55 and 56. I direct your attention to page 55 of *Foundations of Leninism,* and ask you to read that; then I will ask you a question about it.
> The Witness: I quote from *Foundations of Leninism,* page 55.
> "Marx's qualifying phrase about the Continent gave the opportunists and Mensheviks of all countries a pretext for proclaiming

that Marx had thus conceded the possibility of the peaceful evolution of bourgeois democracy into a proletarian democracy, at least in certain countries outside the European continent (England, America)." Shall I go on?

Defense Counsel: Yes.

The Witness: "Marx did in fact concede that possibility, and he had good grounds for conceding it in regard to England and America in the seventies of the last century, when monopoly capitalism and imperialism did not yet exist, and when these countries, owing to the special conditions of their development, had as yet no developed imperialism and bureaucracy. That was the situation before the appearance of developed imperialism. But later, after a lapse of thirty or forty years, when the situation in these countries had radically changed, when imperialism had developed and had embraced all capitalist countries without exception, when militarism and bureaucracy had appeared in England and America also, when the special conditions for peaceful development in England and the United States had disappeared—then the qualification in regard to these countries necessarily could no longer hold good." Shall I proceed?

Defense Counsel: Well, that is enough. Now I ask you, does the Communist Party teach or advocate that simply because that exception no longer exists it is not necessary that there be a revolutionary situation before there can be any possibility of a revolution?

Government Counsel: Objected to.

The Court: Objection overruled.

The Witness: No, certainly not; the Communist Party of the United States does not teach that just because these exceptions no longer hold in the sense pointed out in this passage, that it is no longer necessary to have the preconditions of a revolutionary situation. The two propositions have very little to do with each other. One is the tinning to the possibility that Marx did, that under certain conditions in certain countries, like the United States, England, and Holland, a peaceful transition to socialism and communism is possible, and that principle has never been abandoned in the writings of the leaders of the Communist Party of the United States, or the Communist Party of any country.

What is then pointed out is that the conditions for peaceful transition disappeared in certain countries at certain times, but that does not mean that a violent transition should take place in the absence of the conditions of a revolutionary situation. It means that if a violent transition takes place in any one of those countries it can take place only according to the doctrines of Marxism-Leninism, when there are present, one, sufficient breakdown of normal processes of government so that adequate and peaceful elections are no longer possible and, two, when the revolutionary step has the support of the majority.

The reader will meet this situation more than once in following out these issues. Apparently the prosecution had jumped to the conclusion that if Marxists believe that a peaceful transition to Communism is not possible in a certain country at a certain time they must believe that all the conditions of a revolutionary situation exist in that country at that time. But such reasoning is completely lacking in validity.

Marx and Lenin make it clear that a peaceful transition is possible, in their view, where the parliamentary tradition is strong enough to offer dependable means of carrying out the majority will should that will be for a really radical change. And they make it equally clear that the absence of such a condition, such a possibility of peaceful transition, is in no sense enough to constitute a revolutionary situation. As we have repeatedly seen, they insist that for the revolutionary situation to emerge not only must there be an absence of peaceful means to carry out the majority will, if that will should be for a radical change, but the majority will must actually be for the radical change.

It is plain enough that these are two separate conditions. According to the Marxian view, they must both obtain before revolution could take place. All that Lenin and Stalin said was that one of them (the absence of peaceful means) could be inferred at the time they wrote. But one condition is not sufficient for a revolution, and no call to any such action was ever made in the entire history of the party in this country.

The prosecution also seemed to imagine that Lenin and Stalin, in holding that conditions of peaceful transition to Communism did not exist in the United States in their day, were thereby making an assertion which somehow committed them and their followers to the same judgment for the entire future. But anyone will realize upon a moment's reflection that, just as Lenin and Stalin pointed out that Marx was right for the time he wrote but that conditions subsequently changed, so someone else at a later day might point out that conditions had changed again, and a peaceful transition was once more possible. The political history of every country has ups and downs in matters of this kind.

Also, it would be impossible to argue that a leader's view could never be changed, for the very premise here is that Marx's view was changed. In the terminology of the Communist movement, the "exceptions" which Marx made for the United States, England, and Holland, where he felt the conditions of peaceful transition were present in his day, became known as the doctrine of "exceptionalism." Thus the questioning continued in the following vein:

> Defense Counsel: There are those in the Communist Party who have recognized the fact that Lenin discarded the doctrine of exceptionalism, previously stated by Marx; that is so, isn't it?
>
> The Court: Do you know whether there are those in the Communist Party?
>
> The Witness: I know, Your Honor, that—
>
> The Court: All right.
>
> The Witness:—the leaders of the Communist Party of the United States of America, who have emphasized that this exceptionalism noted by Marx has now disappeared, that none of those leaders of the Communist Party of the United States of America have claimed that that means that it is no longer necessary to have a revolutionary situation.
>
> Defense Counsel: Or does it mean, either, that a peaceful evolution is not possible?
>
> Government Counsel: Objected to....
>
> The Court: Objection overruled....
>
> The Witness: It is quite true that this does not in any way mean that in the view of the Communist Party of the United States a peaceful transition might not be possible in the future. One of the fundamental principles of the teachings of Marxism-Leninism, emphasized and restated by the Communist Party of the United States, is that all those conditions change, social conditions change, and that we cannot take the situation which exists in any one country at any one time as a static model for situations in other countries. May I quote a passage in that respect?
>
> Defense Counsel: If you will.
>
> The Witness: In *"Left-Wing" Communism, an Infantile Disorder,* on page 73 we have the following statement from Lenin:

"As long as national and state differences exist among peoples and countries—and these differences will continue to exist for a very long time even after the dictatorship of the proletariat has been established on a world scale—the unity of international tactics of the Communist working class movement of all countries demands, not the elimination of variety, not the abolition of national differences (that is a foolish dream at the present moment), but such an application of the *fundamental* principles of Communism (Soviet power and the dictatorship of the proletariat) as will *correctly modify* these principles in *certain particulars,* correctly adapt and apply them to national and national-state differences. The main task of the historical period through which all the advanced countries (and not only the advanced countries) are now passing is to investigate, study, seek, divine, grasp that which is peculiarly national, specifically national in the *concrete manner* in which each country *approaches* the fulfillment of the *single* international task, the victory over opportunism and 'Left' doctrinairism within the working class movement, the overthrow of the bourgeoisie, and the establishment of a Soviet republic and a proletarian dictatorship." (Italics in original.)

In the same work, speaking to the same point, Lenin says on page 42: "Of course, no parallel can be drawn between conditions in Russia and conditions in Western Europe."

Defense Counsel: This revolutionary situation that you talk about as being a precondition for revolution, does the Communist Party teach that such a revolution can be brought about by it, or by classes, or by people?

The Witness: No, the teaching of the Communist Party of the United States is that the fundamental preconditions of a revolutionary situation are independent of the will not only of parties, but of classes, as I quoted previously from *The War and the Second International,* by Lenin, on page 13....

Defense Counsel: Doctor, at page 520 of the record the prosecution introduced a quotation from the book *Strategy and Tactics,* Government's Exhibit No. 17. I hand you that book at page 20, and ask you to read the part marked.

The Witness: I quote: "From a study of the objective processes of capitalism in their development and decline, the theory of Marxism arrives at the conclusion that the fall of the bourgeoisie and the seizure of power by the proletariat, and the replacement of capitalism by socialism, are inevitable. Proletarian strategy may be considered truly Marxist only when it makes this fundamental conclusion of the theory of Marxism the basis of its operations."

Defense Counsel: What relationship does that have to whether or not the Communist Party of the United States advocates force and violence?

Government Counsel: Now, if the Court pleases, that is objected to. Again there is no possible foundation for the witness.

The Court: Objection overruled.

The Witness: This passage has the following relationship, in the teachings of the Communist Party of the United States, to the advocacy of force and violence to overthrow the government. The understandings of the Communist Party of the United States in its teachings—

Government Counsel: Excuse me just a moment. Doctor, I beg your pardon. Are you using notes at this point?

The Witness: No, I am not using notes.

Government Counsel: I wasn't sure, because you were looking down.

The Witness: No, I have the book in front of me from which I quoted. The teaching of the Communist Party of the United States, following the principles laid down by Marx, Engels, Lenin, and Stalin, emphasizes that before these events take place, which are mentioned in this passage—the fall of the capitalist system, the seizure of power by the proletariat, and so on—before these events take place, there would have to be a revolutionary situation, one aspect of which is that the existing government would have reached the point where it was no longer capable of carrying on normal functions and normal electoral procedures, and where the majority were in support of the revolutionary step.

Defense Counsel: I now direct your attention to Government's Exhibit No. 12, Lenin's *State and Revolution,* a quotation from which the prosecution offered in the record at pages 611 and 612. Page 53 of *State and Revolution* is marked. Will you read the passage as it has appeared in that book, and as previously read in evidence?

The Witness: I quote the passage, which is itself a quotation from Engels.

" 'Have these gentlemen ever seen a revolution? Revolution is undoubtedly the most authoritative thing possible. It is an act in which one section of the population imposes its will on the other by means of rifles, bayonets, cannon, *i.e.,* by highly authoritative

## "EVIDENCE" OF FORCE AND VIOLENCE 65

means, and the victorious party is inevitably forced to maintain its supremacy by means of that fear which its arms inspire in the reactionaries. Would the Paris Commune have lasted a single day had it not relied on the authority of the armed people against the bourgeoisie? Are we not, on the contrary, entitled to blame the Commune for not having made sufficient use of this authority? And so: either—or: either the anti-authoritarians do not know what they are talking about, in which case they merely sow confusion; or they do know, in which case they are betraying the cause of the proletariat. In either case they serve only the interests of reaction.'"

That is the end of the inner quote from Engels.

Defense Counsel: My question is, does the Communist Party of the United States treat that and use that as an advocacy of violence?

Government Counsel: If the Court pleases, that is asking a specific question as to what the Communist Party of the United States uses in its teachings.

The Court: Objection overruled.

The degree of irony in this line of objection by the prosecution will be appreciated if the reader reflects upon the fact that the prosecution itself never claimed anything was taught by the Communist Party besides the doctrines found in the books under discussion! It was the prosecution who brought these books into court. It was they who said the Communist Party was teaching these books. It was they who selected these passages and who exhibited them as the "evidence" (the only evidence) of intent to overthrow the government by force.

Then, when the passages are analyzed by an expert witness in terms of their context and meaning and it is shown that that meaning does not include any necessity that the United States government be overthrown by force, the prosecution talks as if there were some doubt "as to what the Communist Party uses in its teachings," as if some secret or esoteric teaching materials were in question. If such were the case, where would be the evidence to prove what *those* teachings were? But the prosecution never even alleged that there were any such special teachings. The only teachings they alleged were those they indicated in the passages they themselves selected.

Thus their reasoning followed this strange pattern: The accused are guilty of criminal conspiracy because they teach and accept these doctrines. You say these doctrines do not necessitate any criminal conspiracy? But how do you know what doctrines they teach? It was almost as if the prosecution had forgotten that they themselves had placed in evidence the pages and pages of doctrine taught by the accused.

Since the "evidence" thus reduced itself to the teachings in the Marxian books, it was necessary to take account of the books as a whole and to judge each passage in relation to its context. Hence my answer to the question about the selection quoting Engels was as follows:

> The Witness: No, the Communist Party of the United States does not teach this passage as an advocacy of violent overthrow of the government of the United States. The Communist Party of the United States teaches that this passage of Engels correctly outlines the conditions and happenings when a revolution takes place. The passage emphasizes that when a revolution takes place, a revolution of this character, a violent revolution, there is the use of rifles and bayonets and cannon and so on and so forth; and that did take place in the violent revolution which is historically known as the Paris Commune.
>
> At the same time, there is no abandonment of the principle of the revolutionary situation within this passage or in any other writings of the Communist Party of the United States which have any doctrinal significance. There is no abandonment of the principle that before any of these revolutionary events takes place there must be what is known to them as a revolutionary situation, and that revolutionary situation means there must be present the breakdown of normal governmental processes to the point where normal elections are not possible, and there must be support of the majority for a revolutionary step.
>
> Defense Counsel: Has any Communist writer of any significance in the United States of America taken the position that any such conditions exist in the United States as would warrant what Engels is talking about here?
>
> The Witness: No.
> Government Counsel: Objected to.
> The Court: Objection overruled.
> The Witness: There is no such Communist writer in the United States.

Defense Counsel: I next direct your attention to Government's Exhibit No. 30, Lenin's *Proletarian Revolution and Renegade Kautsky,* quotations of which appear on page 1048 of the record, and it is on page 21 of that book, *Renegade Kautsky.* It starts down from the words "The revolutionary dictatorship" and ends with "America now."

The Witness: I see. "The revolutionary dictatorship of the proletariat is violence against the bourgeoisie; and the necessity for such violence is *particularly* created as Marx and Engels have repeatedly explained in detail (particularly in *The Civil War in France,* and in the Preface to it) by the existence of militarism and bureaucracy. But it is precisely these institutions that were nonexistent in England and America in the seventies of the nineteenth century when Marx made his observations (they do exist in England and America now)." (Emphasis in original.)

The reader will recognize here the same point that concerned us a while earlier in relation to the doctrine of "exceptionalism." The prosecution, in introducing this passage, had evidently relied on the same reasoning which we examined in the earlier instance. Thus the questioning proceeded along similar lines:

Defense Counsel: Now, in respect of that excerpt, Doctor, does the Communist Party in America teach that a revolutionary situation need not exist as a precondition for revolution if those conditions [militarism, bureaucracy] do?

Government Counsel: Objected to.

The Court: Objection overruled.

The Witness: The Communist Party of the United States does not teach that because these conditions have ceased to exist in the United States—that is, the conditions that made possible in the past a peaceful transition—the Communist Party of the United States does not teach that because of those changes a revolutionary situation is no longer necessary in order to have a proletarian revolution.

Defense Counsel: Does any Communist writer of any responsibility in America take the position that the mere existence of militarism and bureaucracy, if it does exist in America, is sufficient to warrant a revolution?

Government Counsel: Objected to.

The Witness: Absolutely not.

The Court: Objection overruled.

Defense Counsel: Will Your Honor indulge me for a moment while we bind these things up? Doctor, I call your attention to Government's Exhibit No. 40, Lenin's *The Paris Commune,* an excerpt from which appears on page 1735 of the record, the excerpt being from page 51 of that Government's Exhibit No. 40, reading "Why do we need," etc.

The Witness: "Why do we need a dictatorship when we have a majority? And Marx and Engels explain: In order to break down the resistance of the bourgeoisie; in order to instill the reactionaries with fear; in order to maintain the authority of the armed people against the bourgeoisie; in order that the proletariat may forcibly suppress its enemies!"

Defense Counsel: Does that, according to the teaching of the Communist Party of the United States, represent an abandonment of their position as to the necessity of the revolutionary situation that you have described?

The Witness: No, it does not represent an abandonment of that position. In understanding this passage, what is above all necessary is to understand the meaning of the term "dictatorship" to the Communist Party of the United States. The meaning of this term "dictatorship" is as follows: It is a synonym, as they use it, for any form of government which relies upon an enforcement apparatus.

As they use the word "dictatorship," therefore, it is not the case that some governments are dictatorships and some governments are not. All governments which rely upon an apparatus of enforcement—the police, jails, prison, army, and so on—are called dictatorships, because the use of force, legal force, is a form of physical dictation rather than moral or intellectual persuasion.

Consequently, when they say "We need a dictatorship even though we have a majority," what they are saying in their own view is "Even though we have a majority we need an apparatus of enforcement, because there are those who break the law."

They feel that the bourgeoisie will be impelled to break the law when there is a proletarian government in power, and they contemplate the necessity of using an apparatus of force, a dictatorship, police, jails, etc., in order to enforce the law against those who would be impelled to break the law.

Defense Counsel: Does the word "dictatorship" in and of itself mean the same thing when it is used as dictatorship of the bourgeoisie and as dictatorship of the proletariat?

## "EVIDENCE" OF FORCE AND VIOLENCE

The Witness: Yes, the term has a common meaning, modified, of course, in one case by the succeeding phrase "of the bourgeoisie," and, in the other, "of the proletariat"; but "dictatorship" means in their literature a governmental apparatus of enforcement. Consequently, it does not have the connotation of a minority. Whether the government represents the will of the minority or majority, in their view as long as it uses an apparatus of physical enforcement through the police and jails it is a dictatorship—in one case, a dictatorship of the majority, in another case a dictatorship of the minority.

It is very necessary to understand that general usage of the word "dictatorship" in their culture, because in this country and in England—in the English-speaking countries—the word "dictatorship" has other connotations, of a minority.

Government Counsel: If the Court pleases, I think we are getting far away from the teachings of the Communist Party.

Defense Counsel: Well, we are defining the words as they use them.

Here again the reader will find it difficult to see how a valid construction could be placed upon the government's reasoning in making such an objection. If the evidence being presented is the teachings of the Communist Party, it would seem to be the most obvious requirement of logic that the terms used in those teachings should be defined, especially terms likely to be misunderstood because they have different meanings in the popular mind. In fact, it had been my responsibility to do a considerable amount of work of that kind in connection with UNESCO projects, and in such books as *Soviet Philosophy* and *The Philosophy of Peace*. The evident need for that sort of thing is the premise of educational effort. On this occasion the Judge also felt the necessity of pursuing this type of analysis, and himself joined in the examination.

The Court: Well, let me ask you: In their understanding would you say the republican form of government in the United States was a dictatorship?

The Witness: Yes, Your Honor, in their understanding the form of government in this country is a dictatorship, and their form of government in their country is a dictatorship. The difference is, as they conceive it, in whose interests primarily they govern.

The Court: Who is the dictator?

Defense Counsel: Well, it isn't used that way.

The Witness: They take it in terms of a class rather than an individual leader. The usage of the word "dictatorship" in the sense of the individual leader was more characteristic of the nazi and fascist usages of the word.

The Court: How about the Russian type?

The Witness: The Russian Soviet conception is that the dictatorship which they have is the dictatorship of a class rather than of any individual.

The Court: They would not conceive of Stalin as a dictator?

The Witness: No, they would not, Your Honor. This is the contrast between the Soviet teaching and the nazi-fascist. For the nazi-fascist, the proud declaration of the philosophers of nazism was that Hitler was a dictator. They invented the term *Führerprinzip,* a German word meaning "principle of individual leadership." That principle is quite absent from Soviet teachings.

The Court: All right.

Defense Counsel: In the Communist view, particularly the Communist Party of the United States, which dictatorship represents in their view the dictatorship in the interests of the majority?

The Witness: The proletarian dictatorship.

Defense Counsel: Which, in their view, represents a dictatorship in the interests of the minority?

The Witness: A capitalist dictatorship, in their view.

Defense Counsel: Now, was the Communist Party of the United States, in speaking of any dictatorship, using that term so as to centralize power in any one man, or any one small group?

The Witness: May the question be repeated?

(Question read by the reporter.)

The Witness: Well, they might if they were talking about a dictatorship that had those particular conditions attached to them, but in simply using the word dictatorship there would be no necessary connotation of power being centralized in the hands of any one small group or any one single individual.

Defense Counsel: When they use, say, "dictatorship of the proletariat," do they mean rule by the majority?

The Witness: They do.

Defense Counsel: When the word "revolution" standing alone is used in the Communist Party of the United States, does it have a specific meaning?

"EVIDENCE" OF FORCE AND VIOLENCE 71

The Witness: It does.

Defense Counsel: What does it mean so used?

The Witness: It would be impossible to say without an examination of the context in which it was used in a particular case, because the word "revolution" is used by the Communist Party of the United States in the same variety of ways that it is used in our ordinary language. On one occasion it can be used to signify a possible social transformation such as the industrial revolution or the mechanical revolution. It can be used to signify a great fundamental change in scientific developments, such as the Copernican revolution—the revolution in our conception of the universe accomplished by the astronomer Copernicus, who established the theory that the earth moves around the sun rather than the sun moving around the earth.

They use the term in that sense, and in the sense of insurrection, violent revolution taking place in the social order in terms of which some radical transformation of the governing control of society is effected, so that you would have to examine the context of any particular passage to establish the sense in which they are using the term "revolution."

And the same situation obtains in the Russian language, and it therefore works its way into these translations. In the Russian language there is a general term for revolution, *revoliutsia,* which covers all the different connotations of the term. There is another term, *vosstanie,* which means, specifically, insurrection or violent revolution, and that distinction is in the English language in those terms, too.

Defense Counsel: In *State and Revolution,* the book written by Lenin, which of those two Russian words to indicate revolution was used?

The Witness: *Revoliutsia.* The title in Russian is *"Gosudarstvo i Revoliutsia,"* "State and Revolution."

The next topic of questioning proved to be one which, as the reader will see, was to arise in a number of different ways. Though it was subsequently to be dealt with in more detail, a basis was laid at this point.

Defense Counsel: There has been testimony here, Doctor, that the Communist Party, although stating that it can sanction revolution only when there is a majority, arrogates to itself the right to determine when and if there is a majority. Is there any writing by any authoritative member of the Communist Party of the United States who says that the Communist Party arrogates to itself the right to say when there is or is not a majority?

The Witness: No. The fundamental teaching on that point was decisively laid down by Lenin, and is taught by the Communist Party of the United States in terms expressed by Lenin in *The War and the Second International,* page 13, part of which we have previously quoted. I quote again. Lenin says:

"Without these objective changes"—objective changes—"which are independent not only of the will of separate groups and parties but even of separate classes, a revolution as a rule is impossible. The co-existence of all these objective changes is called a revolutionary situation."

And consequently, any party that arrogated to itself the right arbitrarily to determine on some subjective basis, irrespective of objective facts, when a revolutionary situation exists and when a revolution should take place would be violating the teachings laid down in the principles of Marxism-Leninism, emphasized by the Communist Party of the United States. It is objective conditions and facts which determine, not the arbitrary or subjective judgment of any group made irrespective of facts.

Defense Counsel: Doctor, what is the relationship between the theory of the Communist Party of the United States as to the right of revolution and the right of revolution stated in the Declaration of Independence?

Government Counsel: That, of course, is objected to, sir.

The Court: Objection sustained.

Defense Counsel: Cross-examine.

Thus our Declaration of Independence was once more pronounced *persona non grata* in a trial which took place in the city of Philadelphia, and in which the issue turned on the doctrine of revolution. After leaving the Federal Building I passed by Independence Hall, where that Declaration had been so proudly signed just one hundred and seventy-eight years before, in the same month of July. Not more than two long lifetimes had elapsed. In the Hall were carefully preserved for solemn display the mementos of that occasion—furnishings, trappings, the original Liberty Bell. In fact, plans were being consummated for the renovation of the building and the improvement of the grounds.

But what about the idea of the Declaration? What about its meaning? While the physical surroundings of its birth were thus being tended with loving care and the material objects involved were being treated as sacred relics, the idea of the Declaration was being denied entrance to a United States courtroom. To express it, to analyze it, even to quote a passage from it was being forbidden. It seemed grimly ironic that good people were so willing to do anything for the Declaration of Independence except declare it.

# 4   The Prosecution Persists

## Cross-examination by Government Counsel

Opposing counsel have, of course, full opportunity to cross-examine witnesses in regard to anything brought forward by them in the course of their testimony. I could therefore be sure that government experts would now do their best, in questioning me, to try to refute my analysis of the passages and quotations on which the government's case was based. I could also be sure that in this process they would bring into play and emphasize whatever they considered their strongest points.

The first of these that offered anything new came from page 20 of Stalin's *Problems of Leninism,* where Stalin was quoting from an article by Lenin—from the same article a portion of which I had earlier translated on the stand, as described at the beginning of Chapter II. Actually, the whole of the passage used by the prosecution consisted of Lenin's words, as cited with approval by Stalin. The latter enters into the wording of the excerpt only by way of supplying italics in order to emphasize certain phrases he evidently considered especially important. The reader will observe that in the first paragraph of the passage Lenin is summarizing a viewpoint with which he disagrees, while in the second paragraph he is expressing his own position. The excerpt was presented as follows:

> Government Counsel: Now I want to read you this passage:
> " 'First let the majority of the population, while private property is still maintained, that is, while the power and oppression of

capital are maintained, declare itself for the party of the proletariat. Only then can it, and should it, take power. That is what is said by' "—and here are italics—" *'petty-bourgeois democrats who call themselves "socialists" but are really the henchmen of the bourgeoisie.'* " That is followed by "[My italics.—J. S.]" which stands for Joseph Stalin, does it not?

The Witness: Yes, sir ...

Government Counsel: Then it goes on to say:

" *'But we say'* "—in italics, followed at the end by "[My italics.—J. S.]"—" *'But we say:* Let the revolutionary proletariat first overthrow the bourgeoisie, break the yoke of capital, break up the bourgeois state apparatus. Then the victorious proletariat will speedily gain the sympathy and support of the majority of the toiling nonproletarian masses by satisfying their wants at the expense of exploiters"

Now, Doctor, do you feel that there is more than one interpretation of those two paragraphs taken together?

The Witness: No, sir; I feel there is only one interpretation.

Government Counsel: All right.

The Witness: Shall I give it to you?

Government Counsel: All right, let me have it.

The Witness: The only interpretation you can make from those passages is that there is not a single word in them which would justify seizure of power by a minority of the population. Let us take it sentence by sentence.

Government Counsel: Yes, let's.

The Witness: In the first paragraph the writers whom Stalin (along with Lenin) is rejecting say: "First let the majority of the population, while private property is still maintained, that is, while the power and oppression of capital are maintained, declare itself for the party of the proletariat." ...

He goes on to say: "Only then can it, and should it, take power. That is what is said by petty-bourgeois democrats" and so on. He means that it is an impossible demand for anybody to make to say that the proletariat should never revolt until it demonstrates by a formal ballot that it has a majority, because that would mean that under the conditions where a formal ballot is impossible but a majority of the people want to revolt, they could not.

Government Counsel: Let me stop you there just a moment.

The Witness: Yes, sir ...
Government Counsel: You are saying that the words "declare itself" mean a formal vote by constitutional ballot in that context, are you?

The questioner, evidently, had correctly sensed that if the passage did refer to formal balloting under regular governmental auspices it would not strengthen his case. In other words, Lenin would be ruling out (under the conditions with which he was confronted) not any method of the majority "declaring itself" but only one kind of method—the conventional form of parliamentary balloting. (There are, of course, other ways in which the majority can make their wishes felt, if and when formal balloting is not possible for them.)

That Lenin had in mind precisely the conventional form of parliamentary balloting can be clearly seen from the context of the passage. On the same page (p. 482, Vol. VI, *Selected Works*), preceding the portion quoted, Lenin expresses the same thought in the following words:

> "In fact, all the representatives and supporters of the Second International, and all the leaders of the so-called German 'Independent' Social-Democrats, are thus deserting to the side of the bourgeoisie, inasmuch as, while giving verbal recognition to the dictatorship of the proletariat, they in practice, in their propaganda, inculcate the idea into the proletariat that it must obtain a formal expression of the will of the majority of the population under capitalism *(i.e.,* a majority of votes in the bourgeois parliament) before political power can pass into the hands of the proletariat."

Lenin's parenthesis toward the end of the sentence is, of course, an express clarification of the question that was raised. My reply to the inquiry about whether I was taking Lenin to mean a "formal vote" was therefore in the affirmative.

The Witness: I am, sir.
Government Counsel: Then let us take the following sentence and see how that fits in with it: "But we say."
The Witness: Now he says, "But we say: Let the revolutionary proletariat first overthrow the bourgeoisie"—and he does not say "while we have minority support."
Government Counsel: Let us finish that.

The Witness: Yes, but that is not the implication. He says: "Let the revolutionary proletariat first overthrow the bourgeoisie, break the yoke of capital, break up the bourgeois state apparatus." Not one word so far about doing this only with the minority. "Then," he says, "the victorious proletariat"—that may even be the majority—"Then the victorious proletariat will speedily gain the sympathy and support"—of whom? Of the majority of the population? No.—"of the majority of the toiling nonproletarian masses…" That is to say, nonproletarian groups in the population, the majority of those. The nonproletarian groups in the population may well be in the minority.

And he goes on to say that they will speedily gain the sympathy and support of the majority of the toiling nonproletarian masses by satisfying their wants and so on…. If he begins with the support, as he assumes, of the proletariat and a minority of the non-proletarian masses, he might well have a majority of the population. Therefore, there is not one word in these two paragraphs which would say that any revolution by force is justified when they have only minority support….

It would appear from this exchange that the questioner or his advisers must originally have formed the impression that the words "will speedily gain the sympathy and support of the majority of the toiling nonproletarian masses" meant the same as "will speedily gain the sympathy and support of the majority of the population." But there is, of course, a great difference between the two.

Interestingly enough, in the same volume (Vol. VI) of Lenin's *Selected Works* containing the article from which the prosecution quoted in this instance, there is also an article entitled "Marxism and Insurrection," actually a letter written by Lenin to the Central Committee of his party just about two months before the Bolshevik revolution of November 7, 1917. In it he further emphasizes his view that majority support is a precondition of any valid revolution. Speaking of conditions as they were during July, he says:

"We still lacked the support of the class which is the vanguard of the revolution.

"We still did not have a majority among the workers and soldiers of the capitals."

But of the time at which he is writing he says: "The picture is now entirely different."

"We have the following of the majority of a *class,* the vanguard of the revolution, the vanguard of the people, which is capable of carrying the masses with it.

"We have the following of the *majority* of the people...." (Lenin's italics.)

Of the earlier period Lenin says: "However, to have concluded that we could have seized power at that time would have been wrong because the objective conditions for a successful insurrection did not exist." He goes on to maintain that such conditions have now come about, stressing the changed attitude of the majority.

The questioning then shifted to another point.

> Government Counsel: I wonder if you would mind referring to Stalin's *Foundations of Leninism?*
>
> The Witness: [I have it here.] Yes, sir.
>
> Government Counsel: Page 22.
>
> The Witness: Yes, sir ...
>
> Government Counsel: Government's Exhibit 11. Now, you recall these passages here having to do with seizure of power starting ... at the bottom of page 22 ... It reads as follows, does it not?
>
> "The opportunists of the Second International have a number of theoretical dogmas to which they always revert as their starting point. Let us take a few of these.
>
> "First dogma: concerning the conditions for the seizure of power by the proletariat. The opportunists assert that the proletariat cannot and ought not to take power unless it constitutes a majority in the country."
>
> Now, that is what you say, is it not, is one of your conditions for the violent revolution?
>
> The Witness: No, sir; this sentence says or talks about the proletariat constituting a majority of the country.
>
> Government Counsel: Exactly.
>
> The Witness: It doesn't talk about the proletariat having the support of the majority.
>
> Government Counsel: Well, now, were we talking about support, or were we talking about being a majority?
>
> The Witness: We were talking about having the support of the majority. There is in social science well-known discussion as to whether in a given country the proletariat as a class is in a majority or not. In some cases, some countries, the proletariat—that

means the industrial working class—is in a majority as a class. In some countries, the proletariat, the industrial working class, is not as a class in a numerical majority, simply quantitatively, demographically, in terms of the population.

Government Counsel: Well, yes. All right, now, let me just—

The Witness: May I—I could add a word of clarification.

The Court: Yes, let the witness finish.

The Witness: Some of the "opportunists" were of the school of thought which felt that a revolution was inconceivable unless the country had progressed industrially to the point where the proletariat, that is, the industrial working class, were actually in the numerical majority of the population.

Government Counsel: I think that is clear.

The Witness: But that is a very different question; that has nothing to do with the Marxist-Leninist doctrine of the revolutionary situation. The Marxist-Leninist doctrine of the revolutionary situation does not say that the proletariat as a class must constitute a majority of the population. It says that the proletarian revolution must have the support of the majority of the population, partly from the proletariat, partly in some cases from the nonproletarian toiling masses, to use that weird terminology.

Government Counsel: That point was just exactly what we are coming to, Doctor.

The Witness: Yes, sir.

Government Counsel: Now, the next sentence reads:

"No proofs are adduced, for there are no proofs, either theoretical or practical, that can justify this absurd thesis. Let us assume that this is so, ... Lenin replies to these gentlemen of the Second International; but suppose a historical situation has arisen (a war, an agrarian crisis, etc.) in which the proletariat, constituting a minority of the population, has an opportunity to rally around itself the vast majority of the laboring masses; why should it not take power then?"

The Witness: Exactly.

Government Counsel: That is what it says, isn't it?

The Witness: Yes, sir; that is the very point.

Government Counsel: Yes; it is my point, too.

The Witness: I imagine one of us misunderstands. I say it is my point, in the sense that he is clearly saying there that even though the proletariat numerically might constitute a minority of the population by count, it could very well have the support of a sufficient group of nonproletarians to constitute majority support for its program.

Government Counsel: Well, Doctor, that passage does not say that it does have the support of the majority, does it?

The Witness: The whole passage is hypothetical. Nothing is said—it is all if. If this is the case, then what will we do? And if that is the case, should we wait? It is all hypothetical.

Government Counsel: Well, sometimes a hypothetical case is a clear way of teaching, isn't it?

The Witness: It certainly is, and I think he is putting his point across very clearly.

Government Counsel: Let me just ask this again, about the part wherein the "situation has arisen ... in which the proletariat, constituting a minority of the population, has an opportunity to rally around itself the vast majority of the laboring masses; why should it not take power then?"

The Witness: Yes, sir. Then it would have majority support, you see. Then it would have—

Government Counsel: When?

The Witness: Beg your pardon?

Government Counsel: Do you think that an opportunity to rally around itself a majority means that it has the support at that time?

The Witness: Yes, I think in the political sense in which he is speaking, an opportunity to rally around itself means an opportunity to count on the support of the vast majority of the laboring masses.

Government Counsel: An opportunity to rally around itself?

The Witness: Yes, sir.

Government Counsel: Wouldn't it be an opportunity to get support? Isn't that what it says?

The Witness: Well, it doesn't say an opportunity to attempt to rally around itself. It says it has an opportunity to rally around itself the vast majority.

Government Counsel: All right. And what is "it" in the sentence, "Why should it not take power then?"

The Witness: I think it is the proletariat.

Government Counsel: Which by hypothesis is in the minority of the population, is that correct?

The Witness: In this case.

Government Counsel: All right.

The Witness: But, of course, I think he is referring there to the group that would exercise the actual functions of the party.
Government Counsel: Doctor, I think you have answered my question.
The Witness: Yes, sir.

Again it would seem likely that the questioner had formed rather strange impressions of the passages he was citing. He seemed to have overlooked the distinction between "constituting" a majority of the population and "having" majority support. He also seemed to think that anyone who spoke of "an opportunity to rally around" himself "the vast majority of the laboring masses" must necessarily be presuming that he did not at present have the support of those masses.

However, it is plain enough that one might have the support of a group simply in the sense that their will and desire were for a certain proposed step. But that might be very different from an actual opportunity to rally the group around oneself in the complex cooperative activity of carrying out the step. And that is exactly the sort of thing Lenin and Stalin were talking about when they spoke of the proletariat having an opportunity to rally around itself the majority of the laboring masses—the opportunity to *count* on their support in *action,* in the complex business of carrying out a revolution.

However, majority support for such a step, in the sense of desire and consent, was clearly, in their view, a precondition to embarking on the step at all, as the whole trend of their writings and those of the other leaders shows. But the questioner was not convinced, as his next question revealed.

Government Counsel: Now, Doctor, would you say that there is no other passage anywhere in the writings of Lenin and Stalin which puts revolution first, majority next, on the order of the day?
The Witness: Well, sir, I say there is not even one passage in the writings of Lenin, Marx, Engels, or Stalin which puts violent insurrection first and support of the majority second. And there are at least forty passages—
Government Counsel: All right.
The Witness:—which put majority support first, before any violent insurrection.
Government Counsel: Let me refer you, Doctor, to Volume X of Lenin's *Selected Works*.

The Witness: Yes.
Government Counsel: Do you have that?
The Witness: No, sir; I do not have it here.
Government Counsel: That is among the writings of Lenin you have read, I take it, Doctor?
The Witness: Yes, sir.
Government Counsel: I want to read you this passage. It starts—have you found page 163?
The Witness: Yes, I have.
Government Counsel: It starts as the first sentence under that heading, you see in the middle of the page ...

"The victory of Socialism (as the first stage of Communism) over capitalism requires that the proletariat, as the only really revolutionary class, shall fulfill the three following tasks. First-overthrow the exploiters, primarily the bourgeoisie as the principal economic and political representatives of the latter; utterly rout them; suppress their resistance; make it utterly impossible for them to attempt to restore the yoke of capital and wage slavery. Second—win over and bring under the leadership of the revolutionary vanguard of the proletariat, of its Communist Party, not only the whole of the proletariat, or the overwhelming, the enormous majority of the latter, but also the whole mass of toilers and those exploited by capital; educate, organize, train, and discipline them in the very process of the supremely bold and ruthlessly firm struggle against the exploiters; tear this overwhelming majority of the population in all capitalist countries from its dependence on the bourgeoisie; imbue it by means of its practical experience with confidence in the leading role of the proletariat and of its revolutionary vanguard. Third— neutralize, or render harmless, the inevitable vacillation between the bourgeoisie and the proletariat, between bourgeois democracy and Soviet power, of the class of small proprietors in agriculture, industry, and commerce—which is still fairly numerous in nearly all advanced countries, although it comprises the minority of the population—as well as the stratum of intellectuals, office employees, etc., which corresponds to this class.

"The first and second tasks are independent tasks, each requiring its own special methods of action toward the exploiters and toward the exploited. The third task emerges from the first two and merely requires the skillful, timely and flexible combination of the first and second types of method in accordance with the concrete circumstances in each separate case of vacillation."

CROSS-EXAMINATION BY GOVERNMENT COUNSEL

Now, the first and second tasks are said to be independent and—we turn back to the preceding page—the first was overthrow the exploiters; second, win over and bring under the leadership of the revolutionary vanguard those sections of the population mentioned, is that right?
The Witness: Yes, sir. May I comment upon that?
Government Counsel: I am just about to ask a question, Doctor.
The Witness: Yes, sir.
Government Counsel: Do you feel that that is more consistent with Stalin's statements in *Problems of Leninism over* your view that you have expressed?

The reader will easily detect in such a formulation a clear case of a "loaded question," that is, one which really assumes the point at issue. In this case, the issue is whether there is any difference between the analysis I gave of the Lenin-Stalin position and the view taken in this passage by Lenin. But the question was such that whether I answered it yes or no I would seem to be admitting that my own analysis was faulty. Thus, if I answered yes, I would be saying that my analysis of the Lenin-Stalin position was out of line with Lenin's own meaning. If I answered no, I would appear to be saying that Lenin's position was not the same as Stalin's on this point, in contradiction of my previous testimony.

This situation comes close to the classic example of what is known in logic as the fallacy of double question: "Have you stopped beating your wife? Answer yes or no." A man who never did beat his wife would falsely suggest his own guilt whichever way he replied, since yes would mean he has stopped now but did beat his wife in the past, whereas no would mean he is still beating her. To be fair, the "double question" must be broken up into two separate questions: (1) Have you ever beaten your wife? (2) If you answered the first question in the affirmative, have you now stopped?

Thus an objection was called for, and was instantly made.

> Defense Counsel: Well, I object to that, sir, because it assumes that there is a contradiction between the two.
> The Court: I think that is so, yes.
> Defense Counsel: I think that is argumentative.
> The Court: I think that is argumentative. Objection sustained.
> Government Counsel: Now, Doctor, you were asked this morning—

Defense Counsel: Unless there is a question about what was read, I move that the reading be stricken, sir.

The Court: Yes, I think that is well taken. You can't put any evidence in on cross-examination. If you read it, you must ask him about it....

Government Counsel: Do you feel that this passage from 163 to 164 is in agreement with the statement of Stalin quoting Lenin on pages 20 to 21, I believe it is, of *Problems of Leninism?*

The Witness: Yes, sir, I believe that it is. Lenin and Stalin are in absolute agreement on this teaching about revolution; and if you will allow me, I would like, if I may, to make a comment about this.

Government Counsel: I think your comments can go on redirect examination.

The Witness: I am sorry; yes.

Defense Counsel: I think he is entitled to explain what he means.

The Court: Yes, I think he ought to do that. This is pretty pertinent. We will hear your comment.

The Witness: Yes, sir; thank you. It seems to me that the heart of this passage—this rather long passage just read, in so far as the issue before us is concerned, whether Lenin suggests they should seize power with a minority—the heart of it is in this sentence: "Second—win over and bring under the leadership of the revolutionary vanguard of the proletariat, of its Communist Party, not only the whole of the proletariat, or the overwhelming, the enormous majority of the latter, but also the whole mass of toilers and those exploited by capital"; and so on.

A superficial reading of this passage might suggest to a reader unacquainted with the principles of Marxism-Leninism, or one who has not studied those principles to any extent, that he means they should seize power with a minority, with only minority support for that revolutionary step.

But I say there is a great distinction between winning over, bringing under the leadership of the Communist Party a certain group of people, and having the support of those people for a certain step. It is one thing to have the support of a lot of people for a certain step. They may give you their support but they may not really be won over, and they may not be considering themselves under your leadership, though they are willing to support your action in this particular. And I believe that is what he means: they have the support, in the sense of the consent. But to win them over to participation in a program, to bring them under the leadership of that party may be quite a different matter. So when he says we will win them over and bring them under our leadership, he is talking about a very much more complex process than the process simply of giving support or consent for one particular step.

Government Counsel: Is that your explanation, Doctor?

The Witness: Yes, sir.

If the reader will consider this situation from a logical standpoint, he will probably experience as much difficulty as I did in following the prosecution's reasoning. That is to say, even if the prosecution had been able to find one or two passages which seemed to justify revolution with only minority support, how much weight or significance would they have in the face of the overwhelming preponderance of passages which point to the necessity of majority support? In deciding what is the view of a given school of thought on any issue, judgment must of course be based on the great bulk of statements which point in one direction rather than upon some few exceptions which may seem to point the other way.

Not only must the factor of preponderance be taken into account. Judgment must also be based on which passages, if any, are *unequivocal* and permit of no possible ambiguity. As we have seen, each of the few passages advanced by the prosecution, when examined in the light of its context, failed to supply any clear proof whatever that forcible revolution was at any time intended with only minority support.

On the other hand, no possible statement could be clearer or less ambiguous than the kind cited on the other side, wherein Lenin says, for example, "We are not Blanquists; we are not in favor of seizure of power by a minority." *(Selected Works,* Vol. VI, p. 29. *Collected Works,* Vol. XX, p. 96; cited by Carr: *The Bolshevik Revolution,* Vol. I, p. 18.) The same must be said of such a statement as, "If a revolutionary party has not a majority among the front ranks of the revolutionary classes and in the country generally, there can be no question of insurrection." (Lenin: *Selected Works,* Vol. VI, p. 293.) Such passages are unequivocal in the highest conceivable degree, and it is surely significant that the prosecution in no way even tried to cast doubt on them or to explain them away.

Many more passages of that kind can be found in the teachings of Marxism-Leninism. Among additional examples are the following. In Vol. VI of his *Selected Works,* in *A Letter to the Comrades,* page 321,

Lenin says: "A military conspiracy is Blanquism *if* it is not organized by the party of a definite class; *if* its organizers have not reckoned with the political situation in general and the international situation in particular; *if* the party in question does not enjoy the sympathy of the majority of the people, as proved by definite facts..." (Emphasis in original.) As part of this same sentence, which is extremely long, Lenin adds a number of other conditions, any one of which would in his view stamp an insurrection as "Blanquism," and therefore contrary to Marxism, and emphatically to be rejected. Among the conditions which, if present, would make any armed uprising unacceptable in his eyes he puts the following: "...*if* the economic situation in the country offers any real hope of a favorable solution of the crisis by peaceful and parliamentary means." (Emphasis in original.)

In his work written in 1917, printed in the Little Lenin Library under the title, *The April Conference,* Lenin says on page 20:

"The government would like to see us make the first reckless step towards decisive action, as this would be to its advantage. It is exasperated because our party has advanced the slogan of peaceful demonstration. We must not cede one iota of our principles to the watchfully waiting petty bourgeoisie. The proletarian party would be guilty of the most grievous error if it shaped its policy on the basis of subjective desires where organization is required. We cannot assert that the majority is with us; in this case our motto should be: caution, caution, caution. To base our proletarian policy on overconfidence means to condemn it to failure."

The reader will note that these words were written by Lenin but six months before the revolution of November 7, 1917. They were part of an important speech which he delivered on May 7, 1917. The fact that even at that late date he was telling his followers, as a reason why he could not yet sanction any uprising, "We cannot assert that the majority is with us ..." is renewed evidence of how important that consideration was in his teachings. This passage also clearly indicates the reason why Lenin attached such great importance to that consideration. "The government," he says, "would like to see us make the first reckless step towards decisive action, as this would be to its advantage." It would be difficult to exaggerate the significance of that sentence for anyone who wants to understand the Leninist position on forcible revolution. As Lenin sees it, there is absolutely nothing to be gained by his own group from entering into any armed action that does not have majority support, for the simple reason that it has no chance of being really successful. As Lenin sees it, only the other side would gain from such an action.

Precisely the same reasoning was applied to individual or conspiratorial acts of terrorism. As early as 1902 Lenin wrote in his work, *What Is To Be Done?*: "*Svoboda* advocates terror as a means of 'exciting' the labor movement, and of giving it a 'strong impetus.' It is difficult to imagine an argument that disproves itself more than this one does! Are there not enough outrages committed in Russian life that a special 'stimulant' has to be invented?" (P. 75, Little Lenin Library edition, International Pub.) *Svoboda* (Freedom) was a periodical current at the time. Lenin's thesis throughout this work, as throughout his life, was that "what is to be done" is not terrorist acts against individuals, or adventurist uprisings on a minority basis, but the organizing of a strong political party based on a sound doctrine which would entertain the idea of forcible measures only when there were no other means to carry out the majority will, and when there was majority support for the forcible measures.

Indeed, as we have seen in a variety of contexts, this attitude towards the majority is something that runs throughout the history of Marxism, going back to its earliest productions. In *The Communist Manifesto,* for example, written jointly by Marx and Engels in 1848, in the early part of their careers, when the latter was twenty-eight years of age and the former thirty, it is stated: "All previous historical movements were movements of minorities, or in the interest of minorities. The proletarian movement is the self-conscious, independent movement of the immense majority, in the interest of the immense majority." (P. 20, International Pub., 1948.)

Nor, as we have seen, is Stalin in any way behindhand in emphasizing his agreement with this position. Typical of his attitude is the way in which he quotes with complete approval some of the same passages from Lenin which came under our examination. For example, in his *Foundations of Leninism* (p. 44, Little Lenin Library) Stalin repeats Lenin's words from *Left-Wing Communism: An Infantile Disorder,* again stressing their significance: " 'The fundamental law of revolution, which has been confirmed by all revolutions, and particularly by all three Russian revolutions in the twentieth century, consists in the following: it is not enough for revolution that the exploited and oppressed masses should understand the impossibility of living in the old way and demand changes; for revolution it is necessary that the exploiters should not be able to live and rule in the old way. Only when the "lower classes" *do not want* the old way, and when the "upper classes" *cannot carry on in the old* way—only then can revolution triumph'" (Emphasis in original.)

The reader will appreciate that when this passage mentions as a precondition of revolution that "the exploited and oppressed masses should understand the impossibility of living in the old way and demand changes," the group being referred to by Lenin as "exploited and oppressed masses" is the majority of the people in Lenin's teachings. Nothing is made plainer in Lenin's entire work than that he considers that under capitalism the majority of the people are the exploited and oppressed masses, that the upper classes are a minority group, and the lower classes a majority group. (Also, in Leninist terms lower classes=exploited and oppressed masses.) By no possibility could phrases like lower classes, oppressed masses, exploited masses, or toiling masses mean anything other than the majority of the people to Lenin and his followers.

Even one unfamiliar with Marxist-Leninist writings might gather the sense in which Lenin uses these terms from passages like the following, in his work *Can the Bolsheviks Retain State Power?* In the course of argument directed against one of his opponents, Lenin says: "And, most important of all, Mr. Peshekhonov does not understand that when he is forced to admit the justice of Bolshevism, to admit that its demands are the demands of the 'toiling masses,' i.e., of the majority of the population, he is thereby *surrendering* his whole position, the position of the petty-bourgeois democrats." (Selected Works, Vol. VI, p. 289. Emphasis in original.) Quite irrespective of who Mr. Peshekhonov was, or of the nature of his position however strong or weak, it is entirely clear from Lenin's manner of expression that he understands by such a term as "toiling masses" a majority of the population.

These are a few of the many additional excerpts that might be cited along these lines. In fact, a fair-sized book could probably be compiled consisting entirely of passages from the classics of Marxism-Leninism bearing upon the concept and role of the majority in that body of teachings.

The questioning now shifted to an area which was to be dealt with in some detail.

Government Counsel: Now, Doctor, regardless of the interpretation you say should be given to certain language of Stalin or

CROSS-EXAMINATION BY GOVERNMENT COUNSEL 89

Lenin, who determines whether a given majority exists in favor of the revolution?

The Witness: I am sorry; I didn't catch your question.

Government Counsel: Who determines whether a given majority exists in favor of the revolution?

The Witness: I should say objective conditions and facts would have to enter into that determination.

Government Counsel: And who evaluates those conditions and facts according to Communist teaching?

The Witness: The people involved.

Government Counsel: And who are the people involved?

The Witness: They would be in this case the majority of the people.

Government Counsel: You mean the majority itself decides whether it is a majority?

The Witness: In a revolutionary situation it would have to, because by definition in a revolutionary situation in this school of thought there is no possibility of a normal or precise vote. If there were such a possibility you wouldn't have a revolutionary situation.

Government Counsel: I am not asking about voting, Doctor. I am saying, who decides whether there is a majority in favor of this revolution?

The Witness: In asking that question you are necessarily asking about voting, because if there is no possibility of voting, then in this view it is the majority itself who must decide when it is in the majority by the other facts and conditions present in the situation. His point is that just because disordered times would make it impossible—

Government Counsel: Doctor, I am afraid you are volunteering something beyond the scope of my question there.

The Witness: I thought it would throw light.

Government Counsel: I am focusing on who decides. Now, you say that the majority itself decides whether it is the majority; is that your answer?

The Witness: My answer is that the principles of Marxism-Leninism state that when it is impossible, owing to disordered times, civil strife, civil war, or what not—when it is impossible to take an adequate vote, but the people need and want something, and feel that they need and want something, that then the people themselves have to decide when they have a majority, because there is no other alternative.Government Counsel: So he eliminated voting?

The Witness: No, it is only in those cases where—Government Counsel: No, under the situation. The Witness:—conditions have eliminated voting. Government Counsel: Conditions have eliminated voting? The Witness: Yes, sir.

The reader will remark that this is the sort of situation which, because of its very nature, is capable of leading to almost endless discussion. Under conditions where it is impossible to take a precise vote, who exactly decides when the majority is in favor of something? Who decided in the American revolution? Who decided in the French revolution, or in any revolution in history? Of course, were one to say that whenever no precise poll can be taken to show that a majority is really in favor then no revolution should take place, one would simply be saying that no actual revolution, including our own, should ever have taken place.

If one agrees to the principle that a revolution is valid under certain conditions, as long as it reflects the majority will, one cannot logically object to the teaching of that principle on the ground that a mistake might be made by some group as to whether the majority were really in favor of a revolutionary step. If the principle taught is that the revolution is valid only when objective conditions show that existing government has broken down and that the majority desire a radical change, what more can be demanded, in the light of all past history?

In emergencies, everyone must make his own decision; and if he is wrong he will have to pay for his mistake. But we cannot revoke human rights because mistakes might be made. It is quite clear from the content of Communist writings that Communists are not enamored of the idea of staging revolutions which are unsupported by the majority, for the very understandable reason that they would not be likely to be successful. Not only is this clearly seen in the principles of the movement but it is also quite consistent with the actual conduct of the Communists in this country, since they have never attempted even a single revolution.

But the government persisted in its attitude that somehow this was all a trick; a few leaders would be sure to push a button some day and a revolution would be precipitated in the absence of any objective conditions necessitating a revolution. As we have seen before, this amounts to saying: We think they will decide wrongly, so we propose to put them in jail now on the ground that they are taking it upon themselves to make a future decision which may be wrong.

Not only could such a procedure put practically anyone in jail; in this case it also ignores the fact that the group in question teaches that the decision should not be made except in the presence of necessary objective conditions, indicating and including majority support. And yet the whole basis of accusation in the case was nothing but the teachings of the group! Nevertheless, the questioning persisted along the same line.

>   Government Counsel: Now, are there some leaders who decide whether the majority wants it or not?
>   The Witness: They don't go into that in the teachings of the principles. The function of the leader, as opposed to others in this particular situation, I would assume to be the normal function of a leader. He would have to give guidance, he would have to give leadership. He would have to make proposals. I assume the normal functions of a leader are—
>   Government Counsel: Well, isn't the Communist Party teaching that the vanguard decides questions of this kind?
>   The Witness: No, sir. That the vanguard must take initiative action, that the vanguard must take the leadership, must propose, must direct, must raise the question, and so on. But the statement of Lenin, which I quoted earlier today, says these conditions must be objective; they are independent of the will of any particular group or party, or even any particular class. In other words, objective conditions must exist independent of the will of any leaders or of any small group of leaders or anything of that kind.
>   Government Counsel: Doctor, however they arise—someone has to decide whether they happened or not, do they not?
>   The Witness: They do, indeed.
>   Government Counsel: And who decides that?
>   The Witness: I would say the majority must decide it in those conditions, according to the teachings of this school.
>   Government Counsel: Now, do you deny that it is the principle of the Communist Party that the Communist Party decides whether there is a sufficient majority that exists?
>   The Witness: I would deny that it is a teaching of the Communist Party that the Communist Party decides when a sufficient

majority exists independently of objective conditions and independently of a majority of the population; yes, sir.

Government Counsel: Now, you mean, what you are saying is that the Communist Party decides, but they don't decide unless they are right? Is that what you mean?

The Witness: I mean they—I mean they enter into the decision, but it is not their subjective decision which makes a conformity to the teachings of Marxism-Leninism. The only thing that would conform to the teachings of Marxism-Leninism would be the participation of the party in that decision in the light of the objective facts which Lenin mentions, which are independent of the will of parties, groups, or even classes.

Government Counsel: Well, to express that a little more precisely, Doctor, do I understand you that the party does determine whether that majority exists, but that it is so all-knowing in its decision that it is never wrong?

The Witness: Oh, no. I think that would be naive and romantic to feel. I should never say that. But I say that according to the teachings of these principles, as reflected also in the teachings of the American Communist Party, it would never be correct to say that this group has set up the doctrine that the party decides these things in some sense that when the party makes up its mind, then that is that, irrespective of facts, irrespective of objective phenomena. The teaching is that the party can only decide and determine those things when certain objective conditions exist that are independent of the will of any of the parties concerned.

Government Counsel: All right, now, who decides whether those objective conditions exist or not?

The Witness: I would say the majority, according to their teachings. They will say the majority would—the teachings say the majority would have to enter into that decision. The facts, behavior, the conditions present would have to indicate majority support.

Government Counsel: Well, Doctor, the majority can't be articulate through all its mouths, can it? It must have someone to speak for it.

The Witness: Sometimes actions speak louder than words.

Government Counsel: Well, now, Doctor, I want to ask you this: Is this one of the propositions in the philosophy, as you term it, of Marxism-Leninism on which no scholars disagree?

## CROSS-EXAMINATION BY GOVERNMENT COUNSEL 93

The Witness: Which proposition are you referring to?
Government Counsel: With regard to whether or not the Communist Party is the one who decides whether a majority exists.

The Witness: Well, I think everybody would agree with that in a certain sense, that the Communist Party, according to the teachings of Marxism-Leninism, enters into this decision, and should take a leading part in it, and should lend organization and initiative to it; but they would all insist that the teachings of Marxism-Leninism maintain that the party cannot by itself or independently of objective facts arrive at any such decision, according to the principles of this school of thought.

Government Counsel: Do scholars agree or disagree as to whether the party undertakes to make that decision?

The Witness: There would be no disagreement that the party undertakes to participate in that decision, but if you mean by "make that decision"—make it irrespective of and independent of objective facts and conditions, I don't think that anybody would agree with you that that is the position taken in the teachings of Marxism-Leninism....

This was a matter about which the Judge showed special interest. On this occasion he joined in the examination in the following way:

The Court: Well, let me ask you this. Who makes this decision? It must be a human, fallible decision, must it not? On what you have said, must not the Communist Party of necessity make the decision, then, that the objective conditions are all right, that the majority is on their side? There is no hocus-pocus to this, is there? There must be a decision. There must be a fallible, human judgment, must there not?

The Witness: It is certainly a fallible, human judgment, Your Honor.

The Court: Now, who makes that human judgment? Doesn't the Communist Party?

The Witness: I am only afraid, Your Honor, by answering that question without qualification, that it might give rise to the impression that this school of thought makes it legitimate for the leaders of the Communist Party themselves, without any guiding or controlling facts, to make up their mind to that.

The Court: No, I don't see that. I don't see that. You say that the Communist Party aids, it is active on behalf of this movement, but you say it must be in connection with objective conditions that must obtain.

The Witness: Yes, sir.

The Court: Now, I say to you that we live in a realistic world. Who makes that judgment, that fallible human judgment that these conditions obtain?

The Witness: According to the teachings of this school, the people generally would enter into that judgment, the Communist Party members would enter into it, and the leaders of the Communist Party would enter into it, in the light of the conditions as they existed.

The Court: Now, who would say that the people are entering into it, that the majority are entering into it? Who makes the decision?

The Witness: Which specific decision now?

The Court: That the people are entering into it. You say the people must enter into it, that the Communist Party must enter into it?

The Witness: Yes, sir.

The Court: The majority must enter into it?

The Witness: According—

The Court: Now, who makes the judgment? Does the Communist Party make that judgment?

The Witness: Partly, I would say.

The Court: Who makes the other part?

The Witness: The rest of the people involved, the objective conditions involved. May I use an illustration, Your Honor?

The Court: Well, now, just a moment. How does the Communist Party know that? How can they divine that judgment of the majority?

The Witness: Well, I would think from the principles of this school what they have in mind is observation of behavior of the people, analyses of conditions, reports on the sort of thing the people are doing and saying, the kind of—

The Court: That is right. And from all that they make the judgment?

The Witness: From all that they make their part of the judgment; yes, sir. I would think that—

The Court: All right.

The Witness: Yes, sir.

The Court: I think we have to recess here. I have an appointment.

It is hard to see what there is about this particular point which should occasion such great difficulty. It would seem quite clear that if people have rights at all, they must naturally exercise their judgment as to when those rights are to be used. Do you grant people the right of self-defense? Do you grant them the right to smash the windows of a train to escape if there is an accident? If you do, then you are necessarily granting them the right to determine, as best they can, when the conditions have arisen which would warrant the exercise of such rights.

What would be the use of saying you granted them the rights if at the same time you insinuated that it would be a crime for them to take it upon themselves to decide when to exercise the rights? That would obviously be the same as saying they should never exercise the rights, especially in the case of a revolutionary situation, which, by definition, is such that normal voting is physically impossible.

If such a situation should arise, it would certainly follow that all groups, Communists included, would have to decide as best they could whether there was majority support for this or that possible revolutionary action. Were this denied, what meaning would attach to the "right of revolution"? How could it ever be exercised?

Of course, we all wish to guard as much as possible against people making mistakes in the exercise of their rights. We would all like to prevent hasty, irresponsible, or ill-considered decisions. But if "preventive" methods were to go the length of putting into jail everyone who might make an ill-considered decision in the use of his rights, who would remain out of jail? The very meaning of any "emergency" right, such as the right of self-defense, the right to destroy property in order to save life when an accident has occurred, or the right of revolution when normal governmental processes have broken down, is that the people concerned have to rely upon themselves; such is the nature of the situation. That does not mean the action they take will necessarily be right; but it does mean they will have to take upon themselves the responsibility of acting—or, what is sometimes an even graver responsibility—not acting.

The reader will observe that this responsibility falls to his lot and to everyone else's lot when dealing with "emergency rights," even though a mistake on his part may make him guilty of a crime. Fire alarm boxes, for example, usually carry some such wording as "In case of fire, break the glass and pull the handle." But who is to decide when there actually is a fire? Are we to teach people that they should never take it upon themselves to decide? That would obviously be to the detriment of the community. But people thus deciding for themselves might be mistaken. That is a chance we must take. It is better to run that risk than to run the risk of teaching them never to decide for themselves whether an emergency actually exists.

What we do is similar to what the Communists do in their teaching: we tell people they must not go about pulling fire alarms at whim or fancy, or at any slight, unverified suspicion. We tell them there are certain signs of a dangerous fire, certain objective conditions that must be present—considerable smoke in unaccustomed places, increased heat or flame that cannot be normally accounted for, continued crackling sounds, and the like. But who is to determine whether those objective conditions exist? The only possible answer is: you, I, anyone who happens to be around. And we will be held accountable, morally, and sometimes even legally, if we happen to be around and do nothing, when our action might have saved property or life. It will be put to us: You saw the conditions; why didn't you break the glass, and pull the handle of the alarm? You should have taken it upon yourself to make the decision.

It should be emphasized that we say these things to people even though we say at the same time: If you make a mistake in these matters where anything important is involved, you may be subject to penalty. That is a social safeguard we set up, against irresponsible or criminal action—a safeguard that applies both to fire alarms and revolutions. But we all recognize that occasions arise when fire engines ought to be called for, and that occasions arise when revolutions ought to be called for. It would be obvious folly to try to prevent every possible future attempt to call for either one. (It must always be borne in mind that in dealing with the American Communist issue, we are dealing *only* with some *possible future* attempt, since Communists have never in the past actually called for any revolution under the conditions obtaining in this country.)

There are certain differences between calling for fire engines and calling for revolutions, as everyone knows. But there can be no doubt that the analogy applies, insofar as the main point is concerned. Just as we have inscribed on the fire alarm box a directive for all to follow, "In case of fire, break the glass and pull the handle," so we have no less plainly inscribed in our Declaration of Independence a directive for all to follow, "In case of tyranny, overthrow the government and establish a new one." (It is assumed, of course, that under a tyranny there is no way for the will of the majority to be implemented peacefully.)

If people make mistakes in trying to follow these directives, they may be penalized. But we could hardly penalize them beforehand on the ground that they are going to decide for themselves whether or not the conditions are such as to call for action. On the contrary, we insist that each person should and must decide for himself, to the best of his ability.

Specifically, everyone (not only Communists) must decide whether, on a given occasion in which balloting is impossible, there is or is not majority support for revolutionary measures. In such a situation, it would also be the duty of each citizen to try to persuade his fellow-citizens of the rightness of his decision. In arriving at his decision each will naturally be influenced by whatever and whomever he chooses. Again, if he chooses wrongly, he will suffer; but he must choose. He must finally make up his mind what to do (or not to do) himself, and what he will (or will not) tell others to do. From that there is absolutely no escape, and he will in the end be held accountable for whatever his final choice is—action or lack of action.

Under these circumstances, it is impossible, on any logical basis, to see how a special problem could be made out of the question: in a situation where balloting is impossible, who decides when there is a majority in favor of revolutionary measures? The only possible answer to such a question is: you, I, anyone who happens to be around. Everyone would have to decide. It would be impossible for anyone to "abstain," since inaction would be as definite a decision as action. Moreover, in the light of his decision, everyone, non-Communist and Communist, would have not only the right but the inescapable duty either to advise his fellow-citizens to take revolutionary action under the existing circumstances, or not to advise them to take it. (Saying nothing would, of course, be a form of not advising them to take action.) Each person, non-Communist or Communist, would thus have the same right and the same duty to determine whether there is or is not majority support for revolutionary action, and whether to do something or not about the situation. In the end, some, no doubt, would be right, and some would be wrong. But all would decide, by word or lack of word, by deed or lack of deed.

In this regard there is of course no way whatever that we could in advance single out some viewpoint with which we do not agree, and say: Those who hold that viewpoint shall, on the future occasion where adequate balloting is impossible, remain silent and frozen. They shall be forbidden to think, speak, act or take initiative. They shall not decide for themselves; and they shall not try to advise or persuade others how to decide. There is no way to do such a thing in practice; and if there were such a way, it would clearly violate, not only basic principles of morality and legality to which we are unequivocally pledged, but the simplest demands of common sense.

In any case, it was interesting to see how this matter would be taken up again and again. In fact, just before I completed my testimony as a whole, the Judge once more returned to it. In the interest of logical continuity I insert at this point a typical portion of that final colloquy.

> The Court: I would like to clear up in my own mind—it seems to me that I gather from your interpretation of the Communist Party position in this country that before violent revolution would be in order, that the revolutionary conditions that you have emphasized would have to obtain?
> The Witness: Yes, sir....
> The Court: Now, in the determination of the judgment which would have to be made as to whether those revolutionary conditions obtain, in looking at the record, finally you said to me that in part the Communist Party would make that determination.
> The Witness: Yes, sir.
> The Court: I would like to know who besides the Communist Party would make the determination that those revolutionary conditions obtain.
> The Witness: In their teaching, the rest of the majority of the people would take part in it.
> The Court: Now, let us analyze that for a moment. You say the majority of the people determine. Isn't that ... self-contradictory?
> The Witness: No, sir; I don't think so. Presupposing, as they do, that there would be no way of taking a formal poll or vote under those disordered conditions, the majority, by talking to one another, by observing—each segment of it observing the other—might arrive at the conclusion that they did constitute the vast mass of the people and that they, not seeing any considerable

section of the people differing with them, might well arrive at the conclusion that they are the majority....

The Court: Well, I say to you, let us lay it in the context of reality.

The Witness: Yes, sir.

The Court: Take the United States of America. Suppose there was a rail strike; suppose there was a utility strike; but suppose transportation was going on to some degree: Who would say in these forty-eight states that revolutionary conditions obtain, if it were not the Communist Party, if their objective is the overthrow of governments and the eventuation into a classless society? Who would make that judgment that now is the time when these revolutionary conditions obtain?

The Witness: Well, I would say according to their teachings their aim would be the coming of Socialism, but not necessarily the overthrow of government. Sometimes they point to peaceful possibilities, but I think that—

The Court: Well, let us assume they point to peaceful—we will make that assumption without deciding—let us get to that point.

The Witness: Yes.

The Court: It seems to me that is the nub of the inquiry under your interpretation. Who does that? Who makes it?

The Witness: According to their teachings the Communist Party participates in that decision; the rest of the majority of the people participate in that decision.

The Court: How would they know that opinion of the rest of the majority? How would it be brought home to the Communist Party?

The Witness: By observation of conditions, by reports and analyses and evaluations that they would make of the behavior, of the actions, of the opinions, of the growing sentiments of the people.... I think in their view, Your Honor, it is something like how we arrive at a determination of what time it is. Now, of course, there must be someone—

The Court: Well, I hope it is not that easy.

The Witness: No, it certainly is not, but I mean in the principle of the thing. In a certain sense there must be someone to determine what time it is. If nobody determines, and nobody looks at anything to determine, it will never be stated what time it is. But granted there must be someone to determine what time it is, what time it is is not just determined by what he wants it to be; it is determined by objective conditions. The sun must be in a certain position in the heavens in relation to the earth.

The Court: That corresponds to the objective conditions that must obtain.

The Witness: Something like that. They feel that there must be certain conditions objectively present which nobody could wish into existence.

The Court: That is right, but who determines that?

The Witness: Well, in their teachings the majority takes part in that determination, and the membership and the leadership of the party.

The Court: How do you understand that the majority makes that determination besides the party itself?

The Witness: Well, I understand it in this way, Your Honor. The concrete illustrations of this are best taken perhaps from the Russian revolution. I think they have in mind that kind of thing.

The Court: You mean the party here?

The Witness: That sort of thing in general—yes, the party here-having in mind that sort of thing that was manifested, wherein, for example, in those disordered times when there was civil war in Russia, and breakdown of all normal processes, and majority ballots were not possible, and so on, the party was meeting, constantly receiving reports, constantly engaged in discussion as to what was happening among the people. And the people would manifest their will by their statements and conversations, by what appeared in the newspapers, by events that took place, and demonstrations, and so on. And they felt—

The Court: "They" being the party.

The Witness: They being the party.

The Court: Yes.

The Witness:—from the observation of these phenomena and the participation of the people in them, that the people were manifesting their activity, their will, their opinions, and participating in all of these decisions, all of these determinations, as well as the membership of the party and the leadership of the party.

The Court: Well, they determined it, then—the party determined that the people were manifesting their will? The party made that determination; isn't that right?

The Witness: I would not say they made it independently of what the people were doing.

The Court: No, I am saying their judgment is that the people, from what they could gather—their judgment was that the conditions were ripe.

The Witness: I would say that the best, the most accurate way to formulate it is that in their view all these different elements take part in the determination of that decision, each in its different way—the leadership of the party, the membership of the party, and the rest of the majority of the people together with the objective conditions. I do not think there is just a mechanical or flat decision made by one group irrespective or independent of the other elements.

The Court: No, but don't they take it into account, and don't they assess it and evaluate it and say it and so report, from what the people are saying, from what the economic conditions are, that now revolutionary conditions obtain?

The Witness: Yes—well, I think it is equally true that the rest of the majority of the people, non-Communists, also enter into expressing their opinion.

The Court: I mean non-Communist and anybody else.

The Witness: Yes.

The Court: I am asking you whether they don't evaluate that, the party evaluate it and make that determination.

The Witness: In respect to their part of it; but I think also in the light of their teachings if they found that the mass of the people got wind of the fact that the Communist Party is there meeting, and the mass of the people manifested its displeasure or disapproval in some way of any revolutionary step, according to their teachings that would be evidence to them that they have not got the support of the masses.

The Court: I agree with you, but that would be their judgment.

The reader will gather, from the context of discussion, that in the thought expressed by the last sentence the emphasis fell upon the word "their." Let us try to reconstruct the attitude lying at the basis of his whole line of questioning, pressed so frequently by both government counsel and judge. Put bluntly, it would seem to consist mainly of the fear that this group, because it is going to exercise its judgment and make some sort of decision, may try to take advantage of some situation to plunge into revolution when they do not really have the support of the majority for such a step. What evidently seems particularly appalling to those in this frame of mind is that the Communists are going to make their decision and action depend on their judgment.

But what alternative is there, besides the absurd one of trying to forbid a group to make any decision or take any action on its own initiative? The insinuation in the line of questioning which was pursued seems to be that if the members of this group say they are going to use *their* judgment in the making of an important decision, there must be something illegitimate involved.

This situation is exactly analogous to the following, which, the reader will readily appreciate, is not wholly hypothetical. Suppose a man has an enemy and strongly suspects this enemy would be glad to see him dead and gone. Moreover, the man naturally has a very low opinion of the general character and moral status of his enemy. Now suppose the man begins to be disturbed by the thought that his enemy believes in the right of self-defense, that his enemy actually advocates that any person has the right to kill another if that other is advancing upon him with a deadly weapon, intent upon murder.

What particularly appalls the man is the thought that this enemy (who would like to see him dead and gone) is thus in a position to use his own judgment, to make his own determination as to when someone is advancing upon him with a deadly weapon. The man begins to imagine situations in which his enemy might claim that he, the man, was thus advancing upon him when in reality such was not the case. But, reflects the man, if this enemy of mine has the right to act on his own judgment, I might get killed.

He thereupon applies to the police with a request that they put his enemy in jail now. "Don't you see," he says to the police, "this enemy of mine is openly saying he has the right to kill me under certain circumstances?" Well, the police might say, what is the matter with that? It is a fact recognized by the law that if you advance upon him with a deadly weapon in an attempt to kill him, he is entitled to kill you. That's all right, says the man, I have no quarrel with that. But the trouble is he says *he* is going to decide when I am advancing upon him. *He* is going to decide whether or not I have a deadly weapon. *He* is going to decide whether or not I am trying to kill him. *He* is going to make that judgment and determination.

The police might reply that he says he is going to make it, not in the light of subjective wishes but in the light of objective facts and conditions, independent of anyone's will or desire. I know, says the man, but who is going to decide when those objective conditions exist? Don't you see, it gets back to *his* judgment, and you know what enmity he bears me and what a low character he is.

Suppose, under these circumstances, the police say they will investigate. They come back and tell the man no weapons can be found, no plans, nothing to indicate his enemy is preparing to kill him. But must we wait, the man asks, until he has *plans?* Isn't it enough that he says he hates me, that he says he has the right to kill me under certain conditions, and that he will use his own judgment in deciding when those conditions obtain?

It is not enough for two reasons: first, because everyone can say that. It is the statement of a right; and no one can properly be put in jail for that, no matter what we may think of him. Second, if all people who have enemies they would like to see dead and gone and who at the same time believe in the right of self-defense could be put in jail, how could we be sure of anyone being left free? Which judge would still be sitting on the bench? Which member of a jury would remain on a panel? Which counsel would be left to argue at the bar? What witness would be at liberty to take the chair? Everyone has enemies, and everyone can invoke the right of self-defense.

Put in more direct language, those who pursue this line of questioning seem to imagine that if the Communists, acting strictly on their own and not really having the support of the majority, called for a revolution on the *pretense* that they had majority support, they might thus win an undeserved victory. But this reasoning has two fatal flaws, either one of which would be sufficient to invalidate it. In the first place, if the Communists (or any other revolutionary group) did not really have the support of the majority, it is hard to see how they could gain any permanent success by trying to stage a revolution. In the second place, what is even more important is the fact that it is the Communists themselves who teach and emphasize the doctrine that majority support is an absolute precondition, as we have seen again and again.

Before I left the stand on this occasion, defense counsel wished to return to one or two points in the Judge's questioning, points which there was reason to feel might have involved misimpressions.

> Defense Counsel: Does the Communist Party of the United States take the position that their own view covers their action or their part, or that their view governs the action to be taken, if any, by the majority?

The Witness: Their teachings are that their view governs their action, and that in determining their own view they must take into account objective facts which are independent of the will of any party, group, or even class. In their view, in short, the coming about of a revolutionary situation is a vast social and historical phenomenon. It does not come about because some conspiratorial activities are undertaken, and it does not come about at whim or fancy. In their view, it comes about through the movement of gigantic economic, social, and political forces.

Defense Counsel: Now, is there any blueprint for it ... when violent revolution will come in point of time, if it ever does come?

The Witness: No, in their view there is nothing that you could call a static or mechanical blueprint. In their view, the development of economic-social forces governs these things.

Defense Counsel: Let me ask you this. In their view is a paralyzing railroad strike sufficient to warrant revolution?

Government Counsel: Objected to.

The Court: Objection overruled.

The Witness: Not at all.

Defense Counsel: Is the existence of a paralyzing transportation strike enough to undertake a revolution?

The Witness: Certainly not in their view.

Defense Counsel: Are both put together enough to undertake a revolution?

The Witness: Certainly not in their view. There would have to be far deeper social crises, far deeper manifestations of underlying economic forces to make for the revolutionary situation—a far greater degree of breakdown of the normal processes of government.

Defense Counsel: So long as there is open to them or to the people in general a peaceful legislative settlement of the situation as it affects the welfare of the people, do they teach that a revolution would be proper or in order?

Government Counsel: I object.

The Court: Objection overruled.

The Witness: No, they teach that a revolution would come about, the proletarian revolution would come about, only when there is present a revolutionary situation; and that would involve serious breakdown of the existing electoral processes, and the support of the majority of the people as determined by objective conditions independent of the will of any group, party, or class.

Everyone must make up his own mind about these issues; but I will candidly say that it was hard for me to escape the conclusion, as the trial went on, that it was being held against the defendants that they talked about revolution at all. As a psychological fact, it is apparently easy to feel, and to communicate the feeling, that the subject of revolution in itself is a suspect and illicit one, with which no honest American would be concerned, even in the city of Philadelphia, within sight of Independence Hall.

## 5  *The Prosecution Forgets Logic*

### The Problem of Peaceful Transition

The reader may recall that, at several points in the foregoing proceedings, what is known as the problem of "peaceful transition" entered the discussion. This expression, frequently found in Marxist-Leninist literature, has reference to the transition from capitalism to the kind of economic and social system which is held, in Communist literature, to be an improvement upon the capitalist system.

As we have seen, Marx and Engels took the position that this transition could be carried out peacefully in certain countries under certain conditions—that is, where popular electoral and legislative traditions existed, and where the administrative machinery could be depended upon to implement the will of the majority even if that will favored a very radical change. It was brought out several times that these leaders placed the United States, England, and Holland in this category in their own day.

Their general view, however, was that in the light of the conditions which prevailed in most countries a majority desire for a radical change would, in all probability, be violently resisted by the entrenched minority. Thus a contest of force would be precipitated, which the people would eventually win but which would be costly to all concerned during the transitional period.

The prosecution evidently felt that this problem had an important position in the development of its case, for, soon after the resumption of cross-examination, counsel returned to it and dealt with it in considerable detail. It was approached as follows:

Government Counsel: Now, Doctor, is it Communist teaching that the United States of America is an imperialist country?

The Witness: At the present time, yes.

Government Counsel: All right; is it Communist teaching that the United States is the most powerful imperialist force in the world threatening the aspirations of the people for peace, democracy, and progress?

The Witness: I would say at the present time, yes.

Government Counsel: Is it Communist teaching that the government of the United States represents a form of the domination of the exploiter minority?

The Witness: I would say at the present time, yes.

Government Counsel: I suggest to you, Doctor, that it is a basic Communist teaching that in such a government as you have just admitted that the United States is characterized as by those previous questions—that in such a government, and particularly the government of the United States, a peaceful transition to Socialism and Communism is impossible. Is that true or false?

The Witness: That is false. That does not follow.

As the reader is aware, I was under cross-examination at this time and hence had no control over the areas toward which questions were directed. There are in fact many passages in the writings of leaders of the United States Communist Party pointing to various possibilities of a peaceful transition at the present day. These teachings, which necessarily led me to answer the last question in the way I answered it, could not be brought in at this point. I could bring them in only later, which, of course, I did, as the reader will see. For the time being, however, I had to address myself to the passages presented by the prosecution. Thus the questioning went on as follows:

Government Counsel: All right; let us examine, then, some of the writings—most of them which you have already referred to but have not been focused upon in that question.

The Witness: Yes, sir.

Government Counsel: I want to direct your attention first to page 9 of *History of the Communist Party of the Soviet Union*.

The Witness: Is it of the Soviet Union or of the United States?

Government Counsel: *History of the Communist Party of the Soviet Union*.

The Witness: Of the Soviet Union, yes.

Defense Counsel: Suppose we give him that. That is Government Exhibit what?

Government Counsel: Sixteen. (G-16 handed witness.) All right, Doctor, does the paragraph—I will read it to you:

"Marx and Engels taught that it was impossible to get rid of the power of capital and to convert capitalist property into public property by peaceful means, and that the working class could achieve this only by revolutionary violence against the bourgeoisie, by *a proletarian revolution,* by establishing its own political rule—the dictatorship of the proletariat—which must crush the resistance of the exploiters and create a new, classless, Communist society."

Now, does that or does it not say that the teaching of Marx and Engels was that a peaceful means could not get rid of capitalism?

The Witness: It did, as of the date written, 1939—

Government Counsel: Isn't that a rather important point?

The Witness: Yes, and I think it can be decided even in a more binding way upon the Communist Party of the United States. I can show you passages from the chairman of the Communist Party of the United States, written more than ten years after this passage, which point specifically to the possibility of peaceful transition to Socialism in the United States today.

[The reader will note that in Communist terminology the word Socialism is used to designate the initial or lower stage of Communism.]

Government Counsel: Do you suggest that he rises higher than Stalin?

The Witness: No, I do not; but I suggest that since his statement was made later than that of Stalin's it is much more binding upon the Communist Party of the United States.

Government Counsel: When did Stalin die, Doctor?... April, 1953, was it not?

The Witness: I think so. And Stalin, therefore, was alive at the time Mr. Foster

Government Counsel: Yes.

The Witness:—published the writings to which I referred, which I have here.

Government Counsel: And during Stalin's lifetime—

The Witness: And Stalin never repudiated Mr. Foster.

Government Counsel:—and during Stalin's lifetime was he not recognized as the head of the world Communist movement?

The Witness: He was, indeed. Therefore I should expect him to reject Mr. Foster's writing if it did not agree with his own convictions at the time Mr. Foster's writing was published.

Government Counsel: Now, you were suggesting, Doctor, that writings of William Z. Foster after he had been indicted for conspiracy under the Smith Act would overrule something that Stalin wrote?

The Witness: Not overrule. I would say supplement it. Government Counsel: Supplement it. All right.

As the reader will later see, the passages from Foster to which I was here referring are by no means confined to his writings after he had been indicted (in 1948) for conspiracy under the Smith Act— the same sort of conspiracy as that charged against the defendants in this case. But even if the passages had been so confined, what difference would that have made to the issue? If, for example, it were a proven fact that the Smith Act, or prosecutions pursuant to the Smith Act, had been the cause of a change in the party's teachings, should not the government have been satisfied? Presumably, such a causeeffect pattern would be precisely in line with the purpose of the act.

The legal situation is that the prosecution must prove, in a federal case of this character, that the defendants committed the alleged offenses at some time during the three-year period directly preceding the date of the indictment, which in this case was Aug. 18, 1953. In other words, the applicable statute of limitations covers three years. Of course, this would not of itself prevent the prosecution from bringing in evidence of questionable conduct or belief on the part of the defendants prior to the three-year period. However, all would agree that such evidence would have decisive value only if the prosecution could prove, first, that the conduct or belief shown was criminal in character; and, second, that it continued on into the three-year period directly preceding the indictment. In the present case the prosecution was able to do neither of these things.

As it turned out, the government was unable to produce from the writings of United States Communist leaders even during the *twelve* years directly preceding the indictment any passage stating that a peaceful transition was impossible in the United States. Whether the change in teaching was caused by the Smith Act or some other factor, or a combination of factors, has no logical bearing on the root issue of the trial, as long as a change took place. In fact, change is in itself considered natural and inevitable by this school of thought, as I tried to indicate at this point.

The Witness: The principle of the Communist movement is that conditions change, and that new doctrines arise and new positions must be taken in the light of newly developing facts. That is the history of their movement....

Government Counsel: Now, I will refer you, Doctor, to the *Selected Works* of Lenin, Volume X, and I want to refer you to a passage which I do not believe has been read before, and I will try to read it slowly. Page 164.

Defense Counsel: Will you just wait a second? All right, go ahead.

Government Counsel: "In the concrete situation which has been created by militarism, imperialism, all over the world, and most of all in the most advanced, powerful, most enlightened and free capitalist countries—the strangulation of colonies and weak countries, the world imperialist butchery and the Versailles 'Peace'—the very thought of peacefully subordinating the capitalists to the will of the majority of the exploited, of the peaceful, reformist transition to Socialism is not only extreme philistine stupidity, but also downright deception of the workers, the embellishment of capitalist wage slavery, concealment of the truth. The truth is that the bourgeoisie, even the most educated and democratic, now no longer hesitates to resort to any fraud or crime, to massacre millions of workers and peasants in order to save the private ownership of the means of production. Only the violent overthrow of the bourgeoisie, the confiscation of its property, the destruction of the whole of the bourgeois state apparatus from top to bottom—parliamentary, judicial, military, bureaucratic, administrative, municipal, etc., right up to the very wholesale deportation or internment of the most dangerous and stubborn exploiters—putting them under strict surveillance in order to combat inevitable attempts to resist and to restore capitalist slavery—only such measures can ensure the real subordination of the whole class of exploiters."

Has that writing of Lenin's been repudiated?

Defense Counsel: Now, since he speaks of a particular time, may we have the time of that writing, sir?

Government Counsel: I think it is 1920; I am not sure.
The Court: Well, it doesn't make any difference, it seems to me, as to the time, does it?
Defense Counsel: Yes, sir, because the principle is that times change, and this particular quotation refers to a particular time.
The Court: Well, we will find out.

The reader may feel there is a certain piquancy in the fact that the exact date on which the highly colorful writing quoted from Lenin was given to the world was July 4, 1920. In addition to recalling our own revolution, this date indicates that Lenin was writing in the midst of civil war, intervention, and *his* revolution. In any case, one can readily appreciate the tremendous importance of the point raised by defense counsel when one reflects that the principle he referred to is central to the entire philosophy of Marxism-Leninism. It is known as the dialectical method, and there is no possibility whatever that any follower of this school of thought would not be aware of it and would not have been taught it amongst his first lessons as something of basic significance.

This dialectical principle teaches that all things change, including social and political conditions, problems, and policies. Hence there is no one social or economic condition that endures eternally, and there is no one political policy that is eternally correct.

Thus, for example, if Lenin points out that something Marx said in an earlier day is no longer true it is thoroughly understood that such an assertion does not necessarily involve any violation of the principles of Marxism or any betrayal of Marx. Marx himself insisted that his own doctrine must be taken *dialectically*, not statically or mechanically. It was he who took over this method and terminology from the German philosopher Hegel.

We have already seen, in the course of testimony, how such a change of viewpoint came about in an instance of cardinal importance, which, in fact, concerns the very problem under discussion—that of peaceful transition. The point came out several times that Marx had said, in 1872 and 1874, that there were countries, such as the United States, England, and Holland, where there was the possibility of gaining the ends he had in view for the working class "by peaceful means," a thought which was corroborated in 1886 by Engels in his preface to the first English translation of *Capital*.

I myself had set forth these facts in the opening statement which I read from the witness chair. And I had immediately added in the very next sentence of that statement "Lenin and Stalin later maintained that conditions had changed in those particular countries, so that, in their judgment, it could no longer be said that the government would peacefully accede to the wishes of the people if the majority really wanted Communism."

This particular application of the dialectical method concerned the doctrine of "exceptionalism," which was brought into the earlier discussion by the prosecution, as the reader will recall. That is, Marx had made an exception for certain countries where he saw the possibility of peaceful transition, whereas, in the view of Lenin and Stalin, the conditions making that exception valid in Marx's day had later changed.

In fact, it was the prosecution itself which emphasized repeatedly that this change of view must be taken account of. If, therefore, a change of viewpoint from Marx to Stalin can be accepted and insisted upon, what logical objection can be raised to the fact that there is another change of viewpoint from Stalin to Foster? If Stalin himself saw no objection to this change of Communist viewpoint, what possible weight could be given to objections voiced by government counsel?

The conclusion is inescapable that the prosecution wanted to accept the first change of viewpoint on the part of the leaders of the Communist movement because that fitted in with their case but when they came to the second change of viewpoint, which did not fit in with their case, they tried to argue that in the Communist movement the viewpoint of the leaders cannot be changed. This kind of argument is on the same logical level as that of the farmer who, trying to maintain in court that he did not break his neighbor's plow, divided his case into two parts: first, he never saw the plow in his life; second, it was already broken when he borrowed it.

There is another aspect of this matter which is perhaps even more important than what we have just been discussing. That is, the problem of whether there is or is not in a given country the possibility of a peaceful transition is very different from the problem of whether there is or is not a revolutionary situation in that country. The conditions of a peaceful transition could be absent without the conditions of a revolutionary situation being present.

## THE PROBLEM OF PEACEFUL TRANSITION

As had been pointed out over and over again, the preconditions of a revolutionary situation, in Communist teaching, are that vast social crises must have reached a point where the existing order is unable to solve its own problems, where normal governmental processes such as elections are no longer possible, and where there is majority support for a revolutionary step. It is amply clear that a Communist could conclude that such a revolutionary situation was not present in a, given country even if, at the same time, he maintained that the possibility of a peaceful transition also was not present. That, in fact, has been the "normal" conditions of capitalist countries during most of the past history of capitalism, according to Communist teaching—a peaceful transition to any radically new order not having been possible because of the absence of effective parliamentary machinery, and a revolutionary situation not having been present because the existing order had not yet reached a point of acute breakdown and the majority will had not yet crystallized for a radical change.

In other words, there is no logical reason for concluding that because a Communist says that a peaceful transition is not possible in a certain country he is also saying that a revolution should be undertaken in that country. Before any revolution should be undertaken, according to his doctrine, there must not only be the *absence* of the conditions of peaceful transition but there must also be the *presence* of the conditions of a revolutionary situation.

Therefore, from any rational standpoint, it would have availed the prosecution absolutely nothing even if they had been able to prove that United States Communists believe that in the United States today the conditions of a peaceful transition are absent. That would still not prove that these Communists are necessarily advocating a revolution in the United States, either now or at any other time.

Although I thought that these considerations had been amply clarified in the preceding testimony, it was necessary for me to emphasize them once more in response to the court's interrogation at this point. For the Judge followed his last comment, "Well, we will find out," with this question:

> The Court: Let me ask you, then, Doctor: Did Stalin's interpretation or Lenin's change from what Engels said?

At first I supposed the Judge was inquiring in general terms, whereas it developed he really had in mind the specific passage quoted from page 9 of *History of the Communist Party of the Soviet Union,* which entered our analysis at the beginning of the present chapter. Thus my first answer was irrelevant to the specific frame of reference of the question.

The Witness: Yes, Your Honor. In several important doctrines—
The Court: Well, can you point out where he repudiated the violence that is, it seems to me, connoted in that passage that was read before? Not this one.
The Witness: Well, Your Honor, as I have tried to point out in my testimony a number of times, citing these basic documents, there is no espousal of violence in the sense of wishing to use violence contrary to the will of the majority. Therefore, there can be no repudiation of violence as if there was previously an espousal of violence, or wish to use violence.
The Court: Well, let us get basic. Do you think or not the previous passage read in which he referred to Engels, that that in and of itself, in the plain import of the language, the common acceptation of it, the reading of it, does not import violence?
The Witness: It says that violence will occur under certain conditions.
The Court: Read that again, that original one that you read, please.
Defense Counsel: Going back to the other one?
The Court: Yes, we are.
Government Counsel: I have it, Your Honor. "Marx and Engels taught that it was impossible to get rid of the power of capital and to convert capitalist property into public property by peaceful means."
The Court: All right. What do you think that sentence connotes?
The Witness: That connotes, Your Honor, that when the time comes, when an attempt is made to convert private capitalist property into public socialist property, violence will probably be involved under the conditions he has in mind when he is writing.
The Court: Why do you import that consideration into it rather than the consideration that it would be initial?
The Witness: That what would be initial, Your Honor?
The Court: The violence. He doesn't say that in there. You import that consideration in, don't you?
The Witness: No, sir, he says in that passage nothing—The Court: Read that sentence again, please.

## THE PROBLEM OF PEACEFUL TRANSITION

Government Counsel: "Marx and Engels—"

Defense Counsel: May it please the Court, this is a chapter dated 1883 to 1901.

The Court: I am appreciative of that. Will you please just let this witness—I am asking this question. Enter your objection, and then let the witness answer. Counsel and I will handle it. You enter your objection.

Defense Counsel: I will enter my objection by saying that I object to Your Honor or government counsel questioning this witness about a paragraph contained in the book published in 1938, which is historical, and it refers to 1883 to 1901, as though it should be read in complete isolation.

Government Counsel: I move that be stricken, sir.

The Court: No, your motion is denied.... All right. Read it again to the witness, please.

Government Counsel: "Marx and Engels taught that it was impossible to get rid of the power of capital and to convert capitalist property into public property by peaceful means."

The Court: Now, "to get rid of." Do you import into it now—do you want the jury to understand that that only comes after the proletariat have assumed the power?

The Witness: No, Your Honor, I do not mean that; but I do want the jury to understand, and everybody to understand, that the teachings of this school of thought, whatever else they may be, do not involve the idea that they like violence; these teachings do not involve the idea that they will initiate the violence; and these teachings do not involve the idea that this violence is to be undertaken contrary to the will of the majority.

The Court: Well, in other words, you are saying that that is taken and is consonant with the will of the majority?

The Witness: Yes, sir, that is exactly—

The Court: Read the other section.

Government Counsel: "... and that the working class could achieve this only by revolutionary violence against the bourgeoisie—"

The Court: You say that is in the same category?

The Witness: Absolutely, Your Honor. There is no follower of the Marxist-Leninist line of thought who would not as part of the meaning of that passage understand that those things would never happen except in the presence of a revolutionary situation, and that that revolutionary situation involves—

The Court: All right, we have your understanding.

The Witness:—the support of the majority and the breakdown of existing forms of government to the point where the government cannot take normal ballots—

The Court: All right, you said that a number of times.

Defense Counsel: He has to, sir.

The Court: I don't want you to say what he has to do.

Defense Counsel: All right, I object—

The Court: I want you to enter your objection.

Defense Counsel: I object to Your Honor cutting in on the witness in that fashion.

The Court: All right, your objection is overruled. Now, what is the balance of the statement?

Government Counsel: I think I should read the previous context.

The Court: All right.

Government Counsel: "... and that the working class could achieve this only by revolutionary violence against the bourgeoisie, by *a proletarian revolution.*" That is the next clause.

The Court (to the witness): And that is in the same category?

The Witness: Of course, Your Honor.

The Court: All right. Now we basically, I think, understand each other.

The Witness: Yes, sir.

Thus the Judge's line of questioning had taken us back to the point which was basic to the entire case. That is, no matter how many passages can be found which talk about violence, no matter how horrendous they may sound when taken out of context and read in isolation (and some of them sound extremely horrendous, read in that way), the question always remains: In the teachings of this school, when, under what conditions, is this violence to come about? And the answer is always the same: This school teaches that this violence will come about only in a revolutionary situation. And these teachings define the revolutionary situation clearly and emphatically as one in which governmental processes have already broken down to a degree making normal balloting impossible and where a revolutionary step has majority support.

Under these circumstances, it is clear that it would make no difference whatever to the root issue of the case whether United States Communists at the present day did or did not believe that a peaceful

## THE PROBLEM OF PEACEFUL TRANSITION

transition was possible in the United States. That is, even if their teachings were telling them that a peaceful transition is impossible, those same teachings are also telling them that violence is not to be used except where it has majority support and existing government has already broken down.

But the fact is that United States Communist leaders like Foster do take the position in their teachings that a peaceful transition would be possible in the United States today. As I have pointed out, court procedure was such that it was only later that I could present passages to show the position of United States Communist leaders on this matter. Meanwhile, cross-examination continued along the line chosen by the prosecution.

> Government Counsel: Now, Doctor, you mentioned these conditions a moment ago. They are the conditions as to when the revolution can take place, are they not?
> The Witness: They are.
> Government Counsel: And the statement back here in the first of this paragraph, "It was impossible to get rid of the power of capital and to convert capitalist property into public property by peaceful means," means just what it says, does it not, that it is impossible by peaceful means?
> The Witness: Only up to the date written, of course. He is not talking about the future....
> Government Counsel: Let us take something that is in the present tense, just to be sure about it ... Now, *Problems of Leninism* was written by Stalin, was it not?
> The Witness: Yes, sir...
> Government Counsel: Yes. *Problems* is dated January 25, 1926, at the end of the book. Now, Doctor, counsel asked you about this passage, from pages 19 to 20 of *Problems of Leninism* ...
> "Can such a radical transformation of the old bourgeois system of society be achieved without a violent revolution, without the dictatorship of the proletariat?"
> Now, that is in the present tense, is it not?
> The Witness: Yes, sir.
> Government Counsel: And the answer is: "Obviously not. To think that such a revolution can be carried out peacefully within the framework of bourgeois democracy, which is adapted to the domination of the bourgeoisie, means one of two things. It means either madness, and the loss of normal human

understanding, or else an open and gross repudiation of the proletarian revolution."

Now I ask you, Doctor, does or does not that passage reject peaceful means?

The Witness: This passage—

Government Counsel: Can you answer that yes or no, Doctor?

The Witness: Not without giving a misimpression.

Government Counsel: Well, that's right; first you answer whether it is yes or no, and then explain.

The Witness: Yes, sir.

Government Counsel: Does it or does it not reject peaceful means?

The Witness: No, sir.

Government Counsel: It does not, you say?

The Witness: No, sir, especially when those peaceful means are envisaged in the future.

Government Counsel: No, that isn't the question, Doctor.

The Witness: Well, that is the misimpression I want to avoid—

Government Counsel: I want to ask you the meaning of these words: "To think that such a revolution can be carried out peacefully within the framework of bourgeois democracy, which is adapted to the domination of the bourgeoisie, means one of two things. It means either madness, and the loss of normal human understanding, or else an open and gross repudiation of the proletarian revolution."

Is that or is that not a rejection of carrying out the revolution peacefully within the terms of bourgeois democracy? ...

The Witness: This passage denies that, under the conditions which Stalin was writing within, the revolution could be carried out by peaceful means—

Government Counsel: All right.

The Witness: But it does not involve any denial of the possibility of carrying out future transitions—

Government Counsel: I only asked you the one question, whether or not it denied peaceful means.

Defense Counsel: I object to the witness not being—

The Court: Yes, he ought to be permitted to finish his answer.

The Witness: It does not in any way deny the possibility of carrying out transitions to Socialism and Communism in the future by peaceful means.

Government Counsel: Where does it say that, Doctor?

## THE PROBLEM OF PEACEFUL TRANSITION         119

The Witness: It says that in every word and every verb arid every sentence, because it is all in the present tense.

Government Counsel: "To think that such a revolution can be carried out peacefully within the framework of bourgeois democracy ..." Now, you have already said that [according to this doctrine] the United States of America is a bourgeois democracy, have you not?

The Witness: I have ...

Government Counsel: Now, in the 1870's, Doctor, Marx suggested in some writing that peaceful evolution of Socialism in the United States of America was possible, did he not?

The Witness: He did.

Government Counsel: And wasn't that suggestion or qualification of Marx's three times rejected by Lenin and Stalin?

The Witness: The principle underlying it was never rejected.

Government Counsel: Was that qualification or was it not three times rejected by Lenin and Stalin?

The Witness: Now, you must distinguish what you mean by the "qualification."

Government Counsel: Do you misunderstand my question?

The Witness: No. I understand the misunderstanding which may follow from an inaccurate answer to your question.

The Court: Can't you answer that yes or no? And then we will permit you to explain.

The Witness: No, sir; not unless the word "qualification" in that question is clearly understood ...

Government Counsel: Suppose I take the latest of these three rejections I am speaking of—which is in *Foundations of Leninism* on page 55.

The Witness: Yes, sir.

Government Counsel: Let us go all the way through it till there is no question about what I am asking you, what I am stating.

The Witness: Yes, sir. I am very familiar with the passage.

Government Counsel: "In a letter to Kugelmann (1871)"—I am reading—"Marx wrote that the task of the proletarian revolution is 'no longer as before, to transfer the bureaucratic military machine from one hand to another, but to *smash* it, and that is a preliminary condition for every real people's revolution on the Continent,' " giving the citation to Marx. Now I am going on with Stalin's language, am I not, Doctor, with the reading?

"Marx's qualifying phrase about the Continent gave the opportunists and Mensheviks of all countries a pretext for proclaiming that Marx had thus conceded the possibility of the peaceful evolution of bourgeois democracy into a proletarian democracy, at least in certain countries outside the European democracy (England, America). Marx did in fact concede that possibility, and he had good grounds for conceding it in regard to England and America in the 'seventies of the last century, when monopoly capitalism and imperialism did not yet exist, and when these countries, owing to the special conditions of their development, had as yet no developed militarism and bureaucracy. That was the situation before the appearance of developed imperialism. But later, after a lapse of thirty or forty years, when the situation in these countries had radically changed, when imperialism had developed and had embraced all capitalist countries without exception, when militarism and bureaucracy had appeared in England and America also, when the special conditions for peaceful development in England and the United States had disappeared—then the qualification in regard to these countries necessarily could no longer hold good."

Now that is the question I asked you. Did or did not Stalin say that the qualification of Marx could no longer hold good?

The Witness: He said two things. He said—

Government Counsel: I am asking you that first, Doctor.

The Witness: Yes, but the two are connected.

Government Counsel: Well, I ask you to answer mine first.

The Court: All right, let the witness explain. I think that is a fair answer. All right.

The Witness: Yes, Your Honor. The two things are connected in the same passage. Stalin does say, as you have read, that the qualification in regard to these countries necessarily could no longer hold good—

Government Counsel: Just a moment.

The Witness: Yes.

Government Counsel: And these countries are what?

The Witness: Are England and the United States—

Government Counsel: All right.

The Witness:—at the time Stalin is Writing-

Government Counsel: All right.

The Witness:—namely, in 1924 or so. But he also says in the same passage—I direct your attention to the—a few lines down

## THE PROBLEM OF PEACEFUL TRANSITION 121

from the top—"Marx did in fact concede that possibility," namely, the possibility of a peaceful transition, and Stalin adds, "and he had good grounds for conceding it."

Now, that means that Stalin recognizes and does not reject the basic principle that there are times and conditions even in countries like the United States and England, and particularly in countries like the United States and England, when a peaceful transition is perfectly possible. Since there are times and conditions under which it is recognized by Marx, Engels, Lenin and Stalin that a peaceful transition has been possible, there are also times and conditions in which a peaceful transition may be possible, once again in the future.

There is no rejection of the future possibilities here. Stalin does not say—

Government Counsel: Let me ask you this, Doctor—
The Witness: Wait a moment. I haven't finished yet.
Government Counsel: It is quite a long answer, isn't it?
The Witness: Stalin does not say and Lenin does not say that forever in the future a peaceful transition will never be possible in America.... He is saying now, under the conditions in which he is writing, namely, in 1925 or so, that a peaceful transition is not possible in England or America.

The reader will recognize that the lengthy passage from Stalin quoted by the prosecution contains the thought which we have discussed a number of times and to which I had made specific reference in my first statement from the witness stand, when I said: "Lenin and Stalin later maintained that conditions had changed in those particular countries, so that, in their judgment, it could no longer be said that the government would peacefully accede to the wishes of the people if the majority really wanted Communism." In fact, in the passage from Stalin quoted by the prosecution, Stalin is doing nothing more or less than discussing with approval the very passage from Lenin's writing to which I made reference in my opening statement.

Actually, therefore, there was absolutely nothing new in this lengthy excerpt and in the extended examination of it entered into by the prosecution. As we saw a few pages back in the present chapter, the logic of this situation is conclusively settled by three facts. The first is that even if the prosecution could prove that Communists do not believe a peaceful transition possible in the United States at present that would not prove they are necessarily conspiring to overthrow the government now or at any other time.

The second is that it is clearly fallacious to say that Communists must have believed a peaceful transition was impossible in the 1950's because Stalin had said it was impossible in the 1920's or 1930's, especially when that very assertion by Stalin (and Lenin) represented a change of view from what Marx and Engels had said earlier. If one change of view could take place, why not another?

The third fact is that another change of view has taken place, as expressed by Foster and other leaders of the United States Communist Party in the 1940's and 1950's. These writings, however, could be brought in only later.

It is significant to note, in this connection, that in the very work, *Foundations of Leninism,* from which government counsel had just quoted, on the very next page (56), Stalin gave specific recognition to the possibility of future peaceful transitions when he added:

"Of course, in the remote future, if the proletariat is victorious in the most important capitalist countries, and if the present capitalist encirclement is replaced by socialist encirclement, a 'peaceful' path of development is quite possible for certain capitalist countries, whose capitalists, in view of the 'unfavorable' international situation, will consider it expedient 'voluntarily' to make substantial concessions to the proletariat. But this supposition applies only to a remote and possible future. With regard to the immediate future, there is no ground whatsoever for this supposition."

Since 1924, when Stalin wrote these words, it is evident that at least some considerable part of the "capitalist encirclement" has been replaced by a "socialist encirclement," and that this development has had its influence on the "peaceful transition" question.

After a recess had been taken the prosecution returned to the problem with another attempt to deduce what the present beliefs of Communists must be by going back to what Stalin had written more than twenty years ago and ignoring what the Communist leaders are actually writing now. It was developed in this way:

> Government Counsel: Doctor, I think you testified before recess sometime that it is Communist teaching that imperialism does exist in the United States; is that correct?
> The Witness: Yes, sir.
> Government Counsel: Is it Communist teaching that monopoly capitalism exists in the United States?

The Witness: Yes, sir.

Government Counsel: Is it teaching of the Communists that militarism exists in the United States?

The Witness: Yes, sir.

Government Counsel: Is it Communist teaching that bureaucracy exists in the United States?

The Witness: Yes, sir.

Government Counsel: It is?

The Witness: It is.

Government Counsel: All right. Now, Doctor, I suggest to you that it is a basic Communist teaching that Socialism cannot be achieved in any capitalist country by the use of the ballot; is that correct or wrong?

The Witness: I would think under most conditions correct, but it is wrong if you imply by that that there would be no conditions which in their view would allow a transition through the ballot.

Government Counsel: Well, then, aren't you saying yes and no?

The Witness: I certainly am.

Government Counsel: What is correct about it?

The Witness: In respect to most of the conditions obtaining in most of the historical period since the development of monopoly capitalism and imperialism, it would be impossible to make transition by peaceful ballot, but—

Government Counsel: Now, let me ask you this.

The Witness: —but—

The Court: Let the witness answer.

Government Counsel: Yes, sir.

The Witness: —but under certain conditions, and one of them is now, in their view of monopoly capitalism and imperialism, it would be possible to make transition by peaceful ballot.

Government Counsel: Now, Doctor, does the Communist teaching as expressed in Communist documents make any such qualification as you state?

The Witness: Yes, sir.

Government Counsel: Let me refer you to some and see if the qualifications are in them. First of all, I want to refer you to the *Program of the Communist International,* which is Government's Exhibit 6.

The reader will perhaps feel, as I did, how eccentric this procedure was from a logical standpoint. I was saying there are passages in the writings of leading United States Communists of the present day which include the teaching that peaceful transition is possible. Government counsel apparently doubted this was really so; but instead of asking me to show him those passages he said he would show me other passages from an earlier day which do not contain this teaching. Such a response comes perilously close to that of the man who was looking around Times Square late at night for something he had lost in Central Park, and who, when asked why he was searching Times Square, replied: "There's more light here."

An exact analogy would be the situation of two men arguing in 1954 about whether or not a certain company has stated, during the years 1950-1953, that it would be possible to construct certain plants in Alaska. One man readily acknowledges that *fifteen or so years earlier* this company had the view that such construction was impossible; but he offers to present written evidence that it changed its mind around that period, and that it now maintains such construction is possible. The other man, however, does not ask to see this evidence but continues to point to writings *all of which date from fifteen or twenty years back* wherein this company maintained the construction in question was impossible. It is clear that such writings could never settle the issue.

In this connection, it must be emphasized that the prosecution was not even claiming that there were any "nonpeaceful" passages written by United States Communist leaders during the three-year period covered by the indictment (1950-1953). The reader will recall that the federal statute of limitations here applicable sets a term of three years within which the offense must have been committed, and the indictment was drawn in August, 1953. Thus the time factor is necessarily of paramount importance.

The whole issue turns on what the defendants were teaching during the period covered by the indictment, not what they might have been teaching ten or fifteen years before that, unless it could be proved that they went on teaching the same things, which, as we have said, would be impossible in the present instance, where documentary evidence shows a clear change. Thus, it is most significant that every passage presented by the prosecution in this regard was written and was originally published more than a dozen years before the indictment, as the reader will note in following this oddly persistent line of inquiry.

# THE PROBLEM OF PEACEFUL TRANSITION 125

To the last reported remark of government counsel, "...I want to refer you to the *Program of the Communist International,* which is Government's Exhibit 6," I replied, in an effort to emphasize the importance of the time factor:

> The Witness: What is the date?
> Defense Counsel: 1928.
> Government Counsel: 1928. This particular edition is the edition published in 1936.
> The Witness: The edition is 1936. What is the date of the document?
> Government Counsel: I think it is 1928.
> The Witness: 1928?
> Government Counsel: Yes. I am referring to page 36:
> "The conquest of power by the proletariat does not mean peacefully 'capturing' the ready-made bourgeois state machinery by means of a parliamentary majority. The bourgeoisie resorts to every means of violence and terror to safeguard and strengthen its predatory property and its political domination. Like the feudal nobility of the past, the bourgeoisie cannot abandon its historical position to the new class without a desperate and frantic struggle. Hence, the violence of the bourgeoisie can be suppressed only by the stern violence of the proletariat. The conquest of power by the proletariat is the violent overthrow of bourgeois power, the destruction of the capitalist state apparatus"—for instance—"(bourgeois armies, police, bureaucratic hierarchy, the judiciary, parliaments, etc.) and substituting in its place new organs of proletarian power to serve primarily as instruments for the suppression of the exploiters."
> Now, Doctor, does that passage admit of any conditions under which voting and the ballot could be used to achieve Socialism?
> The Witness: Yes, sir; it does.
> Government Counsel: Where does it say so?
> The Witness: If future conditions—
> Government Counsel: Where does it say so, Doctor?
> The Witness: Where does it say that it is not ruling out the future? It says it throughout, because it is only speaking in terms of the present.
> Government Counsel: When it says "does not mean," you think that that refers only to today or yesterday?
> The Witness: It does not rule out a change in the future any more than if I said, "In the city of Philadelphia it is impossible to

enter the court house on Sunday from the Chestnut Street side." That does not rule out the possibility in the future that I may be able to do so.

Government Counsel: Doctor, does this passage say, "But this situation may be changed in the future?"

The Witness: It does not mean to at this point.

Government Counsel: Does it say it?

The Witness: I don't think so....

Government Counsel: Again, Doctor, I am asking whether election was held out as a possibility at all. I am referring to *Problems of Leninism,* written by Joseph Stalin in 1926—

The Witness: Yes, sir.

Government Counsel: Page 22, reading as follows: "Replying to those who confuse the dictatorship of the proletariat with 'popular' 'elected' and 'non-class' government, Lenin states:

'the class which has seized political power has done so conscious of the fact that it has seized power alone. This is implicit in the concept of the dictatorship of the proletariat. This concept has meaning only when one class knows that it alone takes political power into its own hands, and does not deceive either itself or others by talk about popular, elected government, sanctified by the whole people' "

Now, does that say anything about election—at some time in the future?

The Witness: Not at this point.

The reader will observe not only that it is as early as 1926 that Stalin is quoting this passage from Lenin but that the passage itself was written quite a few years before that. Even so, it is certainly worth noting, although the prosecution did not do so, that Stalin immediately adds, after quoting Lenin's words, the following qualifications:

"This does not mean, however, that the rule of this one class, the class of the proletarians, which does not and cannot share this rule with any other class, does not need an alliance with the toiling and exploited masses of other classes for the attainment of its objectives. On the contrary. This rule, the rule of a single class, can be firmly established and exercised to the full only by means of a special form of alliance between the class of proletarians and the toiling masses of the petty-bourgeois classes, especially the toiling masses of the peasantry/'

## THE PROBLEM OF PEACEFUL TRANSITION 127

Stalin then quotes further from Lenin:

" 'The dictatorship of the proletariat is a *special form of class alliance* [Stalin's italics] between the proletariat, the vanguard of the toilers, and the numerous non-proletarian strata of toilers (the petty-bourgeoisie, the small masters, the peasantry, the intelligentsia, etc.), or the majority of these.... It is a special type of alliance which is being built up under special circumstances, namely, in the circumstances of furious civil war.... *It is an alliance between classes which differ economically, politically, socially, and ideologically:*' " (Stalin's italics.)

I have quoted further from Stalin's work at this point in order that the reader may again see how the surrounding context can modify the stark impression of a statement that was presented in sheer isolation. In the first place, one sees that Lenin and Stalin are writing in the atmosphere of a war situation—"furious civil war"—which is, of course, exactly what they lived through during this period. In civil war no government could maintain itself except by force of arms, and, under conditions where people are divided by overt conflict over the very question of what government is entitled to exercise power, no government could honestly claim to be "sanctified by the whole people."

This does not mean that a government cannot and should not have the support of the majority under these conditions. The context shows clearly that Lenin and Stalin are anxious to emphasize that mass support is necessary and that this support must come from the nonproletarian masses, "or the majority of these," as well as from the masses within the proletarian class itself, that is, the industrial working class composed mainly of plant and factory hands. It is incontestable that support from the proletarian class plus a majority of the non-proletarian masses of farmers, white-collar workers, and the like would be support from the majority of the population.

It is also clear that support from certain groups is a different thing from sharing leadership with those groups. The fact that a given class keeps leadership and control within its own hands does not mean that it must lack majority support.

While it is necessary to go into all these considerations in order to place such a passage in its historical setting, which is the only way to begin to understand its content and meaning as a whole, the question of its logical relevancy in the trial can be disposed of much more easily. What was the passage supposed to prove? As the reader is aware, it was introduced by the prosecution as part of the attempt to prove that the Communist defendants, about 1950 to 1953, believed that a peaceful transition to the social system they favored was impossible in the United States.

Here again we have to confront the fact that this whole approach is fallacious, for the three binding reasons already given, any one of which, indeed, would be sufficient to invalidate it. Though perhaps not needed, a final recapitulation of these reasons could be made as follows:

1. Even if the defendants believe peaceful transition is impossible, that does not mean they believe a revolutionary situation is present in this country or ever will be present necessarily.

2. It would be utterly impossible to prove that the defendants believed a certain idea between 1950 and 1953 by reference to what the leaders of the movement said between 1920 and 1926, except on the assumption that once-expressed views of the leaders could never be changed. But the prosecution itself is insisting that such an assumption would be false—as indeed it would—since the prosecution is insisting, in regard to this very point, that the changes made by Lenin and Stalin in the doctrine earlier laid down by Marx and Engels must be accepted.

3. Further changes in the teachings have in fact come about. Numerous passages from writings of leaders of the United States Communist Party published in the 1940's and 1950's (during a period in eluding the whole term of the indictment and ten years preceding) emphasize the possibility of a peaceful transition in the United States.

The prosecution had still a few more passages along this line, which it presented as follows:

> Government Counsel: Now, Doctor, I found a passage I was looking for at page 4677 of the record. You were being asked about the basis for your knowledge as to what the Communist Party taught, and I don't think I need to raise the questions unless the context is not clear to you. You said: "For better or for worse, it has probably fallen to my lot to read literally thousands of documents emanating from the Communist movement and the Communist Party of the United States. And my sum total impression is that each and every one of these documents, and taking them

all collectively, lead to no other conclusion than that this party is trying its best to teach the principles that are found in the classics of Marx, Engels, Lenin, and Stalin."

Now, I will ask you, did you ever read a document in which a Communist Party writer in the United States specifically rejected the use of the ballot to attain socialism?...

The Witness: Yes, sir; the full answer to that question is that in my recollection there are some documents written by Communist leaders in the United States which reject the possibility of transition by ballot at some time; and there are documents written by leaders of the Communist Party in the United States which emphasize the possibility of peaceful transition at a different time.

Government Counsel: All right now, let me ask you if you recall reading, as the basis for your knowledge here in court, the article by V. J. Jerome, which was one of those you mentioned, was he not?

The Witness: Yes, sir.

Government Counsel: In *The Communist,* July, 1934.

The Witness: 1934?

The reader will appreciate that nothing which Mr. V. J. Jerome, one of the leaders of the United States Communist movement, wrote in an article in the journal *The Communist* in 1934 could possibly prove what the defendants believed *after 1949,* since the crux of the whole matter is that a change in the teachings took place between 1934 and 1949. Therefore, I shall not at this point burden the reader's attention with the full quotations from Mr. Jerome's article, which consists of a detailed analysis of a convention of the Socialist Party held in Detroit in 1934.

The same must be said of the single remaining passage presented by the prosecution in this connection, which, ironically enough, turned out to be an excerpt from a work of William Z. Foster. Since Foster is the very man who later became the chairman of the party, it was his work above all which would have to be consulted to understand what the teachings were from 1950 on. But it would naturally have to be consulted to see what he was writing around that general period, whereas the passage presented by the prosecution dated from 1937! (Page 152, *From Bryan to Stalin.* Foster was summarizing Lenin's familiar position.)

Thus, although the sole point at issue, in so far as this entire aspect of the case was concerned, was what the defendants expressed in their teachings during and after 1950, every single passage adduced by the prosecution on the subject of peaceful and nonpeaceful transition had been written not in the 1950's, or even in the 1940's, but in the 1920's and 1930's! Let us therefore turn to the actual teachings about peaceful transition expressed in works of the leaders of the United States Communist Party dtuing the 1950's and 1940's.

# 6   Return to the Facts

## Peaceful Transition in the Teachings of American Communists Today

In what is known as redirect examination, which follows cross-examination, it became possible to deal directly with the teachings of United States Communists at the present time and in the recent past on the subject of "peaceful transition." First I was asked a general question that was of considerable importance to this whole area.

Defense Counsel: ... Doctor, is it or is it not a fundamental teaching of Marxism-Leninism—is it not a fundamental teaching of dialectical materialism that changes take place?

The reader may not be familiar with the fact that the philosophy basic to Marxism is given this rather formidable technical label—"dialectical materialism." However, this terminology, queer as it may seem, is itself of some significance to the point before us, as "dialectical," used in this sense, means nothing more nor less than "characterized by constant change." Materialism, to the Marxist, means the assertion of a naturalistic rather than a supernaturalistic basis for the world and for morality.

Thus dialectical materialism is the view that everything which exists, the entire natural order, is in process of constant change. Hence, when the Marxist speaks of his "dialectical" method, he means a method that bases itself upon, and tries to take account of, the fact that changes are taking place. (Matters of this kind are set forth in considerable detail in my book, *Soviet Philosophy: A Study of Theory and Practice.*) I therefore replied as follows:

> The Witness: There is no doubt that one of the—as I have said a number of times—that one of the central principles of this particular movement is the emphasis on change, what they call the dialectical approach; and they regard these laws of dialectics, laws expressing the basic conditions of constant change, indeed, as absolutely fundamental in their world outlook. So that you never can correctly approach this school of thought by assuming that one position laid down is just going to last forever....
>
> Defense Counsel: You were referred to statements contained in publications by Foster and others in respect of the question of force and violence. In addition to the statements to which your attention was directed on cross-examination, are there others by Foster on the issue of force and violence?
>
> The Witness: Yes, sir; there are.
>
> Defense Counsel: And do they take, generally speaking, the position that the future may hold a situation where no force is necessary?
>
> The Witness: I think they do. May I read those passages?
>
> Defense Counsel: I ask you to.
>
> The Witness: I quote from William Z. Foster, *History of the Communist Party of the United States,* a book published in 1952. On page 551—
>
> Government Counsel: If the Court pleases, there is no foundation for this being used throughout the party, sir, as party teaching.

The reader may feel, as I did, that this was certainly a strange objection to be made by one who but a short while before had presented a passage written by Foster in 1937, with no other qualification than that it was a passage written by Foster, which must therefore indicate the nature of Communist teachings. To make the situation even stranger, in 1937 Foster was not the top leader of the Communist Party, whereas in 1952 he occupied that position. Thus his 1952 book is regarded as far more authoritative in teaching at the present time than his 1937 work. The Court naturally overruled the objection, but another was immediately made.

> Government Counsel: If the Court pleases, one further ground for my objection, and that is because of the position of William Z. Foster at the time it was written. I mean, under the

circumstances, it is a self-serving declaration. He is a co-conspirator in this case.

The Court: No, that is all right.

Defense Counsel: That is why it ought to be more material.

The Court: Objection overruled.

The reader will observe at this point the same situation we commented upon in the preceding chapter. That is, whatever the reasons may be for Foster, as chairman of the party, laying down certain teachings, the fact is he laid down certain teachings and that is what must be taken into account. Whether or not the laying down of these teachings was in any respect "self-serving" makes no difference to the fact, except perhaps, as counsel suggested, to make it more relevant and likely under the circumstances. After all, no accused individual could say or do anything to counter an accusation against himself without being in a sense self-serving. There is nothing necessarily illicit in that.

While Foster was not a defendant in this case, he was considered by the prosecution to be a "co-conspirator" in view of the fact that he was the principal leader of the Communist Party, to which the defendants belonged, so that they would presumably be following his leadership if they were in any conspiracy to teach the violent overthrow of the government.

In other words, it would be presumed that the defendants were not in any criminal conspiracy to teach or use force or violence if such were contrary to Foster's directives and teachings. Hence, the teachings expressed by Foster during the relevant period were of cardinal importance at this point. The quotation I proceeded to read was from his *History of the Communist Party of the United States,* the 1952 publication last referred to.

The Witness: The passage is as follows, page 551:

"Communists are the chief fighters against the two major threats of violence in modern society—imperialist international war and fascist civil war—both of which emanate from the capitalists. The Communist Party's democratic aims are in line with the writings of Marx, Engels, Lenin, and Stalin, with the course of the everyday struggles of the workers and their allies, and with their world experience in establishing socialism. The danger of violence in the daily class struggle, and in the inevitable and indispensable advance of the workers and the nation to socialism could come only from the capitalist class, which, seeing its profits threatened, and itself being deposed from its rich dictatorship, then uses every means possible to thwart the democratic socialist will of the people.

For as the great Marx has truly said, there is no case in history where a ruling class has yielded up its domination without making a desperate struggle.

"Marxist theoreticians, while warning the workers against capitalist violence, have always pointed out possibilities for the peaceful establishment of socialism in countries where the democratic elements are strong. Thus, Karl Marx, three generations ago, before the advent of imperialism, with its highly centralized, heavily armed and bureaucratic state, said that If for example, the working class in England and the United States should win a majority in Parliament, in Congress, it could legally abolish those laws and institutions which obstruct its development.' Lenin also, in mid-1917, outlined a peaceful perspective for the Russian Revolution. And Stalin, writing in 1928, while pointing out the danger of capitalist violence at that time, also said that with the strong growth of world socialism, 'a peaceful path of development is quite possible for certain capitalist countries.' The C.P.U.S.A."—that is, the Communist Party, United States of America—"proceeds upon the basis that such a possibility exists in the United States."

The reader will note in the foregoing passage Foster's emphasis on the danger of violence proceeding from an entrenched and powerful capitalist minority should the will of the majority be for a change to a Socialist economic system, that is, to the first or lower phase of Communism, as he sees it. This situation is not without its evident irony, since it shows that the Communists fear violence from capitalist quarters quite as much as capitalists fear violence from Communist quarters.

In no case, however, could such a view be said to constitute an advocacy of violence or of force by any minority. At the same time, there is the clearest acknowledgment of the fact that other Communist leaders have recognized conditions under which a peaceful transition was possible in certain countries, and there is the bluntest statement that he now considers such a possibility exists in the United States. The way in which such a transition might work out, in his view, is indicated in the passage I next cited.

Defense Counsel: Now, Doctor, have you another book written by Foster, *The Twilight of World Capitalism,* published in 1949?

The Witness: Yes, sir.

Defense Counsel: Will you turn to page 126, and see if there is a reference applicable to the present inquiry?

The Witness: Yes. There is on page 126 a passage devoted to this question.

Government Counsel: If the Court pleases, again I object because of the period in which it was written. I ask Your Honor to take judicial notice that Foster was indicted on July 20, 1948.

The Court: I don't think that makes any difference, not at all. All right.

The Witness: The passage is as follows:

"American socialism, beyond question, will have its own specific forms and methods, but basically it will be the same as socialism in other countries, with monopoly capital completely defeated, the industries and national resources in the hands of the people, production for general use instead of for profit, and the working class the leader of the whole people. Only in this way will this country and the world be finally freed of the dangers of poverty, economic chaos, fascist slavery, and murderous war. These steps could be taken legally by a people's government, notwithstanding the opposition of the capitalists, however violent.

"To promote the election of a progressive, coalition government of this type which, by force of circumstances, would move to the Left, and eventually to socialism, on the general pattern of the European People's Democracies, is obviously not to advocate a program of force and violence, the enemies of the Communist Party to the contrary notwithstanding."

Foster evidently feels that if a progressive or radical government were elected in this country, perhaps out of some third party movement, such a government might move further to the left, take up the position of a "people's democracy," and legally enter upon a full-scale program of Socialism as the initial phase of Communism. Now, Foster may be completely wrong about all this. Certainly many would deny that there is any probability in his premises, or cogency in his inferences from them. But it could not be so easily denied that Foster would think in this way. There is nothing inherently improbable about his entertaining such premises and drawing such inferences from them concerning the possibilities of peaceful transition. And that, after all, is the issue before us, and the whole issue before us in a trial of this kind—not whether his teaching is right or wrong, but what his teaching is and whether it is criminal in nature, however mistaken in fact it might be.

I turned next to a work of Eugene Dennis, another of the top leaders of the United States Communist Party, and one of those convicted in the first Smith Act trial in New York.

> Defense Counsel: Will you turn to a paper or article in *Political Affairs* dated September, 1948, page 815, by Eugene Dennis?
> The Witness: Yes, sir.
> Defense Counsel: Is there a statement there applicable to the present inquiry?
> Government Counsel: Same objection, Your Honor, for the same reason.
> The Court: Objection overruled.
> The Witness: Yes, sir. There is a statement here as follows, from an article by Eugene Dennis entitled *"The Fascist Danger"*:
> "As the vanguard party of the American working class, we condemn and oppose the force and violence of capitalism, of imperialism. We oppose its system, its philosophy and its practice of political reaction, exploitation and oppression. We work for the socialist reorganization of society, when the majority of the American working class and people will be the ruling class, and end forever the exploitation of man by man, and crises, wars, reaction and fascism.
> "Today when the advocates and practitioners of forcible imperialist expansion and atomic war, or of lynching and police violence, maliciously charge us with conspiring to overthrow the Government, we strongly second the observations of Frederick Engels made half a century ago when Bismarck inaugurated the famous 'anti-socialist' and 'anti-revolt' laws of that time."

Then follows an inner quote from Engels:

> " 'The irony of world history turns everything upside down. We, the "revolutionaries," the "rebels"—we are thriving far better on legal methods than on illegal methods and revolt. The parties of order, as they call themselves, are perishing under the legal conditions created by themselves. They cry despairingly with Odilon Barrot: *"La légalité nous tue"*—legality is the death of us; while

we, under this legality, get firm muscles and rosy cheeks and look like eternal life.'"

The reader will note that Dennis here suggests, by indirection, that the reason Communists are charged with illegal conspiracies is fear of their legal, parliamentary successes. He was no doubt thinking in international terms, especially of Communist successes in various elections in countries like France and Italy at the time he was writing. Again, whether he was mistaken, partly mistaken, or wholly correct about the facts in their relation to the United States has little bearing on the issue before us. The point is, it is not at all unlikely that he would think in this fashion, which involves an emphasis on the possibilities of peaceful successes.

The next document brought into reference was a booklet entitled *Twenty-Three Questions about the Communist Party Answered by William Z. Foster,* dated Jan. 11, 1948, containing the reprint of an interview with Foster published by the *New York Herald Tribune.* It will be observed that this was six months before Foster was indicted, along with other leaders, in the first New York trial of Communists under the Smith Act.

Defense Counsel: Is there a statement there applicable to the present inquiry?
The Witness: There is. It reads as follows:
"Q. Does the Communist Party advocate the overthrow of the United States Government by force and violence or by any other unconstitutional means?
"A. [Foster] We'll let the Supreme Court of the United States answer this question for us. In its decision in the Schneiderman case, June, 1943, after examining exhaustively, on the one hand, the charges that the Communist Party advocates a violent seizure of power, and on the other hand, the practices and doctrines of the Party, including the writings of Marx, Lenin and Stalin, the Court said:
" 'A tenable conclusion from the foregoing is that the Party in 1927 desired to achieve its purpose by peaceful and democratic means, and as a theoretical matter justified the use of force and violence only as a method of preventing an attempted forcible counter-overthrow once the Party had obtained control in a peaceful manner, or as a method of last resort to enforce the majority will if at some indefinite time in the future, because of

peculiar circumstances, constitutional or peaceful channels were no longer open.'

"We Communists accept this formulation as a fair statement of our attitude toward the question of political violence. American Communists have always recognized the historical fact that parties with advanced social programs cannot secure governmental power by conspiratorial methods or by minority *coups d'etat*. They must have with them an overwhelming majority of the population. The danger of violence in such situations always comes from the reactionary elements, who refuse to bow to the democratic majority will."

If the reader will at this point think back to the portion of the late Chief Justice Vinson's opinion in the Dennis case which we quoted in Chapter 2, he will find himself in the presence of a logical contrast so sharp that it is startling. Vinson's decision against the Communists, which represented the majority opinion of the Supreme Court, was dated June 4, 1951. The decision in favor of the Communists from which Foster quoted was handed down just eight years before, and also represented the majority view of the Supreme Court as it was then constituted.

How different is the reasoning on the central point of all in the two opinions! As we have seen, Vinson stated:

> "In the instant [Dennis] case, the trial judge charged the jury that they could not convict unless they found that petitioners intended to overthrow the Government 'as speedily as circumstances would permit.' This does not mean, and could not properly mean that they would not strike until there was certainty of success. What was meant was that the revolutionists would strike when they thought the time was ripe."

The opinion in the Schneiderman case stated:

> "A tenable conclusion from the foregoing is that the Party in 1927 desired to achieve its purpose by peaceful and democratic means, and as a theoretical matter justified the use of force and violence only as a method of preventing an attempted forcible counter-overthrow once the Party had obtained control in a peaceful manner, or as a method of last resort to enforce the majority will if at some indefinite time in the future, because of peculiar circumstances, constitutional or peaceful channels were no longer open."

Laying aside legal technicalities, one confronts here a diametric opposition. (The year 1927, by the way, has no particular significance to the issue. In the Smith Act cases, beginning with the Dennis case, and including the ones with which we are concerned, the government has of course never contended that there was any acceptable party doctrine in 1927, or that any unacceptable change took place only after 1927. In fact, as we have seen, the government relied very heavily on passages dating from the 1920's and maintained that the defendants should be declared guilty of criminal conspiracy just because they believed, and taught to others, what was in those passages.) The diametric opposition arises precisely in the judgment as to what is contained in the passages.

Vinson says the passages teach the doctrine that Communists should overthrow the government when they think the time is ripe. He stops at that point and immediately draws the conclusion that therefore they are properly adjudged guilty of criminal conspiracy. The reasoning in the Schneiderman opinion goes further into the Communist teachings and finds, in effect, that these passages do not simply teach that government should be overthrown when the time is ripe. The passages further specify and define what the ripe time is, namely, when constitutional or peaceful channels are no longer open and when revolutionary action is necessary to enforce the majority will, as a method of last resort. Hence, the conclusion was drawn that belief in such a doctrine need not be adjudged criminal. While the court recognized that varying views as to the meaning of Communist doctrine were possible, it thus emphasized that a logically tenable conclusion could be drawn, in the light of the doctrine's conditions and qualifications, that it was legally acceptable.

Which of these two interpretations is the more logical? There can be no doubt that that interpretation is more logical which takes into account all aspects of the doctrine. If the doctrine of any school of thought is to be judged, there can be no compromise with the principle that it must be judged in the light of all the qualifications and conditions that are set down within it. This is the clearest, the simplest, and the most obligatory rule of scholarship, and, one might add, of common sense. It applies not only to the doctrine of schools of thought with which we agree or which we respect but it must be applied equally to the doctrine of schools of thought with which we may completely disagree and for which we may feel nothing but contempt.

It is not the rightness of doctrine that is in any way in question. Let it be assumed, for purpose of argument, that the doctrine under examination is completely wrong. That would not in the slightest degree answer the question whether men should be put behind prison bars. What is at issue here is a conflict of reports as to what is in this doctrine. We have before us two extremely different approaches, both by the highest constituted judicial authority. When this happens, men are not usually sent to jail, because it seems clear that there must be reasonable doubt. That is the least that might be said. In this particular matter, it must be further said, as we have seen, that Vinson's interpretation simply will not stand up under analysis, while the interpretation contained in the Schneiderman opinion is adequate to the facts taken as a whole.

We next turned to a typical editorial in a Communist journal.

> Defense Counsel: Do you have a copy of *Political Affairs* dated September, 1947?
> The Witness: I do.
> Defense Counsel: Will you turn to page 779, and is there any statement apropos of the present inquiry there?
> The Witness: Yes, sir, there is. It reads as follows.
> Defense Counsel: By whom is it?
> The Witness: This is an editorial. This is an editorial of this journal, *Political Affairs*—
> Defense Counsel: And that describes itself as the theoretical organ of the Communist Party, does it?
> The Witness: Yes. Its description is a magazine devoted to the theory and practice of Marxism-Leninism, and the statement in its editorial on page 779—
> Government Counsel: Excuse me. Just a moment please, Doctor. This is just a foundation for the article. This is an unsigned article, is it?
> The Witness: This is an unsigned editorial; yes, sir.
> Government Counsel: Objected to.
> The Court: No. We will hear it.
> The Witness: The statement in this editorial on page 779 is as follows:
> "In a word, to work for socialism is to be profoundly loyal to America. As Americans, we Communists do not want socialism to be limited to the Soviet Union. More than any other nation, America has everything necessary for a free, prosperous, socialist

life for all. But as Marxist scientists, who have always fought anarchist adventurism, utopian schemes and putschism, Communists know that the socialist reorganization of society cannot take place until the American working class and its allies among the broad masses of the people desire it, and are ready to bring it about."

It will be noted that this editorial was published almost a year before the first indictment of Communist leaders under the Smith Act. The next document was published more than a year before that indictment.

>   Defense Counsel: Do you have an article published as of June, 1947—The *Theory and Practice of the Communist Party*—at page 25?
>   The Witness: Yes—I have that—in the Marxist study series put out—
>   Defense Counsel: Is that a teaching outline?
>   The Witness: Yes, sir. It is. It is put out by the National Education Department, Communist Party.
>   Defense Counsel: Does that on page 25 have a statement apropos of the present inquiry?
>   The Witness: Yes, sir. It reads as follows:
>   "3. Although bourgeois democracy in the U.S.A, is formal and limited, and fundamentally 'democracy for the rich,' *it is a matter of vital concern to the working class to defend democratic rights and institutions from the attacks of reaction and the forces of fascism.* [Italics in original]
>   "4. America has rich traditions of struggle for democratic rights. The Bill of Rights, universal suffrage, abolition of slavery, compulsory education and abolition of child labor were all won as a result of the democratic struggle of the people. Our country itself was established in a truly democratic, revolutionary progressive war. America's democratic traditions are powerful weapons in the continuing struggle for democracy, security and peace.
>   "5. The working class is not and cannot be indifferent to the form of bourgeois rule. It rejects the position that there is no difference between bourgeois democracy and fascism merely because both are forms of capitalist rule. It fights together with all democratic elements to protect and extend democratic rights and liberties, and to defend democracy from the attacks of fascism.

"6. Communists do not wage the struggle against fascism and for democracy in order to perpetuate bourgeois rule, but to create better conditions for the fight to establish socialism. The struggle for democracy is an indispensable part of the struggle for socialism."

This is followed by a quotation from Lenin:

" 'It would be a fundamental mistake to suppose that the struggle for democracy can divert the proletariat from the socialist revolution, or obscure or overshadow it, etc. On the contrary, just as socialism cannot be victorious unless it introduces complete democracy, so the proletariat will be unable to prepare for victory over the bourgeoisie unless it wages a many-sided, constant and revolutionary struggle for democracy.' "

The reader will note from this passage that, contrary to a widespread impression, the Communist movement does not maintain in its teachings that democratic institutions are of no value or not worth defending under capitalism. Neither is it maintained that all systems of capitalism are as bad as fascism, nor that a war in defense of a capitalist government would not be worth supporting. The position taken is that the Communist's rejection of capitalism as an economic system does not lead him to weaken whatever democratic forms and institutions may be found under capitalism, but, rather, to strengthen and extend them.

Communist teachings have always insisted on a sharp distinction between the economic system of capitalism and the political or social idea of democracy. Ever since the days of Marx and Engels the view has been not only that a rejection of capitalist economics is not a rejection of democracy, but that it is precisely in the interests of democracy that capitalist economics, after a certain point has been reached, must be supplanted by Socialist economics.

As Marxists evidently see it, capitalism, although it represents a great progressive step beyond feudalism, cannot endure forever. Though it greatly increases productivity—which in their eyes is a good thing—brings into being all sorts of technological advances, and transforms the largest single class from serfs into wage workers, for which it is to be given credit, it comes to generate problems which it cannot solve. In the Communist view, problems like periodic mass unemployment, international wars for markets, colonialism, poverty in the midst of plenty, can be solved only by making a transition to Socialism and Communism. In their reasoning, only when the profit motive is removed, and over-all economic production can be planned harmoniously, both in national and international terms, could such problems be solved.

Here again, one may consider the Marxist economic analysis all wrong. Matters such as those are highly controversial, and are obviously in the domain of opinion. But it is not a matter of opinion that the Marxist doctrine, whether that doctrine is right or wrong, has always maintained that capitalism obstructs the fulfillment of democracy in the economic sphere, because of the power it gives to selfish minority interests. It is not a matter of opinion that Marxist doctrine, whether right or wrong, has always maintained that Socialism is a *more democratic* economic system both in terms of principle (collective ownership by the whole people of basic means of production) and in terms of the practical consequences which are claimed (elimination of involuntary unemployment, of colonialism, and their related problems). It is therefore quite natural and consistent that the Communist should argue for the strengthening and further development of democratic forms and institutions, even though they may exist side by side with (and, as he sees it, be limited by) a capitalist economic system.

This part of the testimony concluded with a statement of teachings on the subject of peaceful transition as set forth by William Z. Foster in 1941. The views it asserts were thus actually held seven years before Foster's indictment under the Smith Act. However, they accord completely with the kind of teaching expressed by Foster on this subject after his indictment, as brought out by the passages quoted previously.

> The Witness: It is a statement in a booklet entitled *Socialism, the Road to Peace, Prosperity and Freedom*—date of publication, March, 1941—The statement reads [page 43]:
> "Charges that the Coipmunists advocate violence in this transition from capitalism to socialism are not true. In order that socialism may be instituted the great masses of the American people must be convinced of the imperative necessity of this change, and undoubtedly a gigantic majority can be made to understand that they stand to gain immediately by the introduction of socialism. The masses, once having decided upon establishing socialism, will inevitably turn to the ways of peace and democracy to achieve their legitimate purpose."

In the light of all these documented data, it is indeed a strange experience to read the text of some of the key decisions in the Communist trials. One of the most important was that handed down by Judge Learned Hand of the United States Court of Appeals in 1950, in United States *v.* Dennis, the first Smith Act case involving the principal Communist leaders. Speaking of Communist doctrine, Judge Hand, in the course of his opinion, made the following assertion: "The violent capture of all existing government is one article of the creed of that faith, which abjures the possibility of success by lawful means."

"Abjures," means, of course, to swear away, to renounce completely, to give up entirely. Thus Judge Hand is actually stating that Communist doctrine recognizes no possibility of success by lawful and peaceful means. Examination of this doctrine, as we have seen, reveals the opposite fact: the possibility of success by lawful and peaceful means is fully recognized wherever governmental machinery exists which will carry out the majority will, even if that will is for a radical change. Marx and Engels repeatedly recognized this possibility in their day. Foster and other United States Communist leaders have repeatedly recognized this possibility during the present period, as we have observed again and again in the fundamental teachings.

Judge Hand is a jurist of great renown. No one who followed his career would deny his many accomplishments and his rich gifts. However, no human being is infallible, and it must be plainly said that the statement he made in the opinion cited is a clear case of error. In fact, it might be said to be *the* error of this whole series of trials. In a sense, it is at the root of all the convictions, because it gives judicial sanction to the distorted, "popular" picture of Communist teachings as a body of doctrine in which there is no recognition of any possibility of success by lawful or peaceful means.

Indeed, from a logical point of view, this assumption concerning Communist doctrine would be an absolute necessity if any justification were to be found for conviction in these cases. For the reader will recall that none of the defendants in any of the trials was charged with physical acts of violence, or physical preparations for any such acts, such as collecting stores of weapons or the like. The defendants were charged with conspiring to teach and advocate a certain doctrine, which, it was alleged, *necessitated* force and violence, and the burden of "evidence" adduced against them consisted of passages

TEACHINGS OF AMERICAN COMMUNISTS TODAY    145

taken from that doctrine. Now if it were to be acknowledged that this doctrine (Marxism-Leninism) fully recognizes possibilities of peaceful, lawful success, and that this doctrine furthermore points out that these possibilities exist in this country in the present period, the entire attempt to make out a *criminal* case against the Communists based on their *doctrine* would naturally collapse.

It would thus be difficult to exaggerate the role played by this assumption concerning unlawful violence in all these prosecutions. It is only by virtue of it that there are any prosecutions of this kind. Yet this assumption is demonstrably false, beyond any shadow of doubt. It says a certain doctrine abjures the possibility of success by lawful and peaceful means, whereas that doctrine specifically teaches that there are possibilities of success by lawful and peaceful means, and that they should be utilized. As we have seen, this doctrine also maintains that even in those cases where a successful transition could be made only through the use of force, no such means should be employed unless such action has majority support, and the existing government is unwilling or unable to carry out peacefully the wishes of the people. Under these conditions such action would, of couse, be recognized as lawful.

It is very interesting to see that Judge Hand himself felt the impact of the problems involved, and showed himself keenly aware of the questions that had to be answered, as the case unfolded in the Court of Appeals. *The New York Times* for June 24, 1950, reported from the courtroom:

> "Judge Hand then asked whether the Smith Act, which was adopted in 1940, would have applied to the eighteenth century 'liberals or democrats' who conspired to overthrow a Government if it 'got oppressive enough.'
> 
> " 'That is what is troubling me,' said the Judge. 'Certainly Thomas Jefferson again and again in his encyclicals advocated the propriety of overthrowing a government that had become utterly offensive....'
> 
> " 'Jefferson,' replied Mr. Ginanne [of Government counsel] 'was a man who had lived under an oppressive government, and his views on the right to revolt were conditioned by his experience. He was always talking in terms of the right to revolt against an oppressive government. It is hard for me to believe that he could have been referring to a right to revolt against a government

which provides, as does ours, opportunity to bring about under the Constitution every conceivable kind of economic and social life.' "

This statement is clearly based on the assumption that Communist doctrine teaches the right to revolt against our government even if our government remains one in which there is an "opportunity to bring about under the Constitution every conceivable kind of economic and social life." This assumption is entirely unwarranted and unsubstantiated. Not a single passage from the Marxist-Leninist teachings was ever brought forward to validate it, whereas dozens of passages refute it. Hence it has no logical standing. It is very evident that government counsel here, and others elsewhere, confused *present teaching* of a right to revolt against a tyrannical government with teaching that the *present government* is tyrannical. It need hardly be pointed out that these two things are very different from each other, as different as a gentleman's *green hat* is from a *green gentleman's* hat.

The teaching in question is that *if and when* the government becomes tyrannical there is a right to overthrow it by force. Such a right, if it is a right, must, of course, be taught during the time the government is not tyrannical, just as any other right is. During that time, it can usually be taught openly on the printed page whereas, when the actual government is tyrannical, it usually can be taught only by word of mouth, or covertly. Jefferson, for example, as well as John Adams, Henry Clay, Lincoln, Thoreau, Grant and others continued to proclaim and teach this right *after* our Constitutional government had been set up. (See in the present work, Chapter 11: Opinion of Mr. Justice Jackson on the right of revolution in the Douds case, where numerous quotations are supplied. On the point under discussion Mr. Justice Jackson's opinion unfortunately fell into the same confusion we have here noted.)

It is very significant that government counsel was quite willing to admit that there is nothing wrong with advocating and teaching that there is a right to revolt against an oppressive government. What he objects to is teaching and advocating that there is a right to revolt against a government willing and able to carry out the majority will even if that will is for a very radical change. Thus government counsel is making a distinction between two possible conceptions of the "right to revolt." The first is the right to revolt against an oppressive government; and he can find no objection to that. (Yet that is precisely the version always taught by Communists.) The second is an alleged right to revolt against a government that is in no way oppressive, a government that is ready and willing to carry out the wishes of the majority, whatever they may be. He quite understandably denies there is any such right. (So do the Communists, as emphatically as he does.)

Yet this second concept of the right to revolt is what government counsel is actually trying to identify with Communist doctrine, as taught by Marx, Engels, Lenin, Stalin, Foster, and Dennis! The fact is, as we have seen, that these leaders whose written works were brought into court by the government side as its principal evidence indicate again and again in those very works that they reject such a concept, and that the other concept of the right to revolt (which presupposes an oppressive government and majority support for forceful action) is what they advocate. Nevertheless, government counsel proceeds as if these passages did not exist, and the Court in the end takes the same attitude.

In other words, Communist doctrine does not advocate the right to revolt against our government, as at present constituted and supported by the majority of people, as it is in its present form. Nor has the Communist Party in all its existence ever called for a revolt against our government, which is surely a significant fact in this connection, though its significance is frequently overlooked. That is, it seems to be assumed frequently that Communists, in teaching that people should rebel against a tyrannical government, are really teaching that they should rebel against our present government, since Communists are so completely opposed to our government that they must consider it some sort of tyranny.

It is true that Communists are very much opposed to our government, and they may well consider it "some sort" of tyranny. But they do not teach that any sort of tyranny calls for violent revolution. In their view, as we have seen, the kind of tyrannical situation that calls for armed rebellion is not simply one wherein the government is *bad*. In addition to the government being bad, the majority must be convinced that it is bad, must see that the government will not or cannot carry out their wishes, and must be willing to support forcible measures to set up a new government.

All seem to agree that when Communists are persuaded such conditions have come about they do not hesitate to issue a call for revolt. All must agree that they never have issued a call for revolt in this country. All should then realize that the conclusion is logically inescapable that the Communists do not consider that such conditions have ever obtained in the United States. In other words, they feel they have experienced no tyrannical situation that would call for armed revolt here. Any attempt to draw a contrary conclusion as to their feelings would be a clear violation of the logical rule known as "denying the consequent." That is, when one says, "If the figure is a square, it must have four sides," and then agrees that the figure does not have four sides, one can no longer maintain it might be a square. ("It must have four sides" is in this case the consequent, since it would necessarily follow from the given antecedent, "the figure is a square," if that antecedent were true. If facts show that the consequent must be denied, there is no way the antecedent could still be true.)

If, in such a case, one tried to maintain that the figure might still be a square, the attempt would usually be made because of some temporary victory gained by one or another sort of emotional stress over one's logical faculties. This is probably what happens in the case of individuals highly qualified for rational thinking who nevertheless on occasion say: "Communists are dangerous because if they think a government is tyrannical, they attempt a revolt. They have never attempted a revolt in this country in all their history. Yet I am convinced they think the government of this country is tyrannical." (In this instance, the reader will easily identify the antecedent, "if they think a government is tyrannical," and the consequent, "they attempt a revolt.")

As we have seen, what is taught by Communist doctrine is the right to revolt against our government (or any other) if and when that government should become unable and unwilling to carry out the majority will, and the majority are in support of forceful action. It is quite clear there is no logically consistent way of branding such a doctrine as criminal conspiracy, and at the same time teaching and approving what Jefferson and his fellow-revolutionaries set forth in their Declaration concerning the right and duty of people to overthrow any government which reaches a point where it is unwilling to carry out the ends for which governments are instituted. It is obviously the same basic principle in either case.

It must be said in all candor that the doctrines of Communism make it as clear as it can humanly be made clear in a school of thought that its leaders and followers believe and advocate that no kind of transition, peaceful or otherwise, could or should be made without the support of the majority. This is, in their own view, the indispensable and common foundation of both their doctrine of peaceful transition and their doctrine of the revolutionary situation. Thus the importance of the role played by the principle of majority support in their teachings could hardly be overemphasized. As it turned out, we were to be taken back to this point in its relation to the revolutionary situation by the prosecution itself in the final phase of the testimony.

# 7 The Central Issue Again

## Importance of the Concept of "Revolutionary Situation"

Toward the end of cross-examination government counsel returned to the Communist doctrine concerning the revolutionary situation. Perhaps they had come to the realization that this concept is, in a sense, the crux of the whole matter. It could hardly have failed to occur to them that if Communists teach, as testimony showed, that there can be no justification for any attempt at overthrow of government except in the presence of a revolutionary situation, then the meaning of this concept is something of cardinal significance. Put in the bluntest terms, if the prosecution were to admit that Communists teach that a revolutionary situation is present only where the existing regime has broken down, and there is majority support for revolutionary action, the government would have no logical foundation whatever for its case, either in this trial or in any similar trial.

I speak of a logical foundation. Of course, what people may do, or may be persuaded to do, under the pressure of fear, hysteria, and like emotions, or out of lack of information or inability to reason, is another matter. Rationally speaking, however, there can be no possible doubt that if a school of thought is teaching that there is no justification for overthrow of government unless that government is unable to carry on normally, and unless the will of the majority is for the revolutionary step, a leader or follower of that school of thought could not properly be jailed.

## THE CONCEPT OF "REVOLUTIONARY SITUATION" 151

Justice is pictured blind, but she is not supposed to be blind to the plain facts of history and the elementary principles of logic. No one could recall the circumstances of our own birth as a nation without realizing that there are some conditions under which we recognize overthrow of government to be right and proper. And no one could apply the simplest rules of logic without reaching the conclusion that those conditions are the very conditions just mentioned: where the established government is no longer able to carry on normally, and the will of the majority is for the revolutionary step.

What justice is supposed to be blind to is popular opinion where that opinion is not supported by fact and logic, no matter how widespread the opinion is and how respectable it may seem to be. Justice is supposed to be blind to the distortions of bigotry, no matter how much sanctified by repetition, and to prejudice that is born of ignorance or selfish motive, no matter how much material power it may at the moment command. Those considerations need to be remembered in the present instance.

The prosecution evidently felt that it had to make a final attempt to bring into question whether the Communist teachings did actually include the principle that valid revolution necessitated majority support. In the effort to do this they had to go back to passages I had previously presented, in order to try to show that my analysis of them might have been mistaken. This line of examination took the following course:

> Government Counsel: Doctor, in your testimony as to the conditions of a violent revolution—sometimes compressed and called "the revolutionary situation"—you used, I believe, as your authority for describing the conditions a passage from Lenin in *The War and the Second International;* is that correct?
> 
> The Witness: That is correct, sir.
> 
> Government Counsel: I am going to take the liberty of reading you that. This is on page 13 of *The War and the Second International.*
> 
> The Witness: Yes, sir.
> 
> Government Counsel: "For a Marxist there is no doubt that a revolution is impossible without a revolutionary situation; furthermore, we know that not every revolutionary situation leads to revolution. What are, generally speaking, the characteristics of a revolutionary situation? We can hardly be mistaken when we indicate the following three outstanding signs: (1) it is impossible

for the ruling classes to maintain their power unchanged; there is a crisis 'higher up' taking one form or another; there is a crisis in the policy of the ruling class; as a result there appears a crack through which the dissatisfaction and the revolt of the oppressed classes burst forth. If a revolution is to take place, it is usually insufficient that 'one does not wish way below' but it is necessary that 'one is incapable up above' to continue in the old way; (2) the wants and sufferings of the oppressed classes become more acute than usual; (3) in consequence of the above causes, there is a considerable increase in the activity of the masses who in 'peace time' allow themselves to be robbed without protest, but in stormy times are drawn both by the circumstances of the crisis and *by the 'higher-ups' themselves* into independent historic action." [Italics in original.]

"Without these objective changes, which are independent not only of the will of separate groups and parties but even of separate classes, a revolution, as a rule, is impossible."

Now, is that the only quotation or writing of Lenin on which you rely for your formulation of those conditions?

The Witness: No, sir; I don't think so. There is one further sentence which was quoted in my—

Government Counsel: Yes; let me read it for you. "The coexistence of all these objective changes is called a revolutionary situation."

The Witness: That is correct.

Government Counsel: I am sorry. I didn't know you read that. But this is the one on which you rely for your formulation.

The Witness: This is the most compact formulation, I think, that I selected for reading. There are others saying just the same basic thought.

Government Counsel: Using any of the same language as here?
The Witness: Yes, sir.

Government Counsel: All right; let me ask you this: The third condition that Lenin mentioned there was: "...in consequence of the above causes, there is a considerable increase in the activity of the masses ..." That does not say that the majority becomes in favor of forcible revolution, does it?

The Witness: No, not at that point. It does—

Government Counsel: Does it say anywhere in that passage that it does?

The Witness: Yes, sir; I think so.

Government Counsel: Where?

The Witness: Further—toward the beginning of the passage;
Government Counsel: Read the part you speak of, please.

The Witness: Yes; where Lenin says, "What are, generally speaking, the characteristics of a revolutionary situation? We can hardly be mistaken when we indicate the following three outstanding signs: (1) it is impossible for the ruling classes to maintain their power unchanged; there is a crisis 'higher up' taking one form or another; there is a crisis in the policy of the ruling class; as a result there appears a crack through which the dissatisfaction and the revolt of the oppressed classes burst forth."

Now I think there is no doubt that this means the existing ruling classes have lost the confidence of a majority of the people. It is impossible for them to go on ruling in the old way because they have lost the confidence and the support of the majority of the people.

Then he goes on to the second condition, "... the wants and sufferings of the oppressed classes become more acute than usual." And he says if the revolution is to take place it is usually insufficient that "one does not wish way below," meaning it is insufficient simply that most of the people, the majority of the people, do not want to go on in the old way. But the very fact that he says it is insufficient that the masses do not want to go on in the old way says as a fact about this condition that it would be a condition wherein they do not want to go on in the old way; they want some change, according to him.

Then he goes on to his next condition: The existing government must not be able to carry on, also. That is when he says one is incapable, up above, to continue in the old way. In other words, there are two conditions: One, the masses, the majority of the people, do not want to go on in the old way; and the ruling government is incapable of going on in the old way.

Government Counsel: Where does it say majority of the people, Doctor?

The Witness: Where he says masses of the people, that means majority.

Government Counsel: Let us just look at that. "... there is a considerable increase in the activity of the masses ..." Now, that is what you point to as saying the majority?

The Witness: That is one point. The other point is where he says, "... one does not wish way below ..."—in other words, the masses of the people down beneath—the oppressed classes, as he conceives of it, do not want to go on in the old way.

Government Counsel: And that is all you can show us to justify your contention that, as you put it, a majority of the people are in favor of such a drastic step as a forcible revolution? ...

The Witness: Well, there are other things one might say in support of that, in respect to this particular passage, and there are certainly many other things in other passages.

The reader will understand that since I was at this point under cross-examination I had to answer the specific questions asked of me, which government counsel continued for a while longer to focus upon this particular passage. Though this one quotation did not happen to use the word majority itself, I should have thought its meaning was amply clear from its use of various synonyms, such as "oppressed classes," "masses," and people "way below." However, if there were any actual thought in anyone's mind that Lenin might be using such terms because he might possibly entertain some kind of doubt, hesitation, or reservation concerning the explicit word "majority," the only thing to do, of course, would be to turn to other portions of his text to see if he made use of the actual term "majority."

As we have seen, Lenin, and other leaders as well, did employ exactly that word on numerous occasions, some of which I wish to recall to the reader's attention in a moment. First let us follow the rest of the prosecution's interrogation concerning the text before us. After my last response, suggesting reference could be made to "other passages" as well, questioning proceeded:

Government Counsel: In this passage, first of all—
The Witness: In this—
Government Counsel: I will ask you if you will just point out the language of the passage itself on which you rely.
The Witness: Yes. Well, he goes on, "(3) in consequence of the above causes there is a considerable increase in the activity of the masses"—and I would take that certainly to mean a majority of the people—
Government Counsel: In other words, just stop there. You say "...a considerable increase in the activity of the masses ..." means a majority is in favor, do you?
The Witness: Well, if you go on with the sentence, it does. Government Counsel: Go ahead, go on with the sentence.

The Witness: You stopped me there.
Defense Counsel: You stopped him.
The Witness:—"who in 'peace time' allow themselves to be robbed without protest…" He is assuming that they are oppressed in peace time, but they do not protest. "… but," he says, "in stormy times are drawn both by the circumstances of the crisis and *by the 'higher-ups' themselves* into independent historic action."

Now, I think what he means by the masses being drawn into independent historic action is that the masses, the majority, manifest their support in some way for the step which they always wanted, but, as he sees it, could not take with any possibility of success in other times.

Government Counsel: And, Doctor, with regard to the quantity of the masses in that particular paragraph that you have been quoting me, the words used are, "… there is a considerable increase in the activity of the masses …" are they not?

The Witness: Yes, I think he means by "the masses" at that point the majority, and I think by those who are "oppressed," "way below," he also means the majority. And when he says that it is impossible for the ruling classes to maintain their power unchanged, I think he means it is because they have lost the confidence of the majority, in his view.

Had the procedure permitted, I would at this point have dwelt anew on the significance of various other passages previously brought into testimony, which emphasize beyond any shadow of doubt that Lenin had no reservation about the particular term "majority," in expressing his thought on this matter, which he does in every possible way—positively, negatively, and by concrete example, until there could not be the slightest element of doubt left.

For example, what could be more explicit than the quotation I had read early in direct examination, as reported in Chapter 2 above? "If a revolutionary party has not a *majority* among the front ranks of the revolutionary classes and in the country generally, there can be no question of insurrection." (Lenin, *Can the Bolsheviks Retain State Power?* Vol. VI, *Selected Works*, p. 293.) Even as he there asserted the absolute necessity of having majority support for any revolutionary step, so he condemned, with equal bluntness, the contrary idea of minority revolution, as I had indicated in my opening statement from the witness chair, reported in Chapter 1: "We are not Blanquists; we are *not* in favor of seizure of power by a *minority*." (Lenin,

*Selected Works,* Vol. VI, p. 29.) In that same opening statement I had also pointed out that Lenin did not hesitate to apply his principle to concrete cases of revolutions which were to be rejected as "bourgeois" (a term of the highest reproach) precisely because they did not have the support of the majority. I repeat his words:

"If we take for examples the revolutions of the twentieth century, we shall, of course, have to recognize both Portuguese and Turkish revolutions as bourgeois. Neither is a 'people's' revolution, inasmuch as the mass of the people, the enormous *majority,* does not make its appearance actively, independently, with its own economic and political demands in either the one or the other." *(Collected Works,* Vol XXI, Bk. II, p. 180. *State and Revolution.* My italics in these three quotations.) It may also be noted in this passage that, as Lenin uses the term "mass of the people," he not only equates it with "majority" but with "enormous majority."

On this matter the position of Lenin is in no way peculiar among Communist leaders. As I had also pointed out in testimony, the leader of the United States Communist Party, William Z. Foster, repeatedly asserted the same principle, and repeatedly used the same word, majority, in expressing his teachings. For instance, in the pamphlet, *Twenty-three Questions about the Communist Party Answered by William Z Foster,* he stated: "American Communists have always recognized the historical fact that parties with advanced social programs cannot secure governmental power by conspiratorial methods and by minority *coups d'etat.* They must have with them an overwhelming *majority* of the population."

In his booklet, *Socialism, the Road to Peace, Prosperity and Freedom,* Foster said: "In order that socialism may be instituted the great masses of the American people must be convinced of the imperative necessity of this change, and undoubtedly a gigantic *majority* can be made to understand that they stand to gain immediately by the introduction of socialism." Having laid down this principle, Foster goes on to voice his confidence that in America it would be physically possible for such a majority will to be implemented peacefully. Thus the passage continues: "The masses, once having decided upon establishing socialism, will inevitably turn to the ways of peace and democracy to achieve their legitimate purpose." As I had stated in testimony, the dates of these two works of Foster were, respectively, 1948 and 1941. (Italics supplied by the present writer.)

# THE CONCEPT OF "REVOLUTIONARY SITUATION" 157

In this connection, it is also significant to recall that the United States Supreme Court, in its majority opinion in the Schneiderman case, stated that it could be concluded that Communist teachings

> "... justified the use of force and violence only as a method of preventing an attempted forcible counter-overthrow once the Party had obtained control in a peaceful manner, or as a method of last resort to enforce the *majority* will ..." (Italics added.)

No one willing to examine Communist doctrine objectively and as a whole could possibly entertain the idea that it does not teach the necessity of *majority* support, or that it does not use the word "majority." The prosecution at this point shifted the focus of interrogation, and entered upon a new but related line of inquiry.

> Government Counsel: Incidentally, Doctor, is it not Communist teaching that every capitalist state, as I think you have already told us, represents an exploiting minority; every capitalist government so represents?
> The Witness: Well, to put it precisely, in their view, any capitalist government would represent a government which is functioning primarily in the interests of the capitalist group.
> Government Counsel: And they call it an exploiting minority—
> The Witness: Yes.
> Government Counsel:—in so many words, don't they?
> The Witness: Yes, an exploiting minority capitalist group.
> Government Counsel: Therefore, in Communist teaching such a capitalist government never is subordinate to the will of the majority, is it?
> The Witness: Never is subordinate to the will of the majority?
> Government Counsel: To the will of the majority of the people.
> The Witness: No, that wouldn't follow.
> Government Counsel: The oppressed majority?
> The Witness: It would not follow.
> Government Counsel: Isn't that Communist teaching?
> The Witness: No, sir, it is not Communist teaching that any given capitalist government is never subordinate to the will of the majority.
> Government Counsel: Well, why is it called an exploiting minority, then?

> The Witness: Because for the most part, in the main, as they see it, that sort of government functions in the interest of a minority rather than a majority, as they conceive of it.
> Government Counsel: They say more than in the main, don't they, Doctor?
> The Witness: Well-
> Government Counsel: Don't they say invariably that is the case?
> The Witness: Not in respect to the absence of any exceptions, no. They say there are exceptions.
> Government Counsel: Don't they say that the exploited majority can never obtain what is due them from that exploiting minority?
> The Witness: No. We just read passages from Marx which said in 1872 in England and in America and in Holland the majority could gain their way by peaceful means.

The reader may feel, as I did, that in this exchange the prosecution had originally entertained the idea of arguing that, according to Communist doctrine, every capitalist government must be one wherein, at all times, the majority would find it impossible to gain their will. Then it might be plausibly deduced that, according to Communists, as least one of the conditions of their revolutionary situation was *always* present in any capitalist country. This idea, however, would be contradicted by the teachings themselves, as pointed out.

In any case, the prosecution dropped this line of interrogation at this point and returned to the long passage from Lenin's *The War and the Second International* which we had been discussing. Referring to that quotation, the next question was:

> Government Counsel: Now, Doctor, this very same passage goes on to mention certain other conditions for revolution, does it not?
> The Witness: This particular passage?
> Government Counsel: Yes.
> The Witness: I don't know. I haven't at the moment studied the rest of it.
> Government Counsel: I was curious to know why we hadn't had them in your direct testimony.
> The Court: I wouldn't make any such comments at all. I think we will recess until 2:30.

# THE CONCEPT OF "REVOLUTIONARY SITUATION" 159

At the resumption of the session, I was glad to see that the prosecution continued with this point, as I was very curious to find out what possible advantage to its case could be imagined from further conditions laid down by Lenin. It would seem clear on the face of it that any further preconditions to a revolutionary situation could only have the effect of making less probable any valid occurrence of that kind of situation.

Our dialogue was resumed as follows:

> Government Counsel: [Prior to] recess we were discussing formulation of the conditions for a revolutionary situation in *The War and the Second International,* by Lenin, and I was asking you whether the same passage did not go on to name certain so-called subjective conditions. Have you had an opportunity to check on that?
>
> The Witness: No, sir. I haven't looked at it again; but I have it here before me.
>
> Government Counsel: Well, suppose I just read on from where you left off, then, and you can verify me, if you will. I will start with the last sentence of the passage ...
>
> The Witness: Yes, sir.
>
> Government Counsel: "The co-existence of all these objective changes is called a revolutionary situation. This situation existed in 1905 in Russia and in all the periods of revolution in the West, but it also existed in the seventh decade of the last century in Germany; it existed in 1859-1861 and in 1879-1880 in Russia, though there was no revolution in these latter instances. Why? Because a revolution emerges not out of every revolutionary situation, but out of such situations where, to the above mentioned objective changes, subjective ones are added, namely, the ability of the revolutionary *classes* to carry out revolutionary mass actions *strong* enough to break (or to undermine) the old government, it being the rule that never, not even in a period of crises, does a government 'fall' of itself without being 'helped to fall.' " [Italics in original]
>
> And that is the subjective situation there referred to, is it, Doctor?
>
> The Witness: Yes, sir.
>
> Government Counsel: And from the context we gathered, did we not, that the government does not fall of itself, but has to be helped to fall?

The Witness: Yes, sir, in quote marks.

Government Counsel: Yes, that is right. Now, I am not sure whether I asked you this morning, but I do want to get clear about it. Whenever the Communists deal with these situations, they are unquestionably talking about the conditions for a violent revolution, are they not?

The Witness: Yes, I think so, in most of the cases, a great majority of the cases, probably.

Government Counsel: Well, is there any kind in which these conditions would not be related to a forcible revolution?

The Witness: In the sense that you just read from the passage that sometimes these conditions that constituted a revolutionary situation may be present but no actual revolution takes place....

Government Counsel: But the objective and subjective conditions are those conditions precedent for a forcible revolution; is that correct?

The Witness: Yes, sir. They must be present before there is a forcible revolution.

Government Counsel: Now, the circumstances or the conditions under which a revolution can take place, and we will put it under which a revolution can take place, are, in fact, those which the Communist Party does teach, are they not?

The Witness: I—I don't know whether I grasp exactly what your questions means. Would you repeat it?

Government Counsel: Well, in Communist teaching and understanding, let us assume that they teach that a forcible revolution can occur only if certain conditions constituting a revolutionary situation exist.

The Witness: Yes...

Government Counsel: Now what those conditions, in fact, are as taught in the party are those which the party actually teaches in its schools; is that correct?

The Witness: Yes, sir; I should think so.

Government Counsel: So that if you, Doctor, being human and fallible, should be wrong in your inference as to what the Communist Party does teach, what the Communist Party in fact, teaches, would govern, would it not?

The reader may be somewhat puzzled as to what counsel could be driving at in asking a question of this kind. Taken in purely logical terms, it is simply asking a person to agree that if he is mistaken then he is mistaken. Each side in any dispute would necessarily agree with such a supposition. But what light would that throw on which side is actually mistaken and which side is not mistaken? It is certainly clear that it would throw no light whatever.

It is also possible that the prosecution meant to suggest by such a question that there might be some teaching within the party which is not only supplementary to the positions laid down in the "classics," but contradictory to those positions. In that case, the government side would need an entirely new body of evidence to sustain its charges against the defendants, since its whole procedure in this trial, and all the other trials of this type, has been to argue that the defendants must be in a criminal conspiracy precisely because they teach, advocate, and believe the doctrines laid down in the "classics" of Marxism-Leninism.

It is therefore being maintained by the government that belief in the teachings found in the classics themselves, not belief in something contrary to those teachings, necessarily involves activity that is criminal. In other words, this is all a battle about Marxist-Leninist books, for the simple reason that the government has produced no evidence save what goes back to those books. As a matter of fact, according to the government's indictments, the very organizing of a school for the teaching of the principles set forth in the works of Marx, Engels, Lenin, and Stalin is an "overt act" of criminal conspiracy.

I need not labor the point that it is strange to find such attitudes being officially taken in this country. Indeed, if the government's contention about what is in these books were correct, it would be impossible to escape the conclusion that they should be removed from general sale and circulation, from bookstores and public libraries, and be made available only to "authorized" persons "cleared" by the government.

At one point in the trial the defense did in fact put on the stand a public librarian and a college librarian to testify that these books are and always have been openly available to all, without any special restrictions. The prosecution, however, did not see fit to let this pass without drawing an analogy to books about poisons, which actually precipitated a courtroom discussion of toxicology.

As I listened to all this, I could not help recalling a prewar visit I had made, at the height of the Nazi power, to the Berlin Museum of the First National Socialist Revolution. This extraordinary institution had somewhat the flavor of a kind of Nazi Smithsonian where one could find historical curiosities, rare documents and relics preserved under glass cases. It included what was evidently regarded as a sort of chamber of horrors, where the loyal Nazi, the then respectable German citizen, could satisfy his curiosity by gazing, through heavy glass panels securely locked, at the outside of actual books written by Marx, Engels, Lenin, Stalin, and Karl Liebknecht. There were proper labelings and safe explanations affixed to the panels to tell the public the nature of what was inside the books, any actual contact with which was reserved, of course, only for persons specially authorized by security agencies of the Nazi government.

Many Americans and other visitors were grimly amused to see such an attitude solemnly taken toward books that were then and are now publicly available in all countries which have developed any extensive educational facilities and which can claim any significant practice of intellectual freedom. Are we now in process of removing ourselves from this class of countries? Is it possible we can learn nothing at all from history?

Defense counsel objected to the self-evident question about whether I, being human, might be wrong, but it was allowed. After I readily agreed that I was human, and that, if the facts were different then they would be different, the questioning proceeded as follows:

> Government Counsel: Now, Doctor, you have testified, and I am trying here to quote exactly your testimony—you have testified that the Communists do take the view that violent overthrow of the government is justified under certain circumstances. That was at page 4710.
>
> The Witness: Yes, sir.
>
> Government Counsel: And you phrased it in other words, "What they are advocating is the right to use force and violence under certain conditions." That is on page 4719. Have I quoted you correctly?
>
> The Witness: Yes, sir. That is part of it.
>
> Government Counsel: Under certain conditions—I am not naming the conditions at the moment... And your testimony was related with respect to these circumstances, to the objective conditions; you didn't bother with subjective ones; is that correct?
>
> The Witness: That may be correct. I don't recall whether the sub—so-called subjective conditions seemed relevant at that point or were brought in.

THE CONCEPT OF "REVOLUTIONARY SITUATION"    163

Government Counsel: The subjective conditions being in simple terms a very strong Communist Party? Is that correct?
The Witness: You might call it that, yes, yes.
Government Counsel: Yes.
The Witness: It might be an added—that would be an added condition which should also be present before any forcible revolution could take place.
Government Counsel: That is right.
The Witness: Yes.

Thus concluded the prosecutions's rather strange effort to gain some advantage from the fact that Lenin had spoken of certain "subjective" preconditions of a revolutionary situation, in addition to "objective" preconditions. What Lenin obviously meant by using the word "subjective" in referring to "the ability of the revolutionary *classes* to carry out revolutionary mass actions *strong* enough to break (or to undermine) the old government" (Lenin's italics) was that this ability is a matter of internal self-discipline and organizational skill. It is not something externally imposed on the people, like physical oppression, political tyranny, or economic misery, things which happen independently of and contrary to the will of the masses.

In other words, there must be a certain amount of political organization, good judgment, group solidarity, and the like if anything as complex as a revolution is to be successfully carried out if and when the time comes. Hence, counsel was to that extent correct in saying that from the Communists' point of view this amounts, in simple terms, to a very strong Communist Party. Naturally, they think that things will go badly if their party is not a good, strong one at such a moment. All this could readily be taken for granted.

The odd thing is that the prosecution should have entertained the idea, as it apparently did, that such an added condition would somehow make the case against the defendants stronger. Actually, it has the opposite effect, since it means that one further requirement must be present before any revolution would be entered upon. In other words, even if the other preconditions were present, but this one were absent, no revolution should be undertaken, according to the teachings of this group. However, this precondition is rather self-evident, since no group could successfully undertake anything without being sufficiently organized.

Before relinquishing its attempt to suggest there might be some doubt about the relation of "majority" to the Communist understanding of the revolutionary situation, the prosecution presented one more passage which did not happen to use the explicit term "majority," though the synonyms that were used were assuredly clear enough. This passage was from Stalin's *Foundations of Leninism,* page 44, and was quoted as follows:

> "At the same time, however, it must be borne in mind that the overthrow of the bourgeoisie can be successfully accomplished only when certain absolutely necessary conditions exist, in the absence of which there can even be no question of the proletariat taking power.
>
> "Here is what Lenin says about these conditions in his pamphlet *'Left-Wing' Communism, an Infantile Disorder:*
>
> " 'The fundamental law of revolution, which has been confirmed by all revolutions, and particularly by all three Russian revolutions in the twentieth century, consists in the following: it is not enough for revolution that the exploited and oppressed masses should understand the impossibility of living in the old way, and demand changes; for revolution it is necessary that the exploiters should not be able to live and rule in the old way. Only when the "lower classes" *do not want* the old way, and when the "upper classes" *cannot carry on in the old* way—only then can revolution triumph. This truth may be expressed in other words: *Revolution is impossible without a nation-wide crisis (affecting both the exploited and the exploiters).* It follows that for revolution it is essential, first, that a majority of the workers (or at least a majority of the class conscious, thinking, politically active workers) should fully understand the necessity for revolution and be ready to sacrifice their lives for it; secondly, that the ruling classes should be passing through a governmental crisis which would draw even the most backward masses into politics ... weaken the government and make it possible for the revolutionaries to overthrow it rapidly.' (Lenin, *Selected Works,* Vol. X, p. 127.)" (Stalin's italics.) Now, in those conditions there laid down, Doctor, there is no statement that there must be a majority of the people in support, is there?

The Witness: I think there is.

Government Counsel: Would you point it out, please?

The Witness: Yes, sir. When Lenin says, toward the beginning of the passage "...it is not enough for revolution that the exploited

# THE CONCEPT OF "REVOLUTIONARY SITUATION" 165

and oppressed masses... " I think he clearly means by "exploited and oppressed masses" the majority. In his view the majority of the people are exploited and oppressed under capitalism.

Then he goes on, "... should understand the impossibility of living in the old way and demand changes ..."—in other words, saying that he has got the support there of the exploited and oppressed masses, the majority. And then again, when he goes on and says, "... the 'lower classes' *do not want* the old way" there is no doubt that in his view the exploited lower classes comprise the majority of the population...

Government Counsel: Well, may I ask you this? When he says: "It follows that for revolution it is essential, first, that a majority of the workers (or at least a majority of the class conscious, thinking, politically active workers) should fully understand the necessity for revolution and be ready to sacrifice their lives for it ..." he is not talking about the majority there, is he?

The Witness: Oh, not there; he is referring to that group that will have reached the point where they are ready to sacrifice their lives, and where they fully understand, and all that sort of thing. That is a different thing from having their support. You may have the support of a lot of people who are not ready to sacrifice their lives, and maybe who do not fully understand all that is involved, but you have got their support ...

Government Counsel: He is not talking about active participation, then, is he, by the exploited and oppressed masses?

The Witness: I don't understand your question.

Government Counsel: Well, you were focusing on this question of having support, were you not?

The Witness: Yes, sir.

Government Counsel: Instead of active participation.

The Witness: No, no; here he is talking about support as contrasted to being ready to sacrifice your life.

Government Counsel: I am sorry; that is what I meant by "active participation."

The Witness: Well, that is a rather extreme form of active participation. There is a distinction there, I think.

The reader will, I believe, agree that even if there were no other relevant passages except these two which the prosecution chose to bring forward at this point, the fact that these passages, written by Marxists, used terms like "exploited and oppressed masses," "lower classes," "oppressed classes," and "masses," would be proof beyond doubt that they were referring to the majority. Anyone possessed even of a slight acquaintance with the teachings of Marxism-Leninism must realize that there is no possibility whatever that the "lower classes," the "exploited and oppressed masses," as Marxists use those terms, could mean anything but a majority of the population.

Surely it is well known, even by the general public, that the whole premise of Marxist economic and political thinking is that, under capitalism, the ruling class is a tiny minority, and the lower, exploited classes a vast majority. In other words, Marxists firmly believe, and never tire of repeating their belief, that under capitalism the majority are exploited by the minority. To them the majority are the exploited and the exploited are the majority.

Therefore when they speak of the "exploited and oppressed masses" or "lower classes" wanting something, demanding something, supporting something, or doing something, it is clearly understood that they are referring to the majority. (If, however, there were still any vestige of doubt left in anyone's mind, he would need only to examine the numerous passages, such as those we quoted above, in which the explicit term "majority" is used over and over again by the leading Marxist authorities.)

What we are here saying does not constitute any evaluation of the teachings of Communists. For example, they could be all wrong in their view that the majority is actually exploited under capitalism. If they were completely wrong about that, it would have as little bearing on the issue before us as if they were completely right. For the issue depends not on whether what they say about the allegedly exploited is right or wrong. That is a matter of opinion. It depends on what they mean by "the exploited" in their teachings. That is not a matter of opinion. It is a matter of ascertainable fact, which can be settled by examining their teachings. The fact is they are talking about the majority.

That this is an important fact—perhaps *the* important fact in all these cases—can be judged from the persistence with which the prosecution tried to suggest that the teachings in question might not include a commitment to majority support. The extent of failure in this attempt measures, possibly more clearly than anything else, the lack of a logically justifiable foundation for the government's case.

# 8  Related Issues

## War, Imperialism, and Revolution

All the main lines of argument on the subject of Marxist-Leninist teachings have now been put before the reader, and have been analyzed. All the key passages on which reliance was placed have been quoted in full and discussed. However, before making a final summary of the issues, we should examine, at least briefly, a few of what might be called secondary passages—that is, excerpts brought in by the prosecution, but not emphasized or developed to any great extent.

One of these concerned the possible relationship of revolution to war, or of war to revolution. It was introduced toward the end of cross-examination, in the following way:

> Government Counsel: Now, Doctor, is it taught by the Communists that the revolutionary situation may arise out of a war in which the capitalist government is engaged?
> The Witness: Yes, sir.
> Government Counsel: It is specifically mentioned several times, isn't it?
> The Witness: Yes, sir. That is one of the situations out of which a revolutionary situation may arise...
> Government Counsel: Do not the Communists teach that in case the capitalist government is engaged in imperialist war the proletarian revolution may be hastened by turning the imperialist war into a civil war?

167

The Witness: That was taught under certain conditions that that would be the case, specifically in the First World War.

Government Counsel: Yes. I would like to refer you to that. I want to read you a very brief passage in the *History of the Communist Party of the Soviet Union* with respect to that.... page 167. We are going to start with the third paragraph.

The Witness: Yes, sir.

Government Counsel: "In opposition to the Menshevik and Socialist-Revolutionary policy of defending the bourgeois fatherland, the Bolsheviks advanced the policy of *'the defeat of one's own government in the imperialist war.*[9] This meant voting against war credits, forming illegal revolutionary organizations in the armed forces, supporting fraternization among the soldiers at the front, organizing revolutionary actions of the workers and peasants against the war, and turning these actions into an uprising against one's own imperialist government.

"The Bolsheviks maintained that the lesser evil for the people would be the military defeat of the tsarist government in the imperialist war, for this would facilitate the victory of the people over tsardom, and the success of the struggle of the working class for emancipation from capitalist slavery and imperialist wars. Lenin held that the policy of working for the defeat of one's own imperialist government must be pursued not only by the Russian revolutionaries, but by the revolutionary parties of the working class in *all* the belligerent countries." (Italics in original.)

That is definitely Communist doctrine, is it?

The Witness: Yes, sir; in respect to the time period that you see at the top of each page of this chapter, 1914-1917. The reference to all belligerent countries pins it down, of course, to those countries at war during those years, the years of the First World War.

Government Counsel: In any of the writings of the American Communists you have mentioned have you seen any reference on their part to this doctrine?

The Witness: Do you mean to this doctrine as applied to 1914-1917?

Government Counsel: No, as applied to the work of the Communists in the United States.

The reader may observe, in the approach here being taken by the prosecution, a certain similarity to one of its attempts previously made. That is, as government counsel had before vainly tried to argue that, according to Communist teaching, every capitalist country would automatically be in a revolutionary situation, so here they were apparently trying to suggest that every case of war would have to be regarded as a revolutionary situation. However, such a view would be true neither to the principles of the teachings nor to the historical facts of actual practice. Thus I answered the last question as follows:

> The Witness: I have never seen any references in any Communist writers of the United States to the effect that this doctrine should apply to all wars.
> Government Counsel: I am going to read to you, Doctor, again from William Z. Foster's book *From Bryan to Stalin,* starting on page 159.
> "Although I was, in 1921, deeply certain that the Russian workers had found the way to Socialism and eventual Communism in Soviet Russia, I was not by that fact alone convinced that the Communist program for achieving Socialism was necessarily the best one for other countries, especially the United States. On the contrary, I weighed every phase of it in the light of American conditions and my own long experience in the class struggle. And the final result was that in Leninism I found the answer to every major revolutionary problem.
> "To begin with, I did not have to be convinced in principle of the necessity for a revolutionary struggle to overthrow capitalism. A dozen years earlier I had recognized the futility of the Socialist Party's policy of trying to transform capitalism into Socialism through piecemeal reforms, and my whole conception of Syndicalism, even in its most opportunistic phases, had been based upon the proposition of smashing the power of the capitalists by the workers' superior force. All my experience in the class struggle fighting the cold-blooded, autocratic and ruthless American trusts had ground into my very being the realization that the ruling capitalist class will never allow itself to be talked, bought or voted out of power, but will proceed to any extreme of violence to maintain its control. But Communism taught me many vital lessons regarding the forms and methods of carrying on this revolutionary struggle, including the policy of transforming an imperialist war into a revolutionary war against capitalism, the combination of revolutionary agitation and struggle with the daily fight of the workers for immediate demands, the united

front of the workers and peas ants; these policies have been so brilliantly illustrated in the Russian revolution, and all of them, with adaptation to local situations, are applicable and indispensable in every capitalist country."
Do you recall that passage?
The Witness: Yes, sir. That says "imperialist wars."
Government Counsel: Yes.
The Witness: That is not all wars.

The reader will observe not only that the passage presented by the prosecution dealt with "an imperialist war" rather than all wars, but that it came from a work written by Foster in 1937 rather than any of his works of recent years, wherein, as we have seen, new and important positions are laid down in his teachings.

These new positions obviously reflect new conditions that have arisen since 1937, both on the world scene taken as a whole, and in this country in particular. Anyone now alive who was seriously dealing with public issues in 1937 need only think back to the differences as between the atmosphere and attitudes of those days and the early 1950's to appreciate this point.

But the prosecution persisted in trying to equate Foster's 1937 statement not only with the present, but even with the future. Thus the interrogation proceeded:

Government Counsel: I think we are aware of that, Doctor. We have had that subject before. Just as a matter of information, though, may I ask you—in Communist parlance any country engaged in war against the Soviet Union is engaged in an imperialist war, is it not?
The Witness: Any country engaged in a war against the Soviet Union would be engaged in an imperialist war? Well, that might be a debatable proposition according to their doctrine.
Government Counsel: Isn't that Communist doctrine, Doctor?
The Witness: No, that might be a debatable proposition according to their doctrine. It might not be quite so simple.
Government Counsel: I will ask you if this—
The Court: Before we leave that, what would be an imperialist war, in your judgment, according to what the Communist Party teaches?
The Witness: As far as one can gather from their writings, Your Honor, in their view an imperialist war would seem to be a

war in which the causes at issue are mainly, almost exclusively or exclusively the redivision of colonies, the expansion or decrease of empires, the quarrel over markets and territories, a war that is almost exclusively concerned with such stakes as these—the redivision of colonial dependencies, of colonial territories, of overseas markets, and that sort of thing.

The Court: That embraces pretty nearly all wars, doesn't it?

The Witness: No, I don't think so, Your Honor.

The Court: Overseas markets?

The Witness: Only where it is almost exclusively concerned—for example, in their school of thought the First World War was declared outright to be an imperialist war. They seemed to think it had to do exclusively or almost exclusively with the redivision of colonial territories, mainly between Britain and Germany, speaking of that time. But the Second World War was different in their point of view. The Second World War was not an imperialist war as such. It became in its course of development to them a patriotic—what they call a patriotic war—because, as they saw it, the future of Socialism became something at stake; so that war had to be treated differently, as they saw it. They made those distinctions, whether they were right or wrong.

The Court: Did Russia's engagement in the Second World War have any weight in the balance?

The Witness: Oh, yes; that was the point, Your Honor. Russia's engagement in it was what made it a patriotic war in their terms. I speak now mainly of the literature of the Soviet Russian Communist writers. To them it was a war in which the future of Socialism was at stake, a patriotic war in that sense, as they saw their situation.

Government Counsel: As a matter of fact, Doctor, before June 22, 1941, before Germany attacked Russia, had there been a slogan of the Communists, "The Yanks Are Not Coming"—this is an imperialist war.

The Witness: Yes, I think so. Up to that point of time, I rather think they thought the future of Socialism was not at stake so much as it was later on. That seemed to be their view.

The prosecution at this point left the subject of war, and did not return to it. There did not, indeed, seem to be much ground for the prosecution to stand upon in this matter. All that could be pointed to was the fact that in a certain war, the First World War, the slogan, "defeat of one's own government in the imperialist war" had been advanced. But it obviously could not be argued that such a slogan would be advanced in every war that was considered an imperialist war, because the prosecution itself, while maintaining that the Communists considered the Second World War purely an imperialist war before the U.S.S.R. was engaged in it, had to recognize that no slogan of that character was advanced by the Communists. Hence, no logical conclusion could be drawn that in a future imperialist war such a slogan would necessarily be put forward.

If the prosecution had gone further into this matter the fact would also have had to be acknowledged that, although the directive to work for the defeat of one's own imperialist government was laid down during World War I, it was very far from being followed by all concerned. In fact, this was one of the issues which caused serious splits as between national parties in the international movement, and within national parties, as between group and group. Indeed, this may have been one of the reasons why no slogan of that type was advanced in the early stages of World War II.

In its full sense, an "imperialist" war as such is a war in which both sides are "imperialist exploiters," fighting exclusively or mainly over the spoils of colonial conquests. But surely one need not invoke such a concept to understand that any country which is at war tries to get the people on the other side to revolt against their own government, because such action may weaken that government.

All history shows that any government, including our own, can be expected to consider such an idea an excellent one. Whenever we are in a war, we naturally make every possible appeal to induce the people on the other side to consider their government a bad one, an evil one which should not be supported in its armed actions against us, which should be overthrown in favor of a just and decent government.

Even as we have taken such a line on past occasions, I should expect that our government would probably take a similar line in any possible future war. I should likewise expect that any government engaged in a war against us would also take that kind of line. Under such circumstances, any group within a country which has sympathetic connections with some other country, whether such connections are racial, ideological, religious, or of any other type, will probably be looked upon with suspicion, justifiably or unjustifiably, when there is fear of a possible war with that other country.

It will be felt that in the event of actual war some persons in such a group might collaborate with the enemy.

Yet who would say that these conditions constitute sufficient reason to throw such a group in jail now? The population of our country represents a great variety of racial, national, religious, and ideological backgrounds and connections. Now that we are a Great Power of the first rank, we cannot expect to be without strong competitors, against whom there is likely to be strong feeling. If we were to try to adopt a policy of throwing those sections of our citizenry into jail who had close ties with our current competitor, we would have to change our Constitution, our entire concept of justice, and the whole character of our national life. I do not think we are prepared to do that.

In any case, there is nothing in Communist teachings to the effect that during a war the preconditions of the revolutionary situation are not necessary. There is absolutely nothing which says that a war automatically brings about this situation. War or no war, the Communist teaching is that forcible overthrow of government is justified only when the existing regime cannot carry out its normal functions, and there is majority support for the revolutionary step. If we are to judge the teaching, this fact is of decisive importance.

Another passage introduced by the prosecution, but not pursued at any great length, was from Stalin's *Foundations of Leninism,* page 35, and was read as follows:

> Government Counsel: "Now we must speak of the existence of objective conditions for the revolution in the entire system of world imperialist economy as an integral unit; the existence within this system of some countries that are not sufficiently developed industrially cannot serve as an insurmountable obstacle to the revolution *if* the system as a whole, or, more correctly, *because* the system as a whole is already ripe for revolution." (Italics in original.)
>
> Is that a statement that objective conditions exist in capitalist countries?
>
> The Witness: That is a statement that the objective conditions may exist in various capitalist countries, even though some other capitalist countries are not as fully developed—yes.
>
> Government Counsel: Well, how do you explain that very last clause, "or, more correctly, *because* the system as a whole is already ripe for revolution"?

The Witness: Well, this passage goes back to an old debate among these Communists about their theory. That really goes back to the days of Marx and Engels. The older view of Marx and Engels was that the revolution would be a kind of—when it came—would be a kind of simultaneous, world-wide revolution, or, at least, a simultaneous revolution in the major capitalist countries of the world. That was the old view that was held in their day by Marx and Engels.

Then Lenin considerably modified that view and thus—
Government Counsel: He had the one-country idea, didn't he?
The Witness: And then came in the one-country idea.
Government Counsel: Yes.
The Witness: I think he is hammering at the same thing, that nowadays, he is saying to his followers, we have got to accept the position that the system as a whole may be in a sense ripe, but the revolution is not necessarily going to be simultaneous in the world or in leading countries—
Government Counsel: I see.
The Witness:—but may occur in one or another separately, yes, sir.
Government Counsel: But he now does say that the objective conditions for a revolution do exist, does he not?
The Witness: Not in all the countries, no, no, no. He is saying, now we have to face the fact that these objective conditions may exist in one country but not in another in the same world system of capitalism.
Government Counsel: What is this, what does it mean—"*because* the system as a whole is already ripe for revolution"?
The Witness: I think he means by that the system as a whole represents a kind of world imperialism. Prior to the latter years of the nineteenth century and the opening years of the twentieth century, lots of the world wasn't explored; and the colonial system had not developed to any great extent. But now the system must be viewed, in his position, as a system of connected world imperialism. But I think he is trying to say we must not think because of that that the revolution is going to burst out everywhere at once, and that—
Government Counsel: I think I see.

Had the prosecution desired to pursue this matter, discussion would have brought out at this point that Lenin's modification of the older "classic" thesis consisted in the new view that the revolution could no longer necessarily be expected to occur first in the most highly industrialized countries. Lenin maintained that the older thesis, while correct for the conditions of Marx's day, had become outmoded since the development of world imperialism.

The Leninist argument, whether valid or invalid, was that the injustices, resentments, and economic oppressions increasingly generated by the world-wide spread of the colonial system had, by the first quarter of the twentieth century, reached a point where revolution might possibly break out in any one of a number of territories where native peoples were held in colonial subjection. In other words, in this view, such conditions were increasingly likely to bring into being a revolutionary situation, wherein the majority of people desired a radical change which the government in control was unwilling to grant.

Thus Stalin puts the point, on the page following the one quoted by the prosecution:

> "Where will the revolution begin? Where, in what country, can the front of capital be pierced first?
>
> "Where industry is more developed, where the proletariat constitutes the majority, where there is more culture, where there is more democracy—that was the reply usually given formerly.
>
> "No, objects the Leninist theory of revolution; *not necessarily where industry is more developed,* and so forth. The front of capital will be pierced where the chain of imperialism is weakest, for the proletarian revolution is the result of the breaking of the chain of the world imperialist front at its weakest link; and it may turn out that the country which has started the revolution, which has made a breach in the front of capital, is less developed in a capitalist sense than other, more developed countries which have, however, remained within the framework of capitalism." (Stalin's italics.)

It is certainly worth noting that, according to this very teaching, stemming from Lenin and carried on by Stalin and subsequent leaders to the present day, the United States would be the last country where a proletarian revolution would be expected to occur, since this country is regarded as the strongest, not the weakest, link in the chain of "world imperialism." In fact, it was the prosecution itself which had insisted, early in cross-examination, on emphasizing that point when, in the course of questioning as reported above, government counsel sought and obtained my agreement that it is "Communist teaching that the United States is the most powerful imperialist force in the world..."

Another passage introduced by the prosecution but not dealt with at any length was a brief excerpt from page 1 of Andrei Vyshinsky's book, *The Law of the Soviet State:*

> "The violent seizure of authority by the proletariat, the demolition of the exploiting society's machinery of state and the organization (in lieu of the old state machinery now reduced to fragments) of a new state is the most important thesis of the Marxist-Leninist doctrine of proletarian revolution."

No doubt one of the reasons why there was no extended examination of this passage by the prosecution is that it would be so readily understandable, in the light of previous discussion, that Communist teaching emphasizes the necessity of a revolutionary situation as a precondition of any of the events mentioned in the passage. That is, in the Communist understanding, none of these happenings should or would take place except where the existing government is no longer able to carry out its normal functions, and there is majority support for the revolutionary step.

We are now in a position to take a reckoning.

# 9  The Continuing Danger

## Roots and Perspectives

The jury brought in a verdict of guilty, and the defendants were sentenced to prison terms varying from two to three years. One could certainly wish, in the interests of social science, that each member of the jury had made a written analysis of the reasoning which led to his decision. Such reports would undoubtedly make significant reading.

While the logic that should be decisive to the issues in a case of this kind is by no means too difficult for the average citizen to grasp, the jurors' task, in the circumstances under which it had to be performed, was an enormously difficult one. To appreciate this fact, the reader need only cast back in his mind over all the quotations from the "classics of Marxism-Leninism" in all the preceding chapters of this book, and ask himself whether, as he read them, they were clear to him at the first reading. Doubtless many of them were not.

If some key passage from Lenin or Stalin was not clear, the reader was able to pause at that point, and go over it as many times as he wished, resuming his reading only after he had come to some conclusions about it. Then, too, in the course of this book, explanatory background is supplied which, unfortunately, it was not possible to supply in the courtroom. Add to this the fact that the reader had to focus his attention on fewer quotations than the jurors, since we have weeded out some that were presented, but upon which no particular reliance was placed in the development of the case, and some that turned out to be repetitive.

If, even under these conditions, the reader experienced difficulty at times in understanding, weighing, and judging the content of the quoted passages, let him imagine how much greater that difficulty must have been for the jurors. They could not read and ponder the text on a printed page as the quotations were introduced. They had to listen to them being read, which is a much harder way to grasp a complex thought. They could not go over a given passage again and again at the time that procedure might have been most needed. They had to shift their attention immediately to the argument or comment which followed the reading.

Little historical or logical background could be given to them. They had to be content with what could filter through, in garbled form, after reference to logically relevant facts, such as the Declaration of Independence, and the right of self-defense, had been forbidden.

Under such circumstances even a professional scholar with years of experience in judging texts containing detailed formulations of complex ideas might find it impossible to form accurate impressions, and arrive at balanced judgments. And, among the jurors who sat in Philadelphia, as well as those in all the other Smith Act trials, there was probably not a single professional scholar. Yet they were expected to decide intricate issues of ideological doctrine.

What previous experience could they bring to this enormous responsibility thus thrust upon them? Had any one of them ever read through a "classic" of Marxism-Leninism, or even a chapter of such a "classic" in his or her entire life? Yet, reflect upon what they were being asked to decide. They had to say whether, when you accepted the principles set forth in those classics, taken as a whole, you were or were not necessarily committed to the violent overthrow of the Government of the United States.

It is self-evident that, in order to make such a decision, you must first know the meaning of the doctrine, taken all in all. To do that you must be prepared to carry out a careful and extensive reading program after a certain amount of preliminary training in economics, philosophy, and political science. If persons have not had the opportunity to fulfill these requirements, how can they be expected to understand the meaning of a total body of ideological doctrine scattered through dozens of heavy volumes written by Marx, Engels, Lenin, Stalin, Foster, and others over a period of more than a century? Yet if they do not understand that meaning, how can they render judgment on whether or not that meaning necessarily entails conspiracy to overthrow by violence our United States Government?

A political and social ideology, like a system of religious beliefs, is an *interconnected* body of doctrine. If any of its statements or teachings is to be understood, it must be taken in the context of its relationships within the system as a whole. Otherwise it will simply not be understood. This is one of the most elementary rules of scholarship. It should be self-evident that no book can receive a fair trial unless those who are asked to render judgment are in a position to understand the contents of the book as a whole.

If by any chance anyone did not realize that books are on trial in these cases, a glance into a courtroom where one of them is in process would bring him to a shocked awakening. The tables for prosecution and defense are groaning under piles of books, sometimes stacked so high one has difficulty identifying the lawyer sitting behind them. Witnesses walk to the stand balancing outsize volumes in one hand, and clutching an overloaded briefcase in the other.

The anterooms reserved to counsel and clients of the respective sides for the duration of a trial become reference and lending libraries, with books indexed and catalogued, instantly available for courtroom quotation or counter-quotation, then carefully replaced so as to be in readiness for the next passage-at-arms. Each side has to assign specially trained personnel to keep track of the books, to see that they are all available and in good order. Library hand trucks resembling large tea wagons are wheeled in and out of the courtroom for each session, stacked with the "reserve" books likely to be used that day.

From beginning to end, it is a battle of books, and from beginning to end, the entire battle goes back to one root question: What is taught concerning violent overthrow of government in all these books written by Marx, Engels, Lenin, Stalin, Foster, and other Communist leaders?

This situation is significantly and almost unbelievably reflected in the indictments drawn against the defendants. The purpose of such a document is to set forth the detailed charges and to list the "overt acts" which the government alleges were committed by the accused. In this case the section of the indictment headed "Overt Acts" lists twenty-eight separate actions, so numbered. Not a single one of them even alleges violence, the making of insurrectionary plans, the acquisition of weapons, military training, or anything of that kind.

The "overt acts" are attendance at Communist Party classes, participation in state conventions of the Communist Party, recruiting members into the Communist Party, attending Communist meetings, rallies, dinners, and even picnics! (All this while the Communist Party was a completely legal organization.) Count 21, for example, states absolutely nothing except that one of the defendants "did prepare and cause to be circulated a press release of the Eastern Pennsylvania and Delaware District of the Communist Party of the United States of America." Nothing wrong is alleged about the content of the press release, which is not quoted or even summarized. The "overt act" is simply that the defendant issued this press release as a Communist Party functionary; therefore his act was presumed to be part of a Communist conspiracy.

The whole of Count 1 is that a defendant "did attend and participate in a class of the Communist Party of the United States of America, held at the Wharton Center, 1708 North 22nd Street, Philadelphia, Pennsylvania." No claim is made about anything taking place in the class.

Count 3 is nothing more or less than that a defendant "did attend and participate in the New York State Convention of the Communist Party, held at Webster Hall, 119 East 11th Street, New York, N.Y." No further charges are made about this convention, which was openly and legally held.

Count 16 is entirely devoted to the statement that a defendant "did attend and participate in a rally at Fred Wrigley Hall, Quakertown, Pennsylvania." One brief sentence; no charge whatever that the defendant did anything unusual at the rally.

Count 19 makes the sole charge that two of the defendants "did attend and participate in an affair sponsored for the purpose of raising and securing funds for the Communist Party, held at the Old Mill Road picnic grounds located near Sellersville, Pennsylvania."

Nothing concrete that happened at any of the classes, meetings, conventions, and rallies is mentioned, detailed, or summarized. It was apparently enough for the prosecution that they were *Communist* affairs. The reasoning is simple: since they were Communist affairs, they were necessarily parts of a criminal conspiracy. Why necessarily? Because a Communist believes in certain alleged teachings, and these alleged teachings are that the United States

Government must be overthrown by force and violence. Where are these alleged teachings which a Communist must believe in, and which are supposed to tell him that such a thing must be done? They are in the books written by the leaders of the movement—principally by Marx, Engels, Lenin, Stalin, and Foster. Such is the prosecution's "reasoning."

In other words, the prosecution is not saying the defendants are guilty because we caught them in an act of violence, or because we found weapons on them, or discovered weapons secreted on their premises, or because we found plans to purchase or manufacture weapons, or because we found plans of military operation, or even plans for military training. The prosecution is saying they are guilty because they believe what is in those books, and we caught them in such "acts" as attending classes to study and teach these books, attending and participating in meetings, conventions, rallies, picnics, sending out press releases, and the like, all for the purpose of helping to carry out the program laid down in those books.

This program is not proved criminal because of the "overt acts" done in its name by the defendants. These "acts" are in themselves quite innocent. In fact, many were open to the public and even advertised. The "reasoning" is in reverse: the "overt acts" are proved criminal because of the program that is allegedly believed in!

How does the prosecution "prove" that the program is in itself a criminal one, that it necessarily involves the believer and the leader, the pupil and the teacher, in a criminal conspiracy? The prosecution selects passages from these books, and reads them to judge and jury, or has witnesses read them to judge and jury. The witnesses attest that these books are taught and used as basic authorities in Communist schools, classes, party instruction, and so on. (The whole world knows this, and has always known it; and no Communist has ever denied it.)

Witnesses and prosecution then claim that in teaching these books Communists are teaching that our government, as at present constituted, should and must be overthrown by force and violence. The alleged proof? The contents of the passages. In the last analysis, the government's case rests on the books, all the books, and nothing but the books.

Put bluntly—and this is of decisive importance—if the prosecution is wrong about what is in those books, it has no case whatsoever. The conclusion is logically inescapable that the prosecution *is* wrong about what is in those books. What is in them, taken as a whole, can be gotten at by analysis, and only by analysis. It is a job that requires patience, scholarship, perspective, and, above all, a certain amount of scrupulousness in dealing with beliefs that you yourself do not share and to which you may even be strongly opposed.

The prosecution is wrong about what is in those books because it is not taking them as a whole. It is taking statements out of context, and trying to close its eyes to the qualifications attached to those statements, as our analysis of the revolutionary situation has shown. Moreover, the prosecution fails to distinguish between doctrines taught in recent years (which are the only ones legally or morally decisive in the proceedings) and doctrines of long ago which are no longer taught, as our analysis of Foster's writings on the problem of peaceful transition has shown. The prosecution also goes so far as to ignore a whole series of passages wherein the linguistic expressions are crystal clear and impeccably explicit concerning some important point, like majority support, and then dwells upon one or two exceptional passages which do not happen to use the precise term itself, such as "majority," as if those passages were the only ones in existence on that particular point.

What especially proves the prosecution wrong, irretrievably wrong from any logical standpoint, is the whole doctrine of the revolutionary situation. The government side is trying to maintain, in this trial and in all similar trials, in the Smith Act and in all similar legislation, such as the McCarran Act and the Communist Control Act, that Communists are necessarily in a conspiracy to overthrow our government by force and violence "as speedily as circumstances would permit," to use the exact phrase that is repeated five times in the Philadelphia indictment.

Now that does not happen to be the doctrine taught by the Communists, as we have seen over and over again in the course of testimony quoted and analyzed in the preceding chapters of this book. Communists do *not* teach that an attempt at forcible overthrow of the government of the United States, or of any country, should be made "as speedily as circumstances would permit," without further qualification. That is nothing more or less than the doctrine known as *"putschism,"* and no Communist leader has ever taught it. In fact, Communist leaders like Marx, Engels, Lenin, Stalin, Foster, and Dennis have repeatedly condemned this doctrine in the most emphatic and explicit terms. The reader will recall that this point was dealt with in detail in the course of our foregoing discussion.

What the Communists teach, and have always taught, is not that an attempt at forcible overthrow of government should be made as speedily as circumstances would permit, irrespective of further conditions, but that such an attempt should be made only if and when there exists what is known to them as a "revolutionary situation." This means a situation in which a regime unwilling to implement the people's will has reached a point of breakdown where it is unable to solve its problems and to carry on normally, where adequate voting procedures are impossible, and where there is majority support for a revolutionary step. These are the only circumstances that "would permit" any attempt at forcible overthrow of government according to Communist teachings. The reader has seen how these conditions were laid down with great precision and clarity, and repeatedly emphasized in the basic Communist writings we quoted above.

The reader has also seen that these conditions are, in their essence, the same as those laid down in our own Declaration of Independence. If we did not agree with the Declaration that it is right and proper to overthrow a government by force when such government refuses to carry out the people's will, when adequate representation by voting is impossible, and where there is indication of mass support for the revolutionary step, how could we justify our own claim to sovereignty and independence? If those conditions are beyond legal recognition, then there is no such legal entity as the United States of America.

It is utterly impossible that the Congress, through the Smith Act, intended to make it a crime to believe in and advocate the teaching laid down in our most fundamental and precious political document. (The author of the Smith Act himself attests to this, as the correspondence we quote below shows.) However, even if through some sorry pattern of circumstances, the Congress did so intend on that occasion, surely the First Amendment, which forbids Congress to abridge freedom of speech, should protect the individual. Doubtless no clearer case of undue abridgment of freedom of speech could be conceived than an abridgment which would make it a crime to teach belief in the very principle on which the legitimacy of our own government depends.

It is logically instructive to put this point in the form of the following question: In order for the prosecution at one and the same time to prove its allegation that Communist teaching is that the government of the United States must be overthrown by force "as speedily as circumstances would permit," and to maintain that it (the prosecution) accepts the First Amendment and the Declaration of Independence, what must the prosecution find in the Communist teachings? In other words, suppose the prosecution were to say: "I want to accept the Declaration, and I want to accept the First Amendment, but I still want to insist that Communist teachings on the subject of revolution are illicit and criminal." In that case, what would the prosecution have to find in the Communist teachings?

The prosecution would have to find passages in predominance stating that minority revolution is what is aimed at, that mass support for the Communist revolution is not necessary or important, that the majority principle is of no account, that the whole idea of democratic values can be brushed aside. The prosecution would have to find that the great movements and thinkers associated with the birth and development of humanitarian democracy, such as John Locke, Thomas Jefferson, Abraham Lincoln, the British revolution of the seventeenth century, the American and French revolutions of the eighteenth century, are condemned, assuming they are evaluated.

The prosecution would have to find statements to the effect that the degree of economic or military strength possessed by a given capitalist government has no bearing on whether a revolution should be undertaken. It would have to find statements to the effect that whether or not the overwhelming majority support a given capitalist government has no bearing on whether a revolution should be undertaken. The prosecution would have to find that the teachings simply say: Try to overthrow the government of the United States *by force and violence* just as quickly as you can.

If the prosecution had been able to find anything of this sort in the Communist doctrines, it would, of course, have been presented to the court. It was not presented because it was not found; and it was not found because it is not there. Such is the truth, a stubborn thing which just goes on being the truth, no matter what it is threatened with, nor by whom.

However, there is a school of thought in existence which does espouse and teach many of the doctrines which the prosecution would need to find in order to prove its allegation in all these trials.

It does not happen to be the Communist, but the Nazi-Fascist school of thought. For example, Hitler wrote in *Mein Kampf,* the very Bible of Nazism:
"The parliamentary principle of decision by majority, by denying the authority of the person, and placing in its stead the number of the crowd in question, sins against the aristocratic basic idea of Nature ..." (Reynal and Hitchcock edition, Vol. I, p. 103.)

It would be as impossible to find a proposition of that kind in the teachings of Marxism-Leninism as it would be to find an argument for divine right of kings in the American Declaration of Independence or the Constitution of the United States. What one finds in Communist teaching is the sort of statement Lenin made in one of his chief works, *State and Revolution,* when, discussing this very issue, he wrote:

"... some one may even begin to fear lest we be expecting the advent of such an order of society in which the principle of the subordination of the minority to the majority will not be respected ..." *(Collected Works,* Vol. XXI, Bk. II, p. 214.)

Lenin was certainly not far wrong in that conjecture. He makes his position immediately clear by adding, with flat emphasis:

"We do not expect the advent of an order of society in which the principle of the subordination of minority to majority will not be observed."

In the same work he says that what he wants is "Democracy for the vast majority of the people...," and equates his program "... with an immense expansion of democracy which *for the first time* becomes democracy for the poor, democracy for the people, and not democracy for the rich folk ..." (P. 219. Lenin's italics.)

It will be understood that we are not here discussing the extent to which principles are subject to violation in practice, both by others and by ourselves, nor are we discussing the question who may have violated his principles more. We are discussing what the principles are, particularly what fundamental attitude toward the majority is taken in these principles.

It is significant that Hitler himself fully recognized the diametric opposition between his own ideology and that of Marxism. In *Mein Kampf* he points out:

"Marxism rejects the aristocratic principle in Nature; instead of the eternal privilege of force and strength, it places the mass of numbers and its deadweight." (P. 38)

Fascism takes the same attitude as Nazism in this matter, and exhibits the same diametric opposition to Marxism. Thus Mussolini, in his fundamental treatise, *The Doctrine of Fascism,* spoke of "The Fascist negation of socialism, democracy ..." (P. 37.) In a note referring to the First World War he wrote:

"The war was 'revolutionary' in the sense that—with streams of blood—it did away with the century of Democracy, the century of number, the century of majorities and of quantities."

This is the situation which serious research reveals all along the line. In a technical article in the journal *Philosophy of Science,* April, 1952,1 took occasion to point out that "Detailed comparison shows that such evaluations [those quoted from Hitler and Mussolini] are as typical and representative of the works of Hitler and Mussolini as they are untypical and unrepresentative of the works of Marx, Engels, Lenin or Stalin." (P. 158.) I also dealt at some length with these matters in the original and revised editions of *The Philosophy of Peace.* (1949. 1954. Liberty.)

I am aware there is a widespread belief that the Communist ideology is the same as the Nazi-Fascist. This is a very unfortunate situation, for such a belief is not founded on knowledge, and could never be held by anyone who had actually read the works of Marx, Engels, Lenin, and Stalin on the one hand, and Hitler and Mussolini on the other. While it might have made more sense, in terms of the indictment, if Nazis and Fascists had been the defendants in these cases, the truth is it makes no sense at all, under our concepts of law and government, to try anyone for his ideas. We can properly try people in criminal courts only on the basis of criminal acts, or physical evidence of preparation for criminal acts. Nothing of that kind was even claimed by the prosecution in this trial or in any of the other trials of this type.

If, none the less, governmental authorities are determined that political trials centering on the doctrines of ideologies held by different groups are to continue, then we should have to face and meet the problems involved far more seriously and responsibly than we have so far done. One question we would have to answer is, how would we avoid conditioning our people to believe that the only safe thing is to have no ideas at all? Another consideration that stands out very plainly is that if judges and juries are to be asked to decide these matters they will have to be educated and trained far more thoroughly in a mastery of the literature of the fields concerned.

And if expert witnesses are to be called in to supply what is lacking, they will have to be given far more time and leeway to do the complex job required.

Nowadays trials of this kind have multiplied, so that we have been increasingly faced with the necessity of maintaining standards of accuracy and scholarship that are indispensable to justice in cases where whole groups of citizens are, or may be, sent to jail. For example, in a decision dated Dec. 23, 1954, handed down by the United States Court of Appeals in a "registration" case involving the Subversive Activities Control Board and the Communist Party (11850), the majority opinion of the Court, which decided in favor of the board, stated:

> "The activities of a world Communist movement such as that described in this statute and of organizations in this country devoted to its objectives constitute a clear and present danger within the meaning of any definition of the point at which freedom of speech gives way to the requirements of government security. The basic theory of Communism that all presently existing nationalist governments be superseded by a stateless world organization under a proletarian dictatorship, the domination of one world power with all its assets by the Communists, the succession of national capitulations to the forces of that group, and the declared intentions of its leaders in respect to the remainder of the world, are reflected in the recitations in this statute, and, moreover, are historic facts which cannot be disputed." (Pp. 11, 12.)

The statute referred to is part of the Internal Security Act of 1950, often called the McCarran Act, the constitutionality of which was upheld on this occasion. If one reads carefully the paragraph just quoted from the majority opinion of the appellate court upholding the act, one may come to the conclusion that its main force lies in the phrase "a stateless world organization under a proletarian dictatorship." This has a sound of definiteness, whereas the rest is relatively vague. In a sense, many groups want to "dominate the world"; "national capitulation" might be other people's choices; and "declared intentions" of current political leaders are usually broad and somewhat ambiguous. But "a stateless world organization under a proletarian dictatorship" sounds like the concrete aim of a clearly criminal conspiracy.

Thus the logical propriety of this decision, and its persuasive force, hangs largely on the premise that Communist doctrine lays down the "basic" aim mentioned—"a stateless world organization under a proletarian dictatorship." But anyone familiar with Communist doctrine will have to point out that such a statement is clearly wrong, since, in Communist terms, it would be an obvious self-contradiction. To Communists "stateless" always means the absence of dictatorship; "dictatorship" means the presence of a state. Thus a "stateless" world organization would have to be a world organization without a dictatorship.

As we have seen in our previous discussion (Chapter 3) the word "dictatorship" in Communist usage is part of the very concept of the state. It is synonymous with that aspect of the state which consists in an apparatus of physical enforcement (jails, police, armies, and the like). Hence, to say that Communists teach that there should be "a stateless world organization under a proletarian dictatorship" is just the same as saying Communists teach there should be a policeless world with a strong police force. Though the appellate court calls this statement a historic fact "that cannot be disputed," it is clearly no fact at all, and must be disputed.

The fact is Communists teach that it is desirable, and in the course of time will be possible, for human society to do without any dictatorship, any state apparatus of physical enforcement whatever. This will be possible, they hold, when there is a world-wide social economy of complete abundance operating so that everyone will have available whatever goods he can use (as many people now have water available), and when everyone will be fully and properly educated. These are the main preconditions of the famous "withering away of the state" (Engels' phrase). In other words, in Communist opinion, the kind of conflicts between person and person, or group and group, that now make necessary police, jails, and armies, will under such conditions disappear.

But Communists emphasize strongly that, in their view, such conflicts can disappear only when class distinctions and classes disappear, when everyone has an abundance of economic goods at his disposal, when there is not a single "proletarian" left. In other words, what they mean by the ideal or theory of the "stateless world" is a world without classes, especially without a proletarian class, and a world without any dictatorship, including proletarian dictatorship.

Now the Communists may be completely wrong about all these possibilities. They may be completely mistaken about their estimate of what will come about in the future. That is an entirely different issue. The question here is not whether they are intellectually or politically right or wrong in what they are saying. The only question here is the meaning and content of what they are saying. That is a fact that can be ascertained by direct scholarly examination. Such examination discloses a situation considerably different from what the Court assumes. The Court thinks they are talking about a stateless world under a proletarian dictatorship, whereas they are talking about a stateless world without dictatorship; to them the world can be stateless only when no dictatorship exists, when people have learned to live harmoniously, without the need of police.

Further references to this point in the course of the decision show that the majority opinion placed considerable reliance upon this erroneous assumption. Thus on page 66 it is stated:

> "The amended answer of the Party says that Marxism-Leninism is basic to the Communist Party USA. And, as we have pointed out, while the tenets of Marxism-Leninism, forcefully set out in the writings of Marx, Lenin and Stalin, permit a wide flexibility in tactics, that is, of intermediate activities and objectives, they admit of no deviation from the ultimate objective, which is a classless, stateless world."

It is clear that the only reason the Court sees anything wrong with this objective, and cites it in this connection, is that the Court is under the impression that in Communist doctrine a "classless, stateless world" means a world forever under a proletarian dictatorship.

Again, on page 67 the same idea is used, with the same implications:

> "In this connection, the Party points to the preamble to its constitution, adopted in 1948, which contains the following sentence: 'the Communist Party upholds the achievements of American democracy, and defends the United States Constitution and its Bill of Rights against its reactionary enemies who would destroy democracy and popular liberties.' But *(sic)* that recitation must be viewed in the light of the established position of Communist leaders that American democracy has gone far in protecting the rights of minorities and of working people and in advancing the

economic status of such people, and that in that respect American democracy receives the plaudits of those leaders. But that position in no way negates the ultimate stateless world objective of the Communist movement."

Here the Court directs attention to the fact that Communists admire, defend, and teach respect for the achievements of American democracy, for the Constitution, the Bill of Rights, the advancement of working people, the protection of minority rights and the like. But, the Court solemnly suggests, all this is in some way canceled out because the Communists believe in the ultimate objective of a classless, stateless world! Such an attitude on the Court's part is very evidently based on its mistaken assumption as to what a "stateless world" means in Communist doctrine. The majority of the Court were plainly under the impression that a "stateless world" to the Communists means a "world organization *under* a proletarian dictatorship," whereas it means a world *without* a proletarian dictatorship or any other dictatorship.

This particular concept, as an ultimate aim of the Communists, is actually a sort of extension of the Jeffersonian idea that that government is best which governs least. In fact, Jefferson said on one occasion (in a letter to Madison, 1787):

"Societies exist under three forms, sufficiently distinguishable. 1. Without government, as among our Indians. 2. Under governments wherein the will of everyone has a just influence ... 3. Under governments of force ... It is a problem, not clear in my mind that the first condition is not the best."

In other words, Jefferson's opinion leaned in the direction that the best condition might be society without government. What he concretely pointed to, "as among our Indians," is, by the way, what Marxist writers have often referred to as an example of "primitive Communism," that is, a society without *private* property in the basic means of production (the land, fisheries, hunting grounds, and the like) and without an *organized* state apparatus of *physical enforcement* (police force, jails, prisons).

The period referred to is one that had its rise before any great division of labor or trade, and before the rise of slavery. Every member of the tribe is a sort of all-around man—producer, councilor, and warrior all in one. The Marxist theory is that the state as an organization for physical enforcement was born when division of labor, increasing trade, and the consequent profitability of slavery destroyed the communal foundation of tribal society inasmuch as these developments led to private ownership of the basic means of production. Once there were slaves and slaveowners, propertied and unpropertied groups, an enforcement apparatus became necessary.

Communist writers reason that if a communal basis for society can be reestablished on a world scale, involving unrestricted economic abundance and full education, the need for a state apparatus of physical enforcement will gradually disappear; it will "wither away." As they see it, not only will the *internal* state apparatus of physical enforcement, embodied in police and prisons, go out of existence through disuse. Even armies, navies, and air forces will gradually become unnecessary, since the conditions which mainly caused their use—conflicts over material interests—disappear. In this regard their view is that future communal society could go far beyond primitive communal society, which did without internal police and jails, but still carried on external warfare.

If the majority of the Court had understood what is involved in the Marxist concept of the "stateless world" it is likely they would have regarded it as quite naive. But it is impossible to see how they could have held it to be inherently illicit, or to have any bearing on "registration" under the McCarran Act.

The Court of Appeals opinion in the present instance, in asserting that Communists identify a stateless world with a proletarian dictatorship in their basic theory, thus presents a picture of Communist theory which does not exist in the teachings of the Communists. What is more important is that this picture, as the opinion points out, is the picture written into the McCarran Act itself. But, of course, non-fact cannot be made fact by "due process of law." In our theory of law, it is the other way around. When a law states unfact as fact, the law must be ruled out as contrary to due process.

I am not here suggesting for one instant that the Communists do not want a Communist world. Neither would I suggest that the capitalists do not want a capitalist world, nor that the Catholics do not want a Catholic world, the Buddhists a Buddhist world, and so on. Anyone who does not understand that every true believer wants the world to go his way does not understand what true faith is. We cannot justifiably penalize people for wanting the world to go their way.

The whole question is, do they teach that the world should be forcibly compelled to go their way *contrary to the wishes of the majority?* Are they preparing to make the world go their way by physical violence, irrespective of majority will? Where would be the evidence that any American Communist ever prepared to do any such thing? With all the resources of the Federal Bureau of Investigation at its disposal, the only "evidence" the government could adduce in any of the trials was belief in the teachings. And the teachings, as we have seen over and over again, emphasize that no revolutionary step of any kind is to be taken without majority support.

Now suppose someone were to say, I admit that American Communists have never attempted forcible overthrow of any government in this country. I admit that no physical evidence has been found, such as weapons, or plans to purchase weapons, or the like, which would indicate preparations of any kind for the overthrow by force of such a strong government as ours. Still, I know that Communists have staged armed revolutions in other countries, and I am convinced they did so contrary to the will of the majority. Therefore, I believe we are justified in concluding American Communists are going to do the same thing. So let us bring legal measures to bear now before they have a chance to do it.

If this approach were suggested (and it seems, at least to a degree, to be implicit in the passage we quoted from the appellate court's decision), the first question that would have to be asked is, how do you prove that where Communist revolutions took place they did not have the support of the majority? It is doubtful that anyone would seriously maintain it is easy to prove that all the Communist revolutions that took place, including the Russian and the Chinese revolutions, were undertaken in opposition to the will of the majority. If he did so maintain, how could he explain the fact that many professional non-Communist scholars in this country and in many other nonCommunist countries are prepared to dispute such a proposition, or are prepared to say, at the very least, that it is debatable? Yet the appellate court, in effect, pronounces this proposition—that Communist revolutions can be generally classed as projects undertaken in opposition to the majority will—to be a "historic fact which cannot be disputed."

If this is not the Court's meaning, what would be the relevancy of citing "the succession of national capitulations to the forces of that [Communist] group" as among the "historic facts which cannot be disputed," which "facts" are cited as part of the proof that belief in Communist doctrine represents a "clear and present danger"?

It is obviously inaccurate to maintain that certain "facts" cannot be disputed when they are disputed by scholars every day. Suppose, however, that these alleged facts were not disputed, and that professional scholarly authorities were unanimously agreed upon them, in the Court's sense. What would be the position then? Put bluntly, the position then would be, we are going to punish the American Communists now for what the Russian, Chinese, and other Communists have done in the past. But how could this be reconciled with our concepts of law and justice?

Could we say, for example, we are going to punish American Catholics for what the Spanish Inquisition did, on the ground that, as Catholics, they want to see Catholicism predominant over the whole world, and, to achieve this objective, they are prepared to do the same thing that has been done elsewhere, in spite of anything they may say or point to in their present teachings? Such "logic" would make a mockery of morality, and a shambles of due process of law.

However, the most remarkable part of the Court of Appeals decision, something not characteristic of past decisions, appears on page 11, where the following statement is made:

> "The right to free expression ceases at the point where it leads to harm to the Government."

If that sentence means what it says, and is upheld by the higher bench, then an era of liberty will have come to an end in this country, and an era of totalitarianism will have begun. For the question immediately arises: who is to decide whether some book, pamphlet, article, lecture, doctrine, or other example of "free expression" is such that it "leads to harm to the Government"? Naturally, the government would decide; and a fatal blow would have been struck at the whole idea that the citizen has a right to differ fundamentally with the government on what is good and bad for the nation. The reader might search a long while before finding a more precise, though probably quite unintentional, formulation of the totalitarian concept.

Under such a dictum, how could the citizen ever argue for a fundamental or radical change in the form of government? The existing government could naturally be expected to view most such possible changes as harmful to itself. Under the concept of liberty, one has the right, for example, to argue, by written or spoken word, in favor of turning back all government-operated services, such as power plants, bus lines, subways, postal facilities, schools, and the like, to private hands wherever they are now in government hands. And one has equal right under the concept of liberty, to argue that all such services and facilities, or any others, now privately managed should be managed by the government. Under the concept of liberty it would not matter whether the existing government was or was not firmly convinced that one (or both) of these ideas would lead to profound harm to itself.

Where freedom of speech exists, the citizen has a right to try to persuade the majority of his fellow-citizens by peaceful means that the existing government is wrong, and that it ought to be changed from top to bottom. It would make no difference how harmful to itself the existing government might consider the change. The majority has the right to an opportunity to hear about ideas, however crackpot they may be or may seem to be. And it has a right to act on them if it wishes to act on them, however mistaken such action might be, or might seem to be, in the eyes of the existing government. That is the historic idea of liberty. The historic idea of paternalism and of totalitarianism is well, though doubtless unintentionally, expressed by the statement that the right to free expression ceases at the point where it leads to harm to the government.

Our Constitution was conceived not in the spirit of paternalism, but in the spirit of liberty. The First Amendment says, "Congress shall make no law ... abridging the freedom of speech, or of the press ..." The Constitution does not say, "Congress shall make no law abridging the freedom of speech or of the press except in those cases where, in the opinion of the government, free expression might lead to harm to the government."

The American constitutional conception is not that freedom of speech and press must be maintained in order to protect the existing government, or only as long as such freedom is compatible with the continued existence of the present government. It is that freedom of speech and press must be maintained in order that the majority may make up its own mind, no matter what that might bode for the existing government. It is clear that the majority cannot make up its *own* mind if the existing government can decide beforehand that some idea, if carried into practice, would be harmful to itself, and, on that ground, penalize or prevent expression of the idea.

Under the principle of liberty the only kind of "harm" to the government which the government can legitimately forestall through penalties on free expression is the kind of harm that would be involved in the committing of a crime. Thus the government has a perfect right to penalize anyone who would say or write: "You should assassinate Senator X," if there is any clear and present danger the words might be taken seriously and acted upon.

But, under the concept of liberty, the government cannot justifiably penalize anyone for saying or writing: "I believe we should have an absolute monarch instead of an elected president in this country. I aim to persuade the majority that this change would be a good one; and I further point out that if the great majority desire this change, and the existing government refuses to carry out their wishes legally and peacefully, they have a right to remove that government by force." The existing government might well consider such a change very harmful to itself. Yet, as long as it believes in liberty, it would not penalize the expression of such a view, because this expression is not telling anyone to commit a crime.

Now if it began to appear that this view (absolute monarchy is best) might be taken seriously by the majority, and might be acted on in practice, would the expression of it then constitute a "clear and present danger"? Certainly not, for the simple reason that "clear and present danger," in its binding sense, applies only to an act which would in itself be criminal in nature. Under the principles of democracy it is not, of course, in any way criminal for the majority to favor some political change, however radical, or however harmful in the judgment of the existing government, and to insist that its will be carried into practice.

Let us take the most extreme possible case. Suppose a majority of the people of this country came to feel that Communism was the best system of social life, and that our whole form of government and economic system should be changed. Would not every believer in the sovereignty of the people, including every judge on the bench, be obliged to agree, however regretfully, that the people would have the right to make that decision, and to carry it into practice? Under the concept of the sovereignty of the people there is, of course, no minority that would have any final right to stop the majority, however mistaken the majority might be.

It follows logically that if no branch of the present government has any right to prevent the majority from deciding in favor of Communism, if the majority should want to do that, then no branch of the present government has any right to prevent or penalize a Communist if he wants to try, by peaceful means, to persuade the majority that Communism should be adopted. The same would apply to a monarchist who would want to persuade the majority that absolute monarchy is the best system.

These are political ideas, however harmful they might be in the eyes of this or that group. It is a fact that many countries have lived and do live by them. They are clearly in the realm of ideological debate. This would not apply, however, to something like murder or grand larceny; and no one is arguing that government should not penalize anyone who tries to persuade others to commit an act of murder or theft. In one sense, the whole meaning of freedom of thought and speech is that ideas are not to be defined as crimes.

There is a theory of liberty which takes the strange view that freedom for radical ideas is to be allowed only up to the point where it begins to appear that the radical idea might possibly be carried into practice. Then, it is suggested, the government has the right to step in and forbid any further expression of the idea. This theory treats the radical idea precisely as if it were in itself a crime.

In fact, this is the way the concept of "clear and present danger" is frequently applied in judicial decisions in the type of case under consideration. The expression of radical belief is put on the same level as the expression of a belief that Jones should be murdered. The only question then left is whether the conditions are such that there is any "clear and present danger" that the idea expressed might actually be carried into practice.

In other words, this concept of freedom reduces itself to the proposition that free expression of radical ideas must cease at the point where there is a clear and present danger that they might be acted on. That is not liberty; it is paternalism. We must choose between that and the First Amendment to the Constitution. We cannot have both, because, in practice, the one cancels out the other.

In connection with this whole class of cases, it is worth while to recall and emphasize the exact language of Mr. Justice Holmes in his famous formulation about "clear and present danger" in the Supreme Court opinion which he wrote in 1919 (Schenck *v.* United States): "The question in every case is whether the words used are used in such circumstances and are of such a nature as to create a clear and present danger that they will bring about the substantive evils that Congress has a right to prevent."

In other words, whatever is expressed must involve a "substantive evil," the doing of something definable as criminal under the law. But it is the majority who make and remake the law, who change it and amend it. If the great majority should want a new social system, that could never be regarded as something falling within "substantive evils that Congress has a right to prevent."

Congress would have a right to prevent the foisting of a new social system upon the people *contrary to the will of the majority*. But that is a very different matter. Such a Congressional right could not properly be applied by way of placing penalties on the expression of Communist teachings, because, as we have seen, no Communist teachings can be found which say that Communism should be imposed *contrary to the will of the majority* and an overwhelming body of Communist teaching can be found asserting, in the most explicit terms, that the support of the majority is an indispensable precondition to any attempt to establish Communism.

Now suppose someone were to say: "But I suspect that these people, *in spite of what they say in their teachings,* are going to try, by force and violence, to foist their system upon us contrary to the will of the majority." What would one have to reply? The first thing that would have to be said is that in such a case the Smith Act trials would make no sense whatever. For, as we have seen, the entire structure of "evidence" in the Smith Act trials consists of what is said in the teachings. Once it is admitted that the teachings do not say anything criminal, however distasteful they may be, what is the sense of bringing them into a criminal court? Other evidence would have to be found, in order to justify criminal proceedings and the imprisonment of citizens.

In any event it is significant to observe that the dissenting opinion in the "registration" case, even assuming, as it did, the government's premise that Communism is a criminal conspiracy, found the McCarran Act logically indefensible. At issue in this case was whether the Communist Party should be compelled to obey the order of the Subversive Activities Control Board to "register" and disclose the names and addresses of all members and officers, also to account for all money received and spent during the preceding twelve months. The dissenting opinion draws the following analogy:

"Suppose an Act of Congress required bands of bank robbers to file with the Attorney General statements of their membership and activities, and imposed criminal penalties upon their leaders and members for failure to do so. Such an Act would compel individuals to disclose their connection with a criminal conspiracy. No argument could reconcile such an Act with the Fifth Amendment's command that 'No person ... shall be compelled in any criminal case to be a witness against himself.'

"The registration provisions of the Internal Security Act of 1950 are similar. They compel individuals, under criminal penalties, to disclose intimate associations with the Communist Party, a disclosure which the Supreme Court has held to be incriminatory ... *Blau* u. *United States* is decisive of this case. The Supreme Court there held that an admission that one is 'employed by the Communist Party or has intimate knowledge of its workings' might furnish a 'link in the chain of evidence needed in a prosecution' under the Smith Act and therefore could not be required." (Pp. 76–79.)

In other words, the dissenting opinion quite cogently points out that if the government maintains—as it does maintain in its prosecutions under the Smith Act—that the Communist movement is a criminal conspiracy, then the movement cannot be ordered to disclose its membership, as that would be a clear instance of trying to compel persons to be prior witnesses against themselves. Thus the McCarran Act, which creates such compulsion through its "registration" provisions, is, in the dissenting judge's opinion (the three judges divided two to one), clearly unconstitutional. If any other view is taken, it would certainly seem that the government is having its constitutional cake and eating it at the same time.

One of the announced motivations for the "registration" procedures in the McCarran Act is to identify groups in this country which are "substantially directed, dominated, or controlled" by a "foreign government or foreign organization." Those taking this approach sometimes argue that they are not saying such groups are necessarily criminal in nature, but that they should be publicly identified, and recognized for what they are. Furthermore, in the interests of security, it is argued, their members can be justifiably deprived of certain privileges, such as holding government or teaching positions, and obtaining passports for foreign travel; they can be made to label their publications, broadcasts, and the like in such a way as to indicate foreign control; and other such measures can be brought to bear.

One of the concrete forms this argument takes is that the Communist is not really a "free agent," because he accepts a "party line," and this party line is laid down in a foreign country. Hence, he is really an "agent of a foreign power." On this ground the debarment or discharge of Communists from teaching positions is often claimed to be justified, even in cases where many years of admittedly capable service have been rendered, and no corruption of the teaching process has ever been observed or alleged. The claim is that no one *should* be teaching who is not a "free agent," as such a person is not fully responsible, and could not be fully depended upon.

If those who advance this argument are serious about defending its principle, and carrying it into practice, it could certainly have catastrophic results in our national life. For there are many groups and individuals among our citizens with strong ties binding them to foreign countries and foreign organizations, ties which could lay them open to the possibility of as much external influence and control as the Communists.

In an article appearing in *The New York Times* of Nov. 4, 1954, datelined Rome, Nov. 3, it is reported:

> "According to Pope Pius XII, the belief that 'the Church's authority is limited to purely religious matters' is an error. Roman Catholics 'must take an open and firm stand' against it, he added.
> 
> "Social problems, whether merely social or sociopolitical, were singled out by the Pope as being 'of concern to the conscience and salvation of man' and thus as not 'outside the authority and care of the Church.'
> 
> "Pope Pius said emphatically at a meeting of cardinals, archbishops and bishops that those who sought to limit the Church's authority to purely religious matters were in error.
> 
> "Far from being thus limited, the Church's power extends to the whole matter of natural law and to the moral aspects of its foundation, its interpretation and its application, the Pope said.
> 
> "By natural law is meant the law implanted by God in the minds of His reasoning creatures, distinguishing for them the good from the evil and bidding them follow the good and shun the evil, the Pope declared.

"Instructions and propositions published on matters within the moral law by the Pope for the whole Church, and by bishops for those in their dioceses, cannot be rejected on the ground that 'the strength of the authority is no more than the strength of the arguments,' the Pontiff added.

"On the contrary, 'even though to someone certain declarations of the Church may not seem proved by the arguments put forward, his obligation to obey still remains,' the Pope continued.

"The Pope's statements were made in an address he delivered yesterday in Latin to twenty-five cardinals and 150 archbishops and bishops who had gathered in Rome.... The Latin text was published today by *L'Osservatore Romano,* the Vatican newspaper. Translations in six languages were made available by the Vatican press service....

"In addition to social questions there are problems not strictly religious—even some political problems—that rightly fall within the authority of the Church because they belong to the moral order, weigh on the conscience, and can and very often do hinder the attainment of man's final end, the Pope said.

"Among these he enumerated the following:

"1. The purpose and limits of temporal authority.

"2. Relations between the individual and society—the so-called totalitarian state, whatever be the principle on which it is based.

"3. The 'complete laicization' [putting under the control of laymen] of the state and of public life.

"4. The complete laicization of the schools.

"5. The morality of war as waged today, and whether a conscientious person might give or withold his cooperation in it.

"6. Moral relationships binding and ruling the various nations.

" 'Common sense and truth as well are contradicted by whoever asserts that this and like problems are outside the field of morals, and hence are, or at least can be beyond, the influence of that authority established by God to see to a just order and to direct the conscience and actions of men along the path to their true and final destiny' the Pope continued.

"He then spoke about ecclesiastical discipline, and condemned in strong terms the tendency among present-day Catholics, both men and women, to 'think that the leadership and vigilance of the Church are not to be suffered by one who is grown up/

"He said such persons 'are unwilling in their final personal decisions to have any intermediary placed between themselves and God, no matter what his rank or title'

"It is right and just that adults should not be treated like children, the Pope said, 'but to be an adult and to have put off the things of childhood is one thing, and quite another to be an adult and not to be subject to the guidance and government of legitimate authority/

"Speaking about the tasks of bishops, the Pope urged them to coordinate their activities by holding frequent meetings among themselves, and to bind themselves closely to the Holy See.

" 'Union and harmonious communication with the Holy See arises not from a kind of desire to centralize and unify everything, but by divine right and by reason of an essential element of the constitution of the Church of Christ' he concluded."

Anyone who thinks it unusual for the ideas and beliefs held by individuals and groups in this country to be subject to influence and control from foreign sources could easily find enough material of this kind to keep him busy for a lifetime. In the example at hand, the Pope explicitly states it is an error to believe that "the Church's authority is limited to purely religious matters." It extends to all sorts of social and political, as well as philosophical and religious, matters, as determined by the Pope himself.

As instances of questions that "rightly fall within the authority of the Church" the Pontiff draws up a list which includes "the purpose and limits of temporal authority," which means principally, of course, the authority of government. The list also includes "relations between the individual and society" and "moral relationships binding and ruling the various nations," subjects which involve an immense field of action as well as of ideas. Among the questions listed which are of concrete and immediate public concern is whether the school system of a country should or should not be completely under the control of laymen (persons who are not clerics); also, whether the government should be fully under the control of laymen. Included in this same category is the question whether the individual "might give or withhold his cooperation" in a war.

In the Pope's view, all such matters "rightly fall within the authority of the Church because they belong to the moral order," as the report indicates, and the position is taken that "instructions and propositions published on matters within the moral law by the Pope for the whole Church, and by bishops for those in their dioceses, cannot be rejected on the ground that," as the Pontiff puts it, "the strength of the authority is no more than the strength of the arguments." The Pope is emphatic and explicit in pointing out that "even though to someone certain declarations of the Church may not seem proved by the arguments put forward, his obligation to obey still remains."

Another article in *The New York Times,* Nov. 22, 1955, referring to the Pope, states:

> "The Vatican released the text of his address yesterday to officials of the Italian Ministry of the Interior. In it the Pope spoke of the 'right, even the duty of non-obedience on the part of citizens' whenever in a state 'some laws should be unjust because they were contrary to the common good, the natural law and positive divine or ecclesiastical law.' "

In view of all this, is the Catholic teacher or government employee a "free agent" in his ideas, beliefs, and actions, or is he accepting a "line" laid down outside this country? If the question is put in that way (which is the way it is so frequently put to justify the discharging or debarring of Communists from teaching and other positions), not only Catholics would cease to be "free agents," but anyone who had a strong faith or belief which was not entirely controlled from within this country.

It is clear enough, for example, that the Orthodox Jew to remain an Orthodox Jew, the Episcopalian to remain an Episcopalian, the Buddhist to remain a Buddhist, the Mason to remain a Mason, must accept certain doctrines, certain teachings, certain principles, many of which come from foreign countries—and the same is true of an endless variety of groups that have definite creeds. We live in an interconnected world, in which ideas are bound to come from all sorts of places.

What kind of intellectual life could we lead if we began to insist that no American teacher should seriously believe any doctrine or associate himself with any movement unless it be entirely under the control of American citizens within the geographical boundaries of our own country? Such insistence might well prevent a teacher from being a Christian or believing in the Bible itself, as he or she might in conscience conceive of Christianity and the Bible.

None of these persons, including the Catholic and the Communist, ceases to be a "free agent" because he accepts or believes in a doctrine, "line," or creed, wherever it happens to come from. The reason is simple but decisive. Any time the particular doctrine ceases to satisfy the individual intellectually, morally, or spiritually the individual is free to abandon it—to leave the Church, resign from the party, the order, or whatever it is. It would be a plain mockery of intellectual freedom to tell people they are "free agents" only as long as they do not believe in any definite doctrine or join any definite party. This would come close to saying that only the agnostic or the opportunist is free.

In other words, it would be absurd to hold that intellectual freedom is to be equated with believing nothing definite. It can be equated, in our tradition, only with full opportunity to make up one's own mind what to believe, however definite. And if there is to be full intellectual freedom there must be freedom to choose not to believe in certain kinds of freedom under certain conditions, and freedom, as a citizen, to try to persuade others peacefully that certain kinds of freedom under certain conditions are bad.

For example, it is clear that where either the Catholics or the Communists have been in full control (this applies also to many other groups) they have not granted the sort of freedoms associated with liberalism. Nor have they claimed to. But that would not be sufficient reason to deny them, as long as they are law-abiding, whatever liberties the state offers to other law-abiding persons. We can hardly claim to believe in freedom of thought if we are determined to penalize those whose thoughts about freedom happen to differ from ours.

The reader will understand thoroughly that I am not *attacking* the right of Catholics to teach in our schools. I am *defending* the right of Catholics to teach in our schools. I have taught side by side with splendid Catholic teachers all my professional life; and in my private life I happen to be united to Catholics by the closest possible ties of blood and affection. Nor am I saying anything so absurd as that Catholic beliefs are the same as Communist beliefs. What I am saying is that we cannot justifiably debar one group from certain positions on the ground that their beliefs are heavily influenced by an international organization or foreign power while at the same time other groups whose beliefs are heavily influenced by international organizations and foreign powers are admitted to the positions in question.

This certainly does not mean that any teacher should be permitted to use the classroom for purposes of partisan propaganda, or to pass off some private belief, however dear to him, as if it were necessary objective truth. It is self-evident that such a rule must be insisted on, whether the belief in question is Buddhism, Methodism, McCarthyism, Catholicism, Communism, or a firm belief in the Republican Party or the Democratic Party.

In this matter, as in all other matters, a person should be treated as innocent until proved guilty, and proof of guilt, to be valid, must include instances of relevant *acts*. It would never be sufficient to say that because this person is a Catholic, or an Orthodox Jew, or a Buddhist, or an Episcopalian, or a Communist, or a McCarthyite or a Socialist he *must* be misusing his teaching position to proselytize or spread partisan propaganda. No matter how convinced a believer he is, and no matter how much the given movement may want to spread its beliefs, and may urge its members to do so, no one should be penalized as if he *had* broken a rule or law until he actually *does* break a rule or law.

There are a thousand different pressures on normal individuals which might possibly lead them to break laws or rules—monetary needs, human passions, and the like. Attachment to doctrinal beliefs or ideas is not the only one. But, even if it were, we could not justifiably debar people from teaching, or from similar positions, on the ground that they *might* be led astray through such attachment. If we did, the only teachers left would be those of no faith and few ideas. This would certainly be a remedy worse than the disease.

In any case, one cannot help concluding that what is decisive in this whole situation is not that people's ideas, beliefs, and actions are influenced by external sources, or that some of these sources are outside this country. In itself, such a condition could hardly be avoided. What is decisive is the widespread feeling that the particular ideas and beliefs contained in Communist teaching make necessary an attempt, or a conspiracy to attempt, overthrow of the United States Government by force and violence.

As we have seen, this feeling is not founded on fact. It cannot survive the process of logical analysis, in the light of the actual content of the actual doctrines found in the actual works of Marxism-Leninism taken as a whole. This feeling is the product of fear, which is in turn often the product of ignorance. It is driven home by constant repetition, in all manner of exaggerated, emotionally powerful, and psychologically effective forms in the daily and weekly press, the picture magazines, on the screen, radio, television, and in a hundred other places. That is what convicted the defendants.

I do not here go into the question of motives. Whatever the motives operative in this whole situation may be, and whatever the social and economic forces in which they may be rooted, I am willing to grant that many of the people in this country who have this misimpression of Communist doctrine—that it teaches indiscriminate violence—are sincere. But sincere ignorance is not a satisfactory substitute for truth.

History shows that truth and logic remain truth and logic no matter what happens. But it also shows, unfortunately, that truth and logic can, for shamefully long periods of time, be ignored, persecuted, and penalized. In the end, there is only one answer: knowledge. How long it may take for that answer to be effectively made depends upon the intelligence and courage of the American people taken as a whole, who, whether they are aware of it or not, are on trial as much as the defendants in the courtrooms.

# 10 Variations on a Theme

## Two 1956 Trials, Cleveland and Philadelphia

The second Philadelphia Smith Act trial was based on the so-called "membership clause" of the act. That is to say, the defendant was not charged with *conspiring* to teach and advocate the violent overthrow of our government. Neither was he *specifically* charged with doing the teaching and advocating *himself.* He was charged with being a *member* of a "society, group and assembly of persons who teach and advocate the overthrow and destruction of the Government of the United States by force and violence."

In most of the Smith Act trials which have taken place to date (May, 1956) the defendants were accused of *conspiring* to teach and advocate, not of actually teaching and advocating, the violent overthrow of our government. In other words, they were charged with *conspiracy* to violate the act. This may be considered a lesser offense than knowingly being a member of an organization of persons who teach and advocate violent overthrow, since the maximum prison term for conspiracy is five years, while for membership it is ten. Actually, however, the original provisions of the act as passed in 1940 included a ten-year maximum for any violation, through conspiracy or otherwise. It was by virtue of the 1948 revision of the criminal code that the maximum penalty for conspiracy was reduced to five years.

This whole situation is, of course, paradoxical in that all those persons who were accused of *conspiring* to teach and advocate violent overthrow on the ground that they helped to organize the

Communist Party could just as well have been charged with membership, as they were all publicly known members and leaders of the party. Also, the "overt acts" of conspiracy with which they were charged were simply the acts of carrying out the functions of a party member or leader—attending meetings, conferences, classes, conventions, and the like.

Why, then, were such persons not tried for the graver offense of membership, since they were in fact admitted members of the Communist Party? The reason may be, as some writers have conjectured, that the prosecuting authorities felt that there was little likelihood of obtaining convictions for mere membership in the Communist Party, since the party had been legal for so long, and had never attempted any violence. However, "conspiracy" fits in with the popular impression of Communists. Thus, by calling their actual membership in the Communist Party a conspiracy to help organize the Communist Party it may have been easier to convince a jury that they were doing something criminal than if they had simply been accused of being party members, in spite of the fact that there was nothing charged under the "conspiracy" indictments save the activities involved in being a member!

That the prosecuting authorities probably had in mind the impact on public opinion might also be inferred from the fact that it was stated on several occasions that the leaders were the ones to be singled out for trial. However, it is clear enough in logic that if the leaders of an organization can be convicted of criminal conspiracy on the basis of what the organization teaches and advocates, everyone who is a member of that organization, knowing what it teaches and advocates, becomes a presumptive criminal liable to prosecution. Paradoxically, in this instance the member can then receive a much longer jail term for membership than the leader received for conspiracy.

In other words, the same evidence, the teachings, which might not convince a jury that the believer in them is a criminal, may seem convincing when the activities of setting up and carrying on the organization devoted to the dissemination of the teachings are called a "conspiracy." But calling these activities a conspiracy adds absolutely nothing to the "evidence" for the alleged crime, since no evidence is adduced and no allegation is made by the prosecution except the teachings themselves. Moreover, most of the activities in question, and all of the doctrines taught, are not only made public by the movement, but are vigorously publicized.

Another reason sometimes suggested for beginning with indictments on the conspiracy basis is that if convictions are obtained the same individuals can later be charged under the membership provision, should they remain members. Were this to come about it would mean in effect that the same body of evidence (the teachings) would be serving as the basis of two separate trials and two separate jail sentences for the same individual. One trial would be for "conspiracy," that is, helping to carry on the functions of the organization which did the teaching. The other would be for "membership" in that same organization, although the first-charged "conspiracy" is itself nothing but the activities of the same "membership." This constitutes as pretty a problem in semantics as any logician is likely to find in the range of contemporary life.

Thus, although the penalty was greater in the membership case which was concluded in Philadelphia in March, 1956, the root issues were exactly the same as in the earlier Philadelphia case. The prosecution's contentions were logically identical in the two trials—that the teachings and doctrines basic to the Communist movement involved advocacy of the violent overthrow of our government as soon as circumstances would permit. The only difference was that in the earlier trial the defendants were accused of *conspiring* to set up and carry on an organization to teach and advocate those doctrines, while in the later trial the defendant was accused of being a *member* of an organization of persons who taught and advocated those doctrines. As stated, the difference seems slight; but the possible penalty was double.

It accordingly turned out that the body of teachings adduced by the prosecution was the same; and the same battle of books was once more fought through. However, while the basic line of questioning pursued by the prosecution remained what it had been, and my analysis remained basically what I had given previously, there were a few interesting and important differences, some of which indeed had a touch of Alice-in-Wonderland incredibility.

For one thing, it was possible to make passing reference to the events of 1776. For example, government counsel, in cross-examining me, read some Communist passages which dated from the early 1930's pointing out that conditions making for a peaceful transition to socialism were not present in this country at that time. When I readily agreed that the passages read reflected the Communist estimate of *1934 conditions* in this country, though not of the conditions from the late 1930's to the present time, which are considered such as to make possible a peaceful transition, the following exchange took place.

> Government Counsel: I thought you said, sir, that that condition [non-advocacy of violence by Communists in this country—J. S.] continues to the present time. Didn't you say there was no change? [The questioner at this point is referring to my testimony that throughout the entire history of the Communist Party in this country there has never been any *advocacy* of violence, that there has been no change in that respect.—J. S.]
>
> The Witness: I did, sir. I said there was no change in the basic position as to whether violence was desired; and there is not one word in all that you have read which would say that violence is desired.
>
> Government Counsel: He says it is necessary, is that it?
>
> The Witness: Whether it is necessary or not to achieve a given end is a very different question from whether it is desired.
>
> Government Counsel: Yes. In other words, the Communists don't like violence but they say they must use it?
>
> The Witness: No, the Communists say they don't like violence but that *the majority* will use it if the government is tyrannical, even as they did in 1776 in the city of Philadelphia.

In this trial, as in the earlier Philadelphia trial, the Judge raised a number of questions concerning how the Communists would determine whether or not they had majority support in a possible future revolutionary situation. In answering some of his questions, reference to the early American experience was not challenged. Parts of the record, which also throw some light on the "majority problem" at this point read as follows:

> The Witness: As they see it, Your Honor, they can only think, even conceive or remotely think of revolution when there is a situation of complete breakdown from the normal, when no balloting is normally possible, no parliamentary machinery could operate. If you had operating parliamentary machinery, you wouldn't have a revolutionary situation.
>
> The Court: I comprehend that, but I say, when that situation does exist, and one of the elements is that they have the support

of the majority, who determines the crucial question of whether they do or don't have the support of the majority of the people in that nation?

The Witness: Under such disordered conditions, each group would have to come to its conclusion, each group would have to make up its mind—the Republican Party, the Democratic Party, the Communist Party. What are we going to do at a time when government is broken down, when no normal balloting is possible? We will all have to decide at that time. There is no recipe given out for the future. They suppose a condition of prior breakdown.

The Court: I realize that, but in the writings of Marx, Lenin, Engels, and Stalin to which we have referred so often and so long, when that condition that you describe exists in a state, there is chaos, no vote can be taken, as I understand it, the proletarian revolution is to come about when the time and the circumstances coincide and the proletarians have the support of the majority of the people. No, I still don't find the answer—and if there isn't any, don't hesitate to tell me so—as to who decides whether they have that majority. Do they just go ahead and say, "Well, boys, after the revolution is over and we are in power, we will then count noses and see if we have the majority," because of the known factor of human beings following a winner, or, "Shall we send out agents or investigators to make nose counts in the sundry communities to see how the people feel about it, whether the majority are for us or not," or is it just left in a vacuum?

The Witness: Well, there is no prior recipe laid down, Your Honor. They treat it in their teachings in the way of an emergency situation. For example, if smoke were to filter in this room at this moment, and we became conscious of more and more smoke, we should have to make up our minds in rather a hurry whether we are going to break the windows, break out of the room, say there is a fire, pull the bell. We would have to make up our minds in view of the concrete situation before us ...

The Court: Suppose ... at that time [1917—J. S.] there had been a Republican Party and a Democratic Party in Russia, and the Republican National Chairman said, "It seems to me that the Republicans have a majority," and the Democratic National Chairman of Russia said, "It seems to me the Democrats have a majority," and Lenin said, "It seems to me the Communists have a majority." Now, do they sit down then among themselves and figure out who really has it, or does the proletarian revolution go on because the group in that state following that belief believes that it has?

The Witness: Your Honor, that is exactly what happened. There were a number of parties and groups in Russia at that time. (That is also exactly what happened in the American Revolution.) A number of parties and groups, and each one claimed and thought that it had the support of the majority. And since normal government had broken down, each group tried to seize and take control of the state; and civil war and revolution ensued; and one group won out. That is exactly what happened, and what happens, indeed, in practically every revolution ... As I say, even in our Revolution here in 1776 there was no method of determining with objective precision each group's support. The Continental Congress had to make up its mind that it had majority support for the armed insurrection. If they hadn't had majority support they probably would have been defeated. And if the Bolsheviks had not had majority support they probably would have been defeated.

While there was no opportunity in court to enter into more detailed consideration of the American Revolution, the reader can note the statement in *Encyclopedia Americana,* Vol. 7, p. 507 (Congress, Continental):

> "It [the first Continental Congress—J. S.] also advised the immediate election of delegates to a fresh Congress in Philadelphia 10 May, 1775; which was carried out by various bodies—legislative assemblies in some cases, popular conventions or committees of safety (q.v.) in others. None of these had any legal power to act for this purpose, and the title of all alike was the will of the *force majeure* of the people; for the loyalist section had equal right to oppose the elections, and it was tacit acceptance of superior fighting force that gave the title."

A greater disadvantage in this trial, and one scarcely understandable, was the ruling not to allow any explanation of the historical background of the right of revolution. It came about in this way:

> Defense Counsel: Doctor, let me ask you this: Based on your studies of the history of philosophy, were Marx and Engels the first leaders of philosophic historic thought to uphold in their writings the right of a majority to carry out a revolution?

The Witness: No, sir. They were far from being the first.

Defense Counsel: Now who were some of the people who preceded Marx, came before him, in upholding the right of the majority to carry out a revolution?

Government Counsel: If Your Honor pleases, what effect does that have on his gleanings from the writings of Marx and Engels? I object to it.

The Court: Sustained.

It would have had the effect, of course, of putting the "gleanings" in their historical relationship to the American tradition. But that did not become possible.

Something that had disturbed me on more than one occasion in the course of testimony in preceding trials was the constant implication made by prosecution counsel that if one did not have personal and physical acquaintance with the leaders of the Communist Party one could not know what the doctrines and teachings of the Communist movement were. A correlative assumption, given great emphasis, was that if a person had not himself physically attended Communist Party schools either as a student or an instructor, he would not be able to say what was being taught in such schools.

To let such assumptions and implications pass unchallenged would have been to acquiesce in an attitude of disparagement toward the great bulk of all scholarship having to do with the doctrines of schools of thought and social movements. Most of such scholarship is, of course, based on careful examination of books, documents, study manuals, and other such printed materials, which are compared, contrasted, and collated as a whole in order to determine the ideas and teachings basic to a given movement. For example, one of the most widely used histories of philosophic schools and movements is that written by Friedrich Ueberweg. If we were to consider as valueless or unreliable all of Ueberweg's accounts of the doctrines taught by different groups except the accounts of those groups at which he had been physically present, or whose leaders he knew personally, most of Ueberweg's information and analysis would have to be pronounced worthless, and his book could hardly be assigned to students.

If such a method were to be followed, how much of any standard reference work or encyclopedia could be considered reliable? The vast bulk of the information found in such works is not written by persons who were physically present at the actual occasions, or who had personal acquaintance with the leaders about whom they are writing. Insofar as the physical and personal elements enter, responsible scholars, of course, utilize eyewitness accounts and reports of persons who had physical and personal contacts. But such elements are usually of minor significance in relation to the meaning of a body of doctrine. What is important is the ideas, the content of the basic teachings, all of which appears in printed form.

Particularly is this the case in all the Smith Act trials, where, of course, the burden of proof is on the prosecution. Now of all the defendants who were tried I do not recall a single instance in which the government brought into court the person who taught that defendant physically and personally. There was not a single item of evidence to connect any individual defendant with any specific "teaching" that took place *only* in a *spoken* form, or by physical and personal contact with some particular teacher. The prosecution never even claimed to know the individual personal teachers of the various defendants, much less what was physically spoken to each defendant by such teachers, whoever they might have been, and still less whether the individual defendants actually listened to, understood and mastered such spoken teachings, whatever they might have been, and agreed with all of them.

What the prosecution connected the defendants with throughout the trials was a body of published works, the classics of Marxism-Leninism. What the prosecution maintained throughout was that the defendants were guilty because they believed the ideas contained in those books. No other kind of evidence was brought into court; and the prosecution's own witnesses testified again and again that all the revolutionary ideas, and all the teachings concerning the force and violence they were talking about appeared in the books, the same books that were openly on sale. There were no *secret* teaching materials, according to the prosecution's own witnesses. The sole basis and the whole content of the teachings were the published works of Marxism-Leninism. So said the prosecution itself, and quite correctly.

Hence, although it was sometimes difficult, because of the form of the interrogation, I tried to keep the facts in perspective in answering questions along this line. I did not want to seem to be accepting implications and assumptions which would have been derogatory and absurd in their effect upon scholarship. On one occasion the discussion developed in this fashion:

> Government Counsel: Now, you have told us that you never attended Communist Party schools of any kind.
> The Witness: Not physically, no, sir ...
> Government Counsel: You accomplished the attendance in spirit in what means?
> The Witness: By knowing exactly the materials, books, and teachings which they use ...
> Government Counsel: You don't consider your conversations with these people other than physical, as being in the same category as a séance?...
> The Witness: No, sir. We very seldom as a serious scholarly endeavor have physical contact with the movements and doctrines that we study. We are not concerned with the color of people's eyes, or the shape of their noses, or whether they are tall or slim. We are concerned with the content and nature of their teachings and doctrines. For this you don't have to look in their eyes physically.
> Government Counsel: No, sir. But isn't it necessary to ascertain—whether or not they actually mean what they say?
> The Witness: You could never do so by looking at them, sir.
> Government Counsel: Or talking with them?
> The Witness: No, sir.
> Government Counsel: I see.
> The Witness: You gain that by their action; the application of their doctrine in practice.

On another occasion the interrogation came around to the same point:

> Government Counsel: Doctor, when you read the printed word, you can't hear that word speak, can you?
> The Witness: Can't hear what?
> Government Counsel: Speak. You can't hear the word speak. It doesn't utter any sound, does it?
> Defense Counsel: Objected to, as frivolous.
> Government Counsel: The doctor made a remark. I don't consider my question at all frivolous ...
> The Witness: It doesn't utter any physical sound.
> Government Counsel: It doesn't have any inflection, does it?

The Witness: It sometimes has a literary inflection, but it utters no physical sound. However, it carries a distinct meaning.
Government Counsel: To you?
The Witness: To anyone who uses the English language with some understanding.
Government Counsel: To you, Doctor, as you read it. That is what we are talking about.
The Witness: I beg your pardon?
Government Counsel: When you read the printed word, you receive a meaning from it, do you not?
The Witness: I should hope so.

This trial was the first occasion on which I had heard of the authorship of ordinary Marxist-Leninist works placed in doubt. The rules of evidence must be mysterious indeed to give rise to a result of this kind:

Government Counsel: Doctor, I show you D-55. I think I have already asked you if you saw it before, but I haven't asked you this question. Can you identify it for us? What is it?
The Witness: Yes, sir; this is a pamphlet written by William Z. Foster entitled *The Road to Peace, Prosperity and Freedom;* it dates from 1941, and is an exceptionally important document.
Government Counsel: Just a minute. I ask that the latter part be stricken.
The Court: Strike out that it was written by William Z. Foster ... And that it was an exceptionally important document, unless the witness also establishes that he has knowledge of by whom it was written. It purports to be written by the person named; all right. Dr. Somerville, just let me explain this to you.
The Witness: Yes, sir.
The Court: If you will listen carefully to the questions and testify to that which is within your personal knowledge, and in the sense of personal knowledge I mean things of which you have knowledge yourself which you didn't derive generally from conversations with others, unless, however, the question asks for your opinion and you are permitted, over an objection if there be one, or without objection, to give your opinion.
The Witness: Well, I don't see how this would apply, Your Honor. If I am asked if a book is written by Bertrand Russell, can I say it is?

The Court: If nobody objects in a court of law you may answer it. If your only information in a court of law is that it is written by Bertrand Russell because that name is printed on it, then the law may require some further proof. We have to try cases in court by rules of evidence, Doctor, and we are all bound by them.

As the reader knows through passages quoted in Chapter 6 above from the official record of the first Philadelphia trial, Foster's well known pamphlet, *The Road to Peace, Prosperity and Freedom,* was used in that trial, and discussed from the witness stand. It has been in existence for fifteen years, has been widely advertised and publicly sold in bookstores. It is utterly inconceivable that Foster would be unaware that this pamphlet has been around for a decade and a half, so that if he were not responsible for its contents, he certainly would have made an issue of it long ago. On the other hand, had Foster or anyone else, by the wildest stretch of imagination, attempted to palm off some recently written work as if it had been published in 1941, he would have been proved an impostor within weeks of the first attempt to utilize the work in public. Actually, it it as plain as anything can be plain that the contents of the pamphlet represent the teachings to which Foster subscribed as of the date it was put out, 1941.

It is precisely the date that is the key to this quite incredible situation. Nineteen hundred and forty-one is seven years before the first indictment of the top Communist leaders (Dennis, Foster, and others) under the Smith Act; and in this 1941 pamphlet Foster clearly sets forth the possibility of a peaceful transition to socialism in the United States. The prosecution has been trying to maintain in these trials, as we saw in Chapter 6, that party leaders talk of peaceful transition only because of the indictments drawn under the Smith Act, and that their statements are thus a product of fear and insincerity, and merely "self-serving." It would therefore help the prosecution's case to cast doubt on the authenticity of the pamphlet. The defense was later able to have it admitted only for the limited purpose of showing part of the readings on which I based my testimony.

If the reader has difficulty in believing that the situation just described could actually come to pass, let him prepare to confront an even greater difficulty along this line. The single defendant in this case was Dr. Albert E. Blumberg, who, in the 1930's, had taught philosophy at Johns Hopkins University, and had written a number of articles, mainly on the theory of logic, which were published in scholarly journals. Later he became identified with the Communist Party, in which he held several offices, and wrote various articles on political subjects for *Political Affairs* and its predecessor, *The Communist,* from around the early 1940's to the present. All this had been well known for years to the public, and to people in academic circles, had appeared in newspaper accounts, and had been discussed from many different angles.

The defense naturally wished to place Dr. Blumberg's own political writings in evidence, since they had appeared in Communist publications, to show that he was not advocating force and violence. There is, in fact, no advocacy whatever of force or violence in them. However, the prosecution objected to their admission as evidence on the ground there was no proof they were written by the actual defendant, Dr. Albert E. Blumberg, present in the courtroom!

I myself had seen Dr. Blumberg give a paper on logical theory before a meeting of the American Philosophical Association at Bryn Mawr in the early 1930's, though I had not been in touch with or seen him again until after he had been indicted in the present case. His writings, however, were known to me and to anyone who read the periodicals involved. The questioning proceeded as follows:

> Defense Counsel: Have you read published articles by Dr. Blumberg other than articles on philosophy?
> The Witness: Yes, sir.
> Defense Counsel: Where were they published?
> The Witness: They were published in *Political Affairs* and in the predecessor of *Political Affairs, The Communist.*
> The Court: Doctor, how do you know it was the same Dr. Blumberg whom you heard speak at Bryn Mawr, not having seen him thereafter?
> The Witness: Because it was well known that the philosopher Dr. Blumberg took up a position of affiliation with the Communist teachings, and began to write in these journals. There is no other Albert E. Blumberg who wrote articles.
> The Court: Then the only information you have is that either it is your own conclusion that it must be the same person or that someone else told you that it is the same Dr. Blumberg whom you had previously met at Bryn Mawr. You never saw the man yourself in the interim, did you?

The Witness: Not in the interim, but Dr. Blumberg has claimed authorship of these articles; and it would be utterly impossible that anyone should claim authorship of those articles under these circumstances if he weren't the author.
The Court: That is your conclusion?
The Witness: Yes, sir, that is my conclusion.

Here again, the lay reader may find it as difficult as I did to visualize any rational way in which it would be possible to avoid the conclusion that the articles in question were the defendant's articles. If they were not, it is clear there would have to be two Albert E. Blumbergs in the Communist movement, both known to the public under the same name, one of them as a writer, the other as a party functionary, over a number of years. That would have been an unusual fact, which certainly would have excited comment. Moreover, in that case, the prosecution could easily have issued a warrant for the other Albert E. Blumberg. In fact, had there been any second Albert E. Blumberg who wrote the articles, it would have been the prosecution's duty as well as advantage to bring the person into court so as to expose a fraud on the part of the defendant. But no such warrant was issued, and no slightest hint of the existence of any other Communist writer by the name of Albert E. Blumberg ever emerged. A Communist "ghost writer" would be pointless.

As a matter of legal strategy Dr. Blumberg, like most defendants in Smith Act trials, did not take the witness stand. Once on the stand, a defendant could be asked to "name names," and persons so named might then have been subject to prosecution, thus setting up a sort of indefinitely extended chain of legal proceedings. On the other hand, if a defendant refused to answer such a question while on the stand, he could be adjudged in contempt of court, and could be separately sentenced for any such refusal. Also, the degree of hysteria against Communists increased the possibility of perjury charges difficult to counter, however unfounded they might be.

On cross-examination in this trial the prosecution questioned me about the passage concerning "Aesopian language," which had figured prominently in the government's case in some of the early Smith Act trials. It occurs in Lenin's *Imperialism, the Highest Stage of Capitalism,* and was quoted as follows:

Government Counsel: Well, Doctor, let me read you the second paragraph and ask you if that isn't, as a result of what you have gleaned from the writings—from reading the writings of Mr. Lenin, Mr. Engels, and Mr. Marx, a principle of Marxism-Leninism:

"This pamphlet was written with an eye to the tsarist censorship. Hence, I was not only forced to confine myself strictly to an exclusively theoretical, mainly economic analysis of facts, but to formulate the few necessary observations on politics with extreme caution, by hints, in that Aesopian language—in that cursed Aesopian language—to which tsarism compelled all revolutionaries to have recourse whenever they took up their pens to write a 'legal' work."

Footnote: " 'Aesopian,' after the Greek fable writer Aesop, was the term applied to the allusive and roundabout style adopted in 'legal' publications by revolutionaries in order to evade the censorship."

Is that a principle of the science and philosophy of Marxism-Leninism?

The Witness: No, sir; that is not a principle.

Government Counsel: It is not? You wouldn't deny the master, sir, would you?

The Witness: I am very quick to deny a great many masters. This is not a principle. This may be called a stratagem under certain particular conditions.

Government Counsel: I beg your pardon; I beg your pardon. Is it a stratagem ... recommended by Mr. Lenin?

The Witness: It is a stratagem, as I say, under certain particular conditions, namely the tsarist censorship, as it says, which is recommended by him under those conditions, not under any others.

Government Counsel: It wouldn't apply to the situation as it now existed after the passage of the Smith Act, would it?

The Witness: I should say no. There is no censorship that I know of in this country, fortunately.

Though the jury returned with a verdict of guilty in this trial, as in the first Philadelphia trial, there was a different outcome in Cleveland. There, four defendants were acquitted out of ten whose cases went to the jury, while an eleventh defendant had been acquitted by directed verdict of the judge in the course of the trial on grounds of lack of evidence presented by the government. This was the first instance in which a jury in a Smith Act trial acquitted any Communist defendant who had not renounced Communism.

The jury's deliberations likewise set a record for length in Smith Act cases, fifty-eight hours. From newspaper accounts it appears the jury took a long time to reach agreement that there had been any criminal conspiracy at all. Had they decided negatively on that point, all defendants would have had to be acquitted, as the judge's charge to the jury had, of course, pointed out.

The Cleveland trial followed the same basic pattern as the Philadelphia trials, as far as the doctrinal testimony went. Logically, the issues were the same in all the cases, but in making their decisions people are of course moved by considerations other than logic, even when they are not supposed to be. Some of the considerations operative in this situation were discussed in Chapter 9. The most important difference between the testimony which I gave at Cleveland and at the two Philadelphia trials lay in the more detailed discussion of the right of revolution, including its expression in the Declaration of Independence, which was made possible at Cleveland.

Following are some portions of the testimony bearing upon this matter:

> Defense Counsel: Did Marxism-Leninism originate the concept of the right of the people to revolt?
> The Witness: Certainly not. That was a very old doctrine, coming down from John Locke, from Thomas Jefferson, from a whole host of people from the 17th and 18th centuries, and it is universally recognized as a democratic right, the right of revolution in the sense that the majority of the people, not a minority, but the majority of the people, have the right and even the duty to use force if necessary when the existing government will not peacefully carry out the wishes of the majority. That is, when the existing government is some form of tyranny or despotism.

In the course of cross-examination this subject came up in the following interchange:

> Government Counsel: Let me ask you whether or not the Lenin theory of democracy is substantially different than, let us say, the American theory of democracy?
> The Witness: I would not say substantially different. I would say different in some particulars.
> Government Counsel: Will you explain that, please?

## TWO 1956 TRIALS, CLEVELAND AND PHILADELPHIA

The Witness: Yes, sir. There is a good deal of common ground as between Lenin's theory of democracy and, say, the theory of democracy expressed by Thomas Jefferson, or the American thinkers, or in the Declaration of Independence. There is some common ground and there are some differences. For example, as respects common ground. Both Lenin and our own Declaration of Independence would say that whenever a majority of people want a certain fundamental change, and the government will not grant that change, it is the right and duty of the majority of people to use force and violence to overthrow the existing government.

Government Counsel: Our constitution says that? I mean, the Declaration of Independence, you say?

The Witness: Yes, sir.

Government Counsel: All right.

It might almost seem as if prosecution counsel had been surprised to find that our Declaration of Independence, the document which underlies the legitimacy of our Constitution, represents an expression of the theory and practice of the right of revolution.

In this connection it is interesting to note that the Judge, in the course of his charge to the jury, made the statement: "Under the law of the United States there is no right of violent revolution against the existing government of this country." Surely the Judge would not want to deny that there is a right of violent revolution against any tyrannical government, whether such tyrannical government happens to be in this country or any other country. The meaning, then, that must be attached to the Judge's statement is that there is no right of violent revolution against our government as it *now* exists, as it *now* functions. But Communist teaching has never said there is any right of violent revolution against our government as it *now* exists and functions. Obviously, Communists have never called for violent revolution against any existing government in this country, nor have they made the slightest preparation for violence. Hence it is amply clear, by reference both to theory and to practice, that the right of violent revolution in which they believe is not a right of violent revolution against our government as it now is, but only against a government that *becomes* a tyranny and is seen as such by the majority. In that right we all believe, even the author of the Smith Act himself, as we shall see in the following chapter.

The indictment in the "membership" case, unlike that of the "conspiracy" cases, was quite brief. The full text of the latter appears in Chapter 12. The wording of the former is as follows.

## TEXT OF INDICTMENT, SECOND PHILADELPHIA SMITH ACT TRIAL, 1956

In the District Court of the United States for the Eastern District of Pennsylvania: United States of America vs. Dr. Albert Emanuel Blumberg. No. 17963 Criminal. U.S.C., Title 18, Section 2385—Membership in an organization which teaches and advocates the overthrow of the Government by force and violence.

## INDICTMENT

The Grand Jury charges:
(1) That from on or about July 26, 1945, and continuously thereafter, up to and including the date of the filing of this indictment, the Communist Party of the United States of America has at all times been a society, group and assembly of persons who teach and advocate the overthrow and destruction of the Government of the United States by force and violence as speedily as circumstances would permit;
(2) That from on or about July 26, 1945, and continuously thereafter, up to and including the date of the filing of this indictment, in the Eastern District of Pennsylvania and elsewhere, Dr. Albert Emanuel Blumberg, the defendant herein, has been a member of said Communist Party of the United States of America, the defendant well knowing during all of said period that said Communist Party of the United States of America was and is a society, group and assembly of persons who teach and advocate the overthrow and destruction of the Government of the United States by force and violence as speedily as circumstances would permit, and said defendant intending to bring about such overthrow by force and violence as speedily as circumstances would permit.

In violation of Section 2385, Title 18, United States Code.
A true copy certified to from the record
Dated October 6, 1954
Robert Criswell, Deputy Clerk United States District Court
W. Wilson White, United States Attorney
E. Louis Bumham, Foreman

# 11  The Right of Revolution

## Correspondence with Author of Smith Act and Opinion of Mr. Justice Jackson

Since the central issue in all the "Smith Act trials" has been the interpretation and application of the provisions of the Smith Act concerning "force and violence," I had long felt it would be of interest and value to put a question directly to the author of that act. The same issue had continued to arise, in one form or another, in so many research projects and studies, that I determined to lay the problem in its logically basic terms before Representative Smith himself, in order to have the benefit of his own orientation to it. On April 19,1955,1 wrote as follows to Representative Howard W. Smith of Virginia:

"Recently I have been working on UNESCO materials and other scholarly projects concerning the interpretation of civil liberties in this country. May I ask your advice on an important point which has arisen?

"The Smith Act, which bears your name, and reflects some of your labors in the public service, provides that it shall be a criminal offense to 'teach the duty, necessity, desirability or propriety of overthrowing or destroying any Government in the United States by force and violence' The problem that has arisen is the relation of this provision to the position expressed in our Declaration of Independence, to wit, that under certain conditions it is the right and duty of people to remove a government by force. That is, 'when a long train of abuses and usurpations, pursuing invariably the same object

223

evinces a design to reduce them under absolute despotism, it is their right, it is their duty to throw off such Government ...'

"In the light of this situation, do you feel that it was the intent of the Smith Act to penalize any teaching that government should be overthrown, irrespective of conditions, or, in your own mind was it taken for granted that exceptions could and should be made for the conditions as laid down in the Declaration of Independence? In other words, to take a hypothetical example, do you feel it was the intention to penalize an individual who might get up and say: 'I teach that whenever any Government in the United States becomes so tyrannical that it repeatedly refuses to carry out the majority will, the people have a right to remove it by force'? In short, is it ever right to teach that there are conditions under which a government *should* be overthrown by force?

"I fully realize this matter is not entirely in the hands of any one person. Let me assure you, however, that any answers with which you might be so kind as to favor me in relation to these questions will be highly appreciated, and will be of great value in my own effort to think through these matters.

"With best wishes, and many thanks for the courtesy of your attention, I am, Sincerely yours ..."

To this letter Representative Smith replied as follows on April 29, 1955. (The text of all his letters is here given in full.)

"I have your letter of April 19. I think my views about the propriety or desirability of revolutionary movements is stated in the Smith Act, of which I am the author.

"It is a subject upon which opinions may differ, but one which I do not have the time at present to write a brief about.

"With kind regards, I am Sincerely yours ..."

My second letter to Representative Smith was dated May 14, 1955, and was as follows:

"Thank you very much for your letter of April 29 in reply to mine of April 19.

"Knowing of the many demands on your time, I have hesitated a great deal before writing you again. Yet the matter is of such importance that I felt I should try to reformulate the question, in case it had been in any way misunderstood in the first instance.

"There would be no need for a brief opposing the desirability or propriety of any teaching that any present government in the United States should be overthrown by force or violence. I am sure there is perfect agreement on that. The only question that confronts me, in UNESCO and other research projects, is this. What explanation can one give to scholars or others when they raise the following query.

'Must we understand that the author of the Smith Act, in addition to desiring to penalize any teaching that present government should be overthrown, also desired to penalize the principle taught in the Declaration of Independence—that *if* a government should *become* in the course of time a clearly oppressive tyranny, it would *then* be right to overthrow it by force, if force were the only means left?'

"If you would but advise me whether or not you in any way intended to repudiate the teaching of our Declaration of Independence, it would help my thinking a great deal.

"Let me beg your indulgence once again for taking the liberty of bringing this matter to your attention, and assure you of my sincere gratitude for the privilege of sharing any of your thoughts on this matter. Respectfully yours ..."

The text of the second letter from Representative Smith, written May 27, 1955, is as follows:

"I have your letter of May 14 in which you ask whether I in any way intended by the provision of the Smith Act to repudiate the principles stated in the Declaration of Independence of the right of the people to overthrow a tyrannical government.

"Personally I had no such intention, nor was it considered as far as I know in the debates in the House. Very sincerely yours ..."

On Dec. 11, 1955, I wrote Representative Smith asking his permission to quote his letters. Under date of Dec. 16, 1955, he replied:

"I acknowledge receipt of your letter of December 11 having reference to my previous letters to you of April 29 and May 27, 1955, and in which you inquire whether I would have any objection to your quoting my letters.

"Certainly I have no such objection, but I agree with you that in event you do the letters should be quoted in full.

"With kind regards, I am, Sincerely yours ..."

Thus it is clear that the author of the Smith Act himself, when he confronted the basic issue, had no desire to penalize teaching or advocacy of the right to revolt under certain conditions. He had no intention, nor, presumably, did anyone else, of repudiating the revolutionary doctrine expressed in the Declaration of Independence. He, too, believes in the right of revolution under certain conditions—"the right," as he puts it, "of the people to overthrow a tyrannical government." Therefore, it would never be correct to say that the author of the Smith Act intended to put Communists in jail simply on the ground that they "believe in revolution." It is quite legitimate to believe in revolution against a tyrannical government.

Once again, this brings the whole matter around to the decisive point. If Communists are to be put in jail under the Smith Act for teaching and advocating a doctrine of revolution, it is perfectly clear that there would have to be evidence that their doctrine teaches and advocates revolution against a *non-tyrannical* government. But where is such evidence? To speak plainly, it does not exist. None was produced at the trials. None is to be found in the books and passages brought into court by the government side as its sole evidence of revolutionary beliefs. All the books and writings on the subject of revolution stress that a forcible revolt is to be undertaken only when it has majority support, and the existing government is unable and unwilling to carry out the wishes of the majority. In other words, the government in question must be a tyrannical one.

In fact, Communist doctrine would insist that not only must it be a tyrannical government, that is, a despotic regime violating the wishes of the people; it must be a tyranny that has already broken down to the point where it cannot fulfill the normal functions of government. The reader will recall in this connection the key passages from Lenin which were analyzed in detail in Chapter 2. Lenin keeps insisting that before any revolution should be undertaken not only must conditions be such that the mass of people wish for a radical change and have no peaceful means of obtaining it; the existing governments must be unable to carry on in the accustomed way.

One gains the impression, from the Philadelphia trial and from others, that government counsel would be inclined to argue in the following manner: If Communists say they teach and advocate, not the right to overthrow any government, but only a tyrannical government under certain conditions, that has no bearing on the case, since Communists (it is alleged) believe our present government is tyrannical and is characterized by those conditions. Hence, in any case, they teach the violent overthrow of *our* government.

This line of argument has at least two fatal weaknesses, one in theory and one in practice. In terms of theory, no Communist teacher or leader has ever claimed that the precondition held to be the most important of all, majority support for revolutionary action against the government, has ever been present in our country. In fact, Communist leaders and teachers have over and over again explicitly pointed out that there is as yet no majority support among the American people for any radical change, of a Communist nature. Consequently, it is impossible to argue that Communists believe our government represents the kind of tyrannical government which should be overthrown by force. In other words, even if Communists believe our government is tyrannical in certain respects, as they probably do, they recognize, and have always recognized, that it is not tyrannical in the most essential respect: it is not refusing to carry out the will of the majority for any radical change, for the simple reason that there is no majority will for a radical change. Nor, obviously, has it broken down to a degree where it cannot carry on normal functions.

From the point of view of practice, how could it be logically maintained that a certain group which believes, as this group certainly does, in the right to overthrow a tyrannical government is showing, by its conduct and practice, that it considers our United States government to be of such a nature when, in fact, this group has never in all its history made a move to overthrow that government? Such a group obviously believes that further conditions must be present. This could be inferred even if the group had no doctrine which was subject to examination.

In this case, however, there is an abundance of doctrine, which the prosecuting agencies themselves brought into court, and which specifies the conditions that must be present: the whole process of social evolution must have reached a point where the existing government, unwilling to meet the people's wishes, is no longer able to solve its problems, to function normally, and where the majority are in support of the revolutionary action. This is the whole drift of Marxism-Leninism. The alternative doctrine of indiscriminate conspiratorial revolt, the doctrine of *putschism,* is overwhelmingly rejected in theory and practice.

It is so patently odd that members of a group should be put in jail in a certain country on grounds relating to force and violence when it has been in existence in that country for decades and has never used force and violence that one is impelled to look for motivating factors in some other context. No doubt many take their cue from what they gather has happened in other countries. But how could we put individuals in jail here on the basis of what *other* individuals may have done in *other* countries?

Even if there were no insuperable legal and moral obstacles to such a course, it must be said that the major Communist revolutions that have actually taken place in other countries—in Russia and China, for example—show that the predominant Communist practice has conformed substantially to the Communist doctrine we have been discussing. In both these major cases the forces of social evolution had certainly reached a point where the existing governments, corrupt and tyrannical, were unable to solve their problems, had lost the confidence and support of the masses, and were unable to carry out their normal functions. In the light of the actual facts it would be difficult indeed to deny that in these cases the masses were ready and willing to support revolutionary measures against corrupt regimes which were trying to maintain an old order, disliked and discredited.

How many of those who have even a slight knowledge of the relevant historical facts would want to argue that people should be put in jail for believing that they have a right to revolt against regimes like those of Tsar Nicholas II of Russia, and Chiang Kai-shek when he was in control of the mainland of China? If conditions should ever deteriorate to such a level in this country it is not at all unlikely that a majority of the American people would be quite willing to support forcible measures to bring about a change.

If there have never been in this country any Communist plans or steps of revolutionary practice, as distinguished from a doctrine of revolt applicable to some possible future time, and if the actual revolutions carried out in Russia and China took place under conditions which, were they to develop in this country, would probably move the majority to revolt, what kind of behavior *is* being imputed to Communists by prosecuting agencies who would argue that they should be put in jail? Professor Francis Wormuth presents the interesting theory that, in the light of key judicial decisions and opinions handed down by the federal Court of Appeals and the Supreme Court, the defendants were actually convicted because it was assumed that they were *likely* to commit seditious conspiracy, whereas of course they were not charged on any such ground, nor could they be, for in our code there is no crime definable as *likelihood* to commit seditious conspiracy, or anything else.

In our conception of law and justice, persons might be picked up for questioning if it were thought by the authorities that they were likely to commit a crime; but such persons could never, on that ground alone, be sentenced to jail terms as criminals. Even if they had long criminal records of actual convictions in the past it would be necessary to prove another criminal act, or physical preparation for another specific criminal act, before they could be justifiably convicted of crime and sent to prison.

In his exceptionally well documented and closely reasoned article in *The Western Political Quarterly* for September, 1953, Professor Wormuth, dealing with the first Smith Act trial of the principal Communist leaders, a trial which set the pattern for later ones, observes:

"Apparently it was only with reluctance that the government brought its prosecution for speech. [That is, for advocating, rather than carrying out, the action. J. S.] It kept the case before the grand jury for more than a year, evidently in the hope of getting an indictment for violation of one of the numerous non-speech offenses of a political character in the federal Criminal Code. It was unable to persuade the grand jury that the defendants were agents of a foreign power, or that they had carried on political activity on behalf of a foreign power, or that they had incited to rebellion or committed a seditious conspiracy, sabotage, or espionage, or that they had conspired to commit any offense whatever against the United States. But it did obtain an indictment for conspiring to advocate revolution in violation of the Smith Act." (P. 543.)

One may wonder whether that grand jury, which set the precedent for indicting Communists for conspiring to advocate revolution in violation of the Smith Act, would have done so if they could have had knowledge of the statement which was later to be made by Representative Smith, in his letter of May 27, 1955, quoted above. In that statement Congressman Smith clearly points out that he had no intention, nor, so far as he knows, did anyone else involved in passing the law entertain any intention, of penalizing advocacy "of the right of the people to overthrow a tyrannical government." Had such a statement then been available and taken into account, it is impossible to see how Communists could have been indicted, since it is precisely "the right of the people to overthrow a tyrannical government" which they advocate, not a right to overthrow a non-tyrannical government.

When the case reached the Court of Appeals Judge Learned Hand wrote the opinion sustaining conviction, a portion of which we have already examined in Chapter 6. Professor Wormuth quotes another passage from that opinion:

" 'By far the most powerful of all the European nations had been a convert to Communism for over thirty years; its leaders were the most devoted and potent proponents of the faith; no such movement in Europe of East to West had arisen since Islam. Moreover in most of West Europe there were important political Communist factions, always agitating to increase their power; and the defendants were acting in close concert with the movement ...

" '... Any border fray, any diplomatic incident, any difference of construction of the *modus vivendi*—such as the Berlin blockade we have just mentioned—might prove a spark in the tinderbox, and lead to war. We do not understand how one could ask for a more probable danger, unless we wait till the very eve of hostilities ... We hold that it is a danger clear and present' " (P. 549.)

Commenting upon this passage, Professor Wormuth writes:

"This is a flat statement that the defendants have organized and command a seditious conspiracy, a conspiracy to revolt, which is a very different thing from a conspiracy to teach the duty and necessity of revolution. Judge Hand does not tell us where he gets his evidence of seditious conspiracy. His summary of the record ... deals solely with the propositions that the defendants conspired to teach Marxism-Leninism, and that Marxism-Leninism teaches the desirability of revolution on some propitious occasion in the indefinite future. There is no word of sedition or of assistance to the Soviet Union ... The advocacy of Marxism-Leninism raises a probable—*i.e.,* imminent—danger because the defendants are 'probably' guilty of seditious conspiracy.

"It was no mere oversight that Judge Hand fails to point to evidence of seditious conspiracy in the record. The case was not tried on that theory, and it appears that the record was altogether barren of such evidence. In the Supreme Court Mr. Justice Douglas summarized the 16,000 page record thus:

" 'If this were a case where those who claimed protection under the First Amendment were teaching the technique of sabotage, the assassination of the President, the filching of documents from public files, the planting of bombs, the art of street warfare, and the like, I would have no doubts ... This case was argued [by the prosecution on appeal] as if those were the facts. The argument [of counsel] imported much seditious conduct into the record ... *But the fact is that no such evidence was introduced at the trial....* (Italics supplied)" (Pp. 549, 550.)

Professor Wormuth adds: "This characterization of the record is not disputed by any of the seven opinions in the Court of Appeals and the Supreme Court." He quotes, for example, from the opinion of Mr. Justice Frankfurter, who, although he upheld the decision of the lower courts for conviction (while Douglas did not), said, in regard to this aspect of the case:

" 'Mr. Justice Douglas quite properly points out that the conspiracy before us is not a conspiracy to overthrow the Government"; 'there are no reliable data tracing acts of sabotage or espionage directly to these defendants'; and 'there appears to be little reliable evidence demonstrating directly that the Communist party in this country has recruited persons willing to engage in espionage or other unlawful activity on behalf of the Soviet Union.' " (Pp. 552, 553.)

"Summarizing the whole process," concludes Professor Wormuth, "it seems fair to say that Judge Hand established a danger resulting from the defendants' conspiracy to advocate Marxism-Leninism by imputing to them guilt of seditious conspiracy. The danger remote in time which is threatened by the defendants' teaching of Marxism-Leninism is an imminent danger resulting from the defendants' seditious conspiracy ...

"In effect we have two revolutions. The first, the Marxist-Leninist, which is remote in time, is the one that is punished. The second, the pro-Soviet revolution imminent of execution, is the one that is dreaded. The first is punished because the second is dangerous." Any danger involved in furthering the Marxist-Leninist doctrine concerning the first revolution "would not sustain a conviction." The second revolution, however, that involving the imputed seditious conspiracy, "is not a doctrine, but a plot imminent of execution. If the defendants were to be convicted for having made such a plot, evidence of the plot should have been introduced, and this evidence should have gone to the jury. Neither of these requirements was met." (Pp. 550, 551.)

There is certainly much that can be said for Professor Wormuth's theory, when all the facts are considered. One might test it, in a sense, in the following fashion: Imagine a person brought into court who believed in all the doctrines contained in the passages from

Communist writings adduced by the government side. But further imagine that, because of some very peculiar circumstances, this person had no knowledge whatsoever of any political party or group, in this or any other country, organized on the basis of these doctrines. In other words, he knows nothing of the fact that the Soviet Union, or any other country, is a functioning Communist power. But he believes in the principles of the doctrines, without connecting them with any particular authors, and is preparing to set up an organization to teach these principles to others in just the way he believes in them.

If there could be any such person or persons, and they were indicted under the Smith Act for criminal conspiracy to teach the violent overthrow of our United States government, it is difficult indeed to picture a jury finding them guilty, in the absence of any possibility of linking the accused with any Communist movement in other powerful countries. In the first place, as Professor Wormuth indicates, if we leave out of account the existence of the Soviet Union and of international Communism, any possible danger involved in the occurrence within the United States of the kind of revolution that is actually expounded in Marxist doctrine is far too remote to justify a conviction. In the second place, when the Marxist-Leninist doctrine is seriously examined in its own terms, the fact emerges clearly that the preconditions attached to the kind of revolution actually expounded would suffice to render such a revolution lawful and justifiable in the eyes of any American who believes in the Declaration of Independence.

There can be little doubt that in the mind of the average juror (or judge) a necessary link in the chain of thought leading to the conclusion that the defendants in the actual trials were really dangerous, and therefore guilty, was the assumption that they were so connected with powerful foreign countries inimical to the United States that, in case of trouble, they would be prepared to betray and sacrifice the United States to the interests of such foreign countries. If that link were not there, it is very unlikely they would be convicted.

What does that link amount to? As Professor Wormuth points out, it amounts to the *assumption* that the accused are guilty of the serious crime of seditious conspiracy—that is, a definite conspiracy to perform acts similar to sabotage or espionage in the interests of a foreign power, or to oppose by force the law or authority of the United States government, as at present constituted. Now if the defendants were thought to be guilty of any such thing, they should have been specifically charged with it, in order that they might have a fair opportunity to defend themselves; and tangible evidence of a specific nature should have been brought forward. Unless and until both these things are done—and neither has ever been done—it is clear that the defendants should not be presumed guilty.

Let us now turn to one of the few recent instances in which a judge, in handing down an adverse decision, has directly and at length confronted the right of revolution in his written opinion. It is that of Mr. Justice Jackson in *American Communications Association* v. *Douds,* 339 U.S. 382, dated May 8, 1950. In this context Jackson was not addressing himself to the Smith Act but to the law establishing the National Labor Relations Board, specifically to that part of it which sets up a requirement of a non-Communist oath for certain officials of labor unions. However, the decisive question was exactly the same as that which is basic to all the Smith Act cases: What is the Communist doctrine concerning revolutionary force and violence? What Mr. Justice Jackson had to say probably constitutes the most concrete judicial attempt ever made to take account of the principles of the Declaration of Independence together with our history, and still justify legal penalties against Communists because of their doctrine on revolution. It is therefore worth examination.

"...we cannot ignore the fact," wrote Mr. Justice Jackson (p. 439), "that our own government originated in revolution and is legitimate only if overthrow by force may sometimes be justified. That circumstances sometimes justify it is not Communist doctrine, but an old American belief." Surely the phrasing in this sentence involved a slip of the pen. What the Justice obviously meant was that it is an old American belief *as well as* Communist doctrine, or that it was an old American belief *before* it was Communist doctrine; in other words, that it is not *exclusively Communist* doctrine. But, as the whole subsequent course of his argument shows, he would never, of course, want to say that the belief in question—that circumstances sometimes justify violent revolution—is not a Communist belief. If this phrasing were not to be regarded as a slip of the pen, it would have to be set down as the clearest and most childish instance of the impossible attempt to assume that anything Americans believe in must be rejected by Communists and *vice versa*. It would then be merely an instance of extreme emotionalism, the result of being so worked up against an opponent that it becomes impossible to acknowledge that one has any belief whatever in common with that opponent—even the belief that two and two make four, or that storekeepers should give correct change.

"The men," continues Mr. Justice Jackson, "who led the struggle forcibly to overthrow lawfully constituted British authority found moral support by asserting a natural law under which their revolution was justified, and they bravely proclaimed their belief in the document basic to our freedom. Such sentiments have also been given ardent and rather extravagant expression by Americans of undoubted patriotism."

At this point Mr. Justice Jackson appends a lengthy and most significant footnote which reads as follows:

"A surprising catalogue of statements could be compiled. The following are selected from Mencken's *A New Dictionary of Quotations,* under the rubric 'revolution':

" 'Whenever any form of government becomes destructive of these ends [life, liberty, and the pursuit of happiness] it is the right of the people to alter or abolish it, and to institute new government, laying its foundation on such principles, and organizing its powers in such form as to them shall seem most likely to effect their safety and happiness' Thomas Jefferson, The Declaration of Independence, July 4, 1776.

" 'The community hath an indubitable, inalienable and indefeasible right to reform, alter or abolish government in such manner as shall be by that community judged most conducive to the public weal' The Pennsylvania Declaration of Rights, 1776.

" 'It is an observation of one of the profoundest inquirers into human affairs that a revolution of government is the strongest proof that can be given by a people of their virtue and good sense.' John Adams, *Diary,* 1786.

" 'What country can preserve its liberties if their rulers are not warned from time to time that this people preserve the spirit of resistance? Let them take arms' Thomas Jefferson, Letter to W. S. Smith, Nov. 13, 1787.

" 'An oppressed people are authorized, whenever they can, to rise and break their fetters' Henry Clay, Speech in the House of Representatives, March 4, 1818.

" 'Any people anywhere, being inclined and having the power, have the right to rise up and shake off the existing government, and found a new one that suits them better' Abraham Lincoln, Speech in the House of Representatives, 1848.

" 'All men recognize the right of revolution, that is, the right to refuse allegiance to, and to resist, the government where its tyranny or its inefficiency are great and unendurable' H. D. Thoreau, *An Essay on Civil Disobedience,* 1849.

" 'This country, with its institutions, belongs to the people who inhabit it. Whenever they shall grow weary of the existing government they can exercise their constitutional right of amending it, or their revolutionary right to dismember or overthrow it' Abraham Lincoln, Inaugural Address, May 4, 1861.

" 'Whenever the ends of government are perverted, and public liberty manifestly endangered, and all other means of redress are ineffectual, the people may, and of right ought to, reform the old or establish a new government; the doctrine of non-resistance against arbitrary power and oppression is absurd, slavish and destructive of the good and happiness of mankind' Declaration of the Rights of Maryland, 1867.

" 'The right of revolution is an inherent one. When people are oppressed by their government, it is a natural right they enjoy to relieve themselves of the oppression if they are strong enough, either by withdrawing from it, or by overthrowing it and substituting a government more acceptable' U.S. Grant, *Personal Memoirs,* Vol. I, 1885.

"Quotations of similar statements," says Jackson candidly at the conclusion of his footnote, "could be multiplied indefinitely."

Now, one wonders, in what way will Mr. Justice Jackson try to reconcile all these statements by famous and respected American authorities with the fact that he wants to penalize Communists when *they* say the same thing? For the reader will bear in mind that Justice Jackson's opinion concurred with the majority of the Court in upholding those provisions of the law under discussion which enacted certain penalties against Communists. The way which he chooses is immediately made clear, as he continues in his text:

"Most of these utterances were directed against a tyranny which left no way to change by suffrage. It seems to me a perversion of their meaning to quote them, as the Communists often do, to sanction violent attacks upon a representative government which does afford such means." Here again one is forced to wonder whether such language, in view of its evident ambiguity, is not a slip of the pen.

Consider the phrase, "to sanction violent attacks." Mr. Justice Jackson is actually talking as if the Communists used such quotations as a justification for taking arms in hand and proceeding to use force and violence against our existing "representative government." He *seems* to be saying that that is the reason why he would penalize the Communists but not the Americans who originally made the statements quoted. But if he were specifically confronted with this point Mr. Justice Jackson would certainly have to admit, as everyone else has to admit, that the Communists never have used, in any instance whatsoever in all their history in this country, those quotations or any others as a justification for taking up arms in force and violence against our representative government.

The reason is simple but decisive: They have never taken up arms against our representative government on any basis at all, with or without justification by quotation from anyone. Whether foreign Communists have ever taken up arms against representative governments in other countries would be matter for debate. They would argue that they have not taken up arms against any government that could be characterized as "representative." They consider such governments as those of the Tsar (or Kerensky) in Russia, of Chiang Kai-shek when he was in control of the Chinese mainland, of the Axis powers in Hungary, Rumania, and other such countries, as far from being "representative." They are, of course, not the only ones who would hold that view.

Suppose, however, that we were convinced some cases could be found in which Communists in certain countries had taken up arms against a truly "representative" government. Would that mean we could justifiably proceed to penalize Communists in our country without further ado? How could we prove they would in future necessarily follow the example of foreign Communists who overthrew "representative" governments rather than the example of foreign Communists who overthrew "unrepresentative" governments, or no governments at all?

In any case, there would be no possibility of saying that the difference between American Communists and the other Americans quoted is that the Communists used the statements to justify a violent revolution against a good and proper representative government whereas the other Americans had in mind only a tyrannical government. The Communists, too, have in mind a tyrannical government. Some of the Americans quoted did, of course, actually engage in violent revolution against a government which they considered tyrannical—that of their British sovereign. The American Communists are like the others quoted, in that they are asserting a right to do something only if and when the conditions of a tyrannical government should arise at a future time.

Hence it is quite plain that when Mr. Justice Jackson used the phrase, "to sanction violent attacks," he did not really mean physical violence. With due respect for simple fact, he could have been referring only to the bitter and abusive language of partisan political speechmaking and the like—"violent attacks" in that sense. But that is no crime.

The Communists are, of course, opposed to our present economic system and to our present form of government insofar as it reflects and legally sanctions the capitalist economic system. In other words they are, as is well known, in favor of various fundamental changes, of a political, economic, and social character. They are without question against the present system in this country; but they are not calling for a violent revolution in this country to overthrow that system, for the plain reason that they recognize it is representative of the *present* will of the people of this country.

They are trying to change that will through their various forms of education, propaganda, and the like, although they may be quite mistaken in their ideas, beliefs, and anticipations. But again, all that is no crime. The language in which they sometimes attack the persons, policies, and institutions they are opposed to may be quite regrettable; but we in the United States take pride in and credit for the fact that we do not try to punish it legally. Justice Jackson himself immediately goes on to point this out and to emphasize it.

"But," he continues, "while I think Congress may make it a crime to take one overt step to use or incite violence or force against our Government, I do not see how in the light of our history a mere belief that one has a natural right under some circumstances to do so can subject the American citizen to prejudice any more than possession of any other erroneous belief."

Again, one must pause to reflect upon the language used in order to do justice to the thought. If one took the word "erroneous" in this context literally and directly, one would have to conclude that Mr. Justice Jackson was actually maintaining that any belief in the right of revolution, even when qualified by "under some circumstances" (that is, a tyranny), may be put in the class of "erroneous belief." But he could not possibly have had such a view; it would mean, among other things, that he was rejecting the Declaration of Independence. Not only would this be unlikely in general, but Mr. Justice Jacksdn has already specifically emphasized, in this very opinion, that "we cannot ignore the fact that our own government originated in revolution, and is legitimate only if overthrow by force may sometimes be justified." (I believe we may take it that Mr. Justice Jackson did not consider that the government in whose highest court he was sitting as judge was illegitimate.)

What Mr. Justice Jackson probably meant by "erroneous belief" was not belief in the right of revolution itself under certain circumstances but belief that this right should be applied by way of carrying out an actual revolution in this country under circumstances which would not justify such an action—for instance, when the government was still able and willing to carry out the wishes of the people. But neither the Communists nor the other Americans quoted propose any such action. They propose it only *if* and *when* government becomes tyrannical. It is difficult, therefore, to see in what precise sense the word "erroneous" could be used in this context.

However, whether the particular belief in the right of revolution be in any way erroneous or not, Justice Jackson is clear and emphatic in his insistence that the area of *belief* must be separated from the area of *overt action*. "...while I think Congress may make it a crime to take one overt step to use or incite violence," as he said, "...I do not see how in the light of our history a mere belief that one has a natural right under some circumstances to do so can subject the American citizen to prejudice ..." In other words, the only group that could properly be subjected to legal penalty or prejudice is composed of those who take at least "one overt step to use or incite violence or force against our Government."

Now it is clear that American Communists cannot be placed in this group, since they have never taken even one overt step to use violence or incite violence against any government that now exists or has ever existed in this country. (Had there been a single scrap of such evidence it would, of course, have been placed in the very forefront of all these trials.) Nevertheless, in some way known finally only to himself, Mr. Justice Jackson concluded that American

Communists should be placed in the group properly subjected to legal penalty!

In this connection the reader will bear in mind that, as we have previously seen, the "overt acts" listed by indictments brought under the Smith Act are not overt acts of force or violence, such as Mr. Justice Jackson had in mind in drawing his distinction between belief and action, or incitement to action. As the reader will recall, the "overt acts" in the prosecutions we have been concerned with are only in the class of "acts" that are necessary to teach and spread *beliefs*—*that* is, acts such as setting up and attending classes, participating in meetings, publishing articles, and the like.

These are obviously not overt acts of violence; they are overt acts of teaching and spreading belief. Nor are they incitements to violence; if they are "incitements" at all, they are obviously incitements to belief. To what belief? That violent revolution should take place against our present government? Clearly not, since these people have never called for violent revolution under any conditions or circumstances existing in this country. Obviously, it was and is the belief not that *present* circumstances justify violent revolution but, in Mr. Justice Jackson's words, "that circumstances *sometimes* justify it," which, as he added with a warm and even belligerent display of pride, unfortunately entirely contradictory to his ultimate decision, is "an old American belief."

# 12  Chapter and Verse

## Text and Analysis of Smith Act and Indictments

The Smith Act, officially known as the "Alien Registration Act, 1940" (H.R. 5138), was passed by the Seventy-Sixth Congress June 28, 1940, at a time when there were widespread feelings of hostility toward aliens. World War II had begun, but the United States had not yet entered the conflict.

The official designation of the act does not reflect its central content; the bill represented a number of measures thrown together. As Professor Zechariah Chafee Jr. of Harvard Law School observed in his classic survey, "Free Speech in the United States," most of the act "is not concerned with registration and the very first part of it has nothing particular to do with aliens." (P. 44.) The sections under which the indictments were drawn read as follows:

"Sec. 2 (a) It shall be unlawful for any person—

(1) to knowingly or willfully advocate, abet, advise, or teach the duty, necessity, desirability or propriety of overthrowing or destroying any government in the United States by force or violence, or by the assassination of any officer of any such government;

(2) with the intent to cause the overthrow or destruction of any government in the United States, to print, publish, edit, issue, circulate, sell, distribute, or publicly display any written or printed matter advocating, advising, or teaching the duty, necessity, desirability, or propriety of overthrowing or destroying any government in the United States by force and violence;

(3) to organize or help to organize any society, group, or assembly of persons who teach, advocate or encourage the overthrow or destruction of any government in the United States by force or violence; or to be or become a member of, or affiliate with, any such society, group, or assembly of persons, knowing the purposes thereof.

(b) For the purposes of this section, the term "government in the United States" means the Government of the United States, the government of any State, Territory, or possession of the United States, the government of the District of Columbia, or the government of any political subdivision of any of them.

Sec. 3. It shall be unlawful for any person to attempt to commit, or to conspire to commit, any of the acts prohibited by the provisions of this title.

Sec. 4. Any written or printed matter of the character described in section 1 or section 2 of this Act, which is intended for use in violation of this Act, may be taken from any house or other place in which it may be found, or from any person in whose possession it may be, under a search warrant issued pursuant to the provisions of title XI of the Act entitled "An Act to punish acts of interference with the foreign relations, the neutrality and the foreign commerce of the United States, to punish espionage, and better to enforce the criminal laws of the United States, and for other purposes," approved June 15, 1917 (40 Stat. 228; U.S.C. title 18, ch. 18).

Sec. 5. (a) Any person who violates any of the provisions of this title shall, upon conviction thereof, be fined not more than $10,000, or imprisoned for not more than ten years, or both.

(b) No person convicted of violating any of the provisions of this title shall, during the five years next following his conviction, be eligible for employment by the United States, or by any department or agency thereof (including any corporation the stock of which is wholly owned by the United States)."

By virtue of the revision of the federal criminal code in 1948 the maximum penalty for *conspiracy* to commit any of the prohibited acts was reduced to five years.

Analyzing the Smith Act against the historic background of American practice and institutions, Professor Chafee observes: "... this statute contains the most drastic restrictions on freedom of speech ever enacted in the United States during peace." (P. 441, "Free Speech in the United States.")

He adds: "Here at last is the federal peace-time sedition law which A. Mitchell Palmer and his associated patrioteers tried to scare the country into passing twenty years ago without success. Not a spark of evidence was introduced in committee or in Congress to show any more need for such a federal statute now than in 1920. No proof was offered of any evil which had to be remedied by the unprecedented provision of section 2. The plain reason for it is, that the persons and organizations who have been hankering for such a measure during the last two decades took advantage of the passion against immigrants to write into an anti-alien statute the first federal peace-time restriction on speaking and writing by American citizens since the ill-fated Sedition Act of 1798.

"So far as I can ascertain, the provisions of section 2 never received a favorable report from any committee of the Seventy-Sixth Congress that had subjected them to the test of a public hearing." (P. 463.)

Referring to the "membership clause," Professor Chafee emphasizes the conflict between this type of legislation and the American tradition: "Special attention must be given to the most drastic portion of section 2, namely clause (a) (3). This makes it a crime for a man to be a member of an organization which is subsequently found to advocate the overthrow of the government by force, regardless of what he himself says or does. This idea that guilt is not necessarily personal, but can result from association, is absolutely abhorrent to every American tradition or conception of criminal justice before 1918." (P. 470.)

In order to analyze the nature of the specific charges in the indictments let us first quote the official text in full.

## INDICTMENT, PHILADELPHIA
## SMITH ACT TRIAL, 1954

In the District Court of the United States for the Eastern District of Pennsylvania: United States of America *vs.* Joseph Kuzma, *et al.,* U.S.C., Title 18, Sec. 10 (1946 ed.); U.S.C., Title 18, Sec. 2385 (1948 ed.); U.S.C., Title 18, Sec. 11 (1946 ed.); U.S.C., Title 18, Sec. 371 (1948 ed.)—Conspiracy to advocate the overthrow of the Government by force and violence. No. 17418 Criminal,

# TEXT AND ANALYSIS OF SMITH ACT AND INDICTMENTS

## INDICTMENT

The Grand Jury charges:

(1) That from on or about April 1, 1945, and continuously thereafter up to and including the date of the filing of this indictment, in the Eastern District of Pennsylvania and elsewhere, Joseph Kuzma, also known as Joe Kuzma; Robert Klonsky, also known as Robert Kirby; Sam Gobeloff, also known as Joseph Roberts; Benjamin Weiss, also known as Ben Weiss; David Dubensky, also known as David Davis; Thomas Nabried; Irvin Katz, also known as "Chick" Katz and Irving Katz; Walter Lowenfels, also known as William Lerner; and Sherman Marion Labovitz, also known as Sherman Labovitz, the defendants herein, unlawfully, wilfully and knowingly did conspire with each other and with William Z. Foster, Eugene Dennis, John B. Williamson, Jacob Stachel, Robert G. Thompson, Benjamin J. Davis, Jr., Henry Winston, John Gates, Irving Potash, Gilbert Green, Carl Winter, Gus Hall, Elizabeth Gurley Flynn, Betty Gannett, and Pettis Perry, co-conspirators but not defendants herein, and with divers other persons to the Grand Jury unknown, to commit offences against the United States prohibited by Section 2 of the Smith Act (54 Stat. 671) U.S.C., Title 18, Section 10 (1946 Ed.) and U.S.C. Title 18, Section 2385 (1948 Ed.) in violation of U.S.C. Title 18, Section 11 (1946 Ed.), being Section 3 of the said Smith Act while said section of said act remained effective, and thereafter in violation of U.S.C., Title 18, Section 371 (1948 Ed.), by (1) unlawfully, wilfully, and knowingly advocating and teaching the duty and necessity of overthrowing and destroying the Government of the United States by force and violence, with the intent of causing the aforesaid overthrow and destruction of the Government of the United States by force and violence as speedily as circumstances would permit; and by (2) unlawfully, wilfully and knowingly organizing, and helping to organize, as the Communist Party of the United States of America a society, group, and assembly of persons who teach and advocate the overthrow and destruction of the Government of the United States by force and violence, with the intent of causing the aforesaid overthrow and destruction of the Government of the United States by force and violence as speedily as circumstances would permit;

(2) It was a part of said conspiracy that the said defendants and their co-conspirators would become members, officers, and functionaries of said Communist Party, knowing the purposes of said

Communist Party, and in such capacities would assume leadership in said Communist Party, and responsibility for carrying out its policies and activities to and including the date of the filing of this indictment;

(3) It was further a part of said conspiracy that said defendants and co-conspirators would cause to be organized groups, clubs, sections, and district, state, city and national units of said Communist Party in the State of Pennsylvania, in the State of Delaware, in the State of New Jersey, in the State of New York, and elsewhere, and would recruit, and encourage recruitment of, members to said Communist Party, concentrating on recruiting persons employed in key basic industries and plants;

(4) It was further a part of said conspiracy that said defendants and co-conspirators would publish and circulate, and cause to be published and circulated, books, articles, magazines, and newspapers teaching and advocating the duty and necessity of overthrowing and destroying the Government of the United States by force and violence as speedily as circumstances would permit;

(5) It was further a part of said conspiracy that said defendants and co-conspirators would write, and cause to be written, articles and directives in publications of the Communist Party of the United States of America, including, but not limited to, *Political Affairs, Daily Worker, The Worker,* and the Pennsylvania edition of *The Worker,* teaching and advocating the necessity of overthrowing and destroying the Government of the United States by force and violence as speedily as circumstances would permit;

(6) It was further a part of said conspiracy that said defendants and co-conspirators would conduct, and cause to be conducted schools and classes in which recruits and members of said Communist Party would be indoctrinated in the principles of Marxism-Leninism and in which would be taught and advocated the duty and necessity of overthrowing and destroying the Government of the United States by force and violence as speedily as circumstances would permit;

(7) It was further a part of said conspiracy that said defendants and co-conspirators would agree upon, and carry into effect, detailed plans for the vital parts of the Communist Party of the United States of America to go underground, in the event of emergency and from said underground position to continue in all respects the conspiracy described in paragraph (1) of this indictment;

(8) It was further a part of said conspiracy that said defendants and co-conspirators would use false names and false documents in order to conceal their identities and activities as members and functionaries of said Communist Party;

(9) It was further a part of said conspiracy that said defendants and co-conspirators would do other and further things to conceal the existence and operation of said conspiracy.

In pursuance and furtherance of said conspiracy and to effect the objects thereof, the defendants and co-conspirators did commit, in the Eastern District of Pennsylvania, and elsewhere, the following overt acts, among others:

## OVERT ACTS

1. On or about June 20, 1946, Sherman Marion Labovitz, also known as Sherman Labovitz, a defendant herein, did attend and participate in a class of the Communist Party of the United States of America, held at the Wharton Center, 1708 North 22nd Street, Philadelphia, Pennsylvania.

2. On or about August 9, 1946, Sam Gobeloff, also known as Joseph Roberts, a defendant herein, did attend and participate in a Communist Party class held at 37 Howe Street, New Haven, Connecticut.

3. On or about July 18, 1948, Sam Gobeloff, also known as Joseph Roberts, a defendant herein, did attend and participate in the New York State Convention of the Communist Party held at Webster Hall, 119 East 11th Street, New York, N.Y.

4. On or about July 18, 1948, Joseph Kuzma, also known as Joe Kuzma; Benjamin Weiss, also known as Ben Weiss; David Dubensky, also known as David Davis; Thomas Nabried; Walter Lowenfels, also known as William Lerner; and Sherman Marion Labovitz, also known as Sherman Labovitz, defendants herein, did attend and participate in a convention of the Eastern Pennsylvania and Delaware District of the Communist Party of the United States of America, held at Chris J. Perry Elks' Hall, 1416 No. Broad Street, Philadelphia, Penna.

5. On or about February 11, 1949, Sam Gobeloff, also known as Joseph Roberts, a defendant herein, did attend and participate in a Communist Party meeting held at Hotel Diplomat, New York, N.Y.

6. On or about April 24, 1950, Irvin Katz, also known as "Chick" Katz and Irving Katz, and Sherman Marion Labovitz, also known as Sherman Labovitz, defendants herein, did formulate and cause to be published and circulated copies of a letter and plan of work for the recruitment of Communist Party members and Communist Party building.

7. On or about June 4, 1950, Joseph Kuzma, also known as Joe Kuzma; Robert Klonsky, also known as Robert Kirby; Benjamin Weiss, also known as Ben Weiss; David Dubensky, also known as David Davis; Thomas Nabried; Irvin Katz, also known as "Chick" Katz and Irving Katz; and Sherman Marion Labovitz, also known as Sherman Labovitz, defendants herein, did attend and participate in a Communist Party conference held at Chris J. Perry Elks' Hall, 1416 North Broad Street, Philadelphia, Penna.

8. On or about December 10, 1950, Robert Klonsky, also known as Robert Kirby; Benjamin Weiss, also known as Ben Weiss; David Dubensky, also known as David Davis; and Thomas Nabried, defendants herein, did attend and participate in a convention of the Eastern Pennsylvania and Delaware District of the Communist Party of the United States of America, held at April Farms, RD #2, Coopersburg, Pennsylvania.

9. On or about January 28, 1951, Walter Lowenfels, also known as William Lerner, and Sherman Marion Labovitz, also known as Sherman Labovitz, defendants herein, did attend and participate in a meeting held at Garvey Memorial Hall, 1611 West Columbia Avenue, Philadelphia, Pennsylvania.

10. In or about February, 1951, in the City of Trenton, State of New Jersey, Joseph Kuzma, also known as Joe Kuzma, a defendant herein, did issue and furnish instructions of a clandestine nature for the purpose of securing funds for the underground apparatus of the Communist Party of Eastern Pennsylvania and Delaware and to promote the program and policies of the Communist Party-USA.

11. On or about February 17, 1951, Robert Klonsky, also known as Robert Kirby; Benjamin Weiss, also known as Ben Weiss; Thomas Nabried; Irvin Katz, also known as "Chick" Katz and Irving Katz; Walter Lowenfels, also known as William Lerner; and Shennan Marion Labovitz, also known as Sherman Labovitz, defendants herein, did attend and participate in a Communist Party meeting held at Heller's Colonial Dining Room, 3729 Spruce Street, Philadelphia, Pennsylvania.

12. Joseph Kuzma, also known as Joe Kuzma, a defendant herein, did cause to be used, on or about February 20, 1951, a safe deposit box located in the Broad Street Trust Company (formerly known as Mid-City Bank and Trust Company) at Broad and Market Streets, Philadelphia, Pennsylvania, for the purpose of carrying out certain financial transactions of the underground apparatus of the Communist Party of Eastern Pennsylvania and Delaware.

13. On or about March 9, 1951, Robert Klonsky, also known as Robert Kirby; Benjamin Weiss, also known as Ben Weiss; David Dubensky, also known as David Davis; Thomas Nabried; Irvin Katz, also known as "Chick" Katz and Irving Katz; Walter Lowenfels, also known as William Lerner; and Sherman Marion Labovitz, also known as Sherman Labovitz, defendants herein, did attend and participate in a meeting held at Chris J. Perry Elks' Hall, 1416 North Broad Street, Philadelphia, Pennsylvania.

14. On or about March 21, 1951, Benjamin Weiss, also known as Ben Weiss, and Sherman Marion Labovitz, also known as Sherman Labovitz, defendants herein, did attend and participate in a meeting held at Rockland Palace, 155th Street and 8th Avenue, New York, N.Y.

15. On or about May 4, 1951, David Dubensky, also known as David Davis, a defendant herein, did attend and participate in a Communist Party rally held at Chris J. Perry Elks' Hall, 1416 North Broad Street, Philadelphia, Pennsylvania.

16. On or about May 5, 1951, David Dubensky, also known as David Davis, a defendant herein, did attend and participate in a rally at Fred Wrigley Hall, Quakertown, Pennsylvania.

17. On or about May 5, 1951, Robert Klonsky, also known as Robert Kirby; Benjamin Weiss, also known as Ben Weiss; Thomas Nabried; and Irvin Katz, also known as "Chick" Katz and Irving Katz, defendants herein, did attend and participate in a meeting held at Heller's Colonial Dining Room, 3729 Spruce Street, Philadelphia, Pennsylvania.

18. On or about May 27, 1951, Benjamin Weiss, also known as Ben Weiss; Thomas Nabried; Walter Lowenfels, also known as William Lerner; and Sherman Marion Labovitz, also known as Sherman Labovitz, defendants herein, did attend and participate in a Communist Party conference held at Chris J. Perry Elks' Hall, 1416 North Broad Street, Philadelphia, Pennsylvania.

19. On or about August 26, 1951, David Dubensky, also known as David Davis, and Sherman Marion Labovitz, also known as

Sherman Labovitz, defendants herein, did attend and participate in an affair sponsored for the purpose of raising and securing funds for the Communist Party, held at the Old Mill Road picnic grounds located near Sellersville, Pennsylvania.

20. On or about September 28, 1951, Robert Klonsky, also known as Robert Kirby, a defendant herein, did prepare and cause to be issued and circulated, a letter and directive to all clubs of the Eastern Pennsylvania and Delaware District of the Communist Party of the United States of America.

21. On or about February 20, 1952, Robert Klonsky, also known as Robert Kirby, a defendant herein, did prepare and cause to be published and circulated a press release of the Eastern Pennsylvania and Delaware District of the Communist Party of the United States of America.

22. On or about May 18, 1952, Thomas Nabried, Walter Lowenfels, also known as William Lerner; and Sherman Marion Labovitz, also known as Sherman Labovitz, defendants herein, did attend and participate in a meeting held at Chris J. Perry Elks' Hall, 1416 North Broad Street, Philadelphia, Pennsylvania.

23. On or about June 28, 1952, Benjamin Weiss, also known as Ben Weiss; Thomas Nabried; and Irvin Katz, also known as "Chick" Katz and Irving Katz, defendants herein, did attend and participate in a meeting held at American Yugoslav Hall, 405 West 41st Street, New York, N.Y.

24. On or about August 1, 1952, Sam Gobeloff, also known as Joseph Roberts, a defendant herein, while acting as a functionary in the underground apparatus of the Eastern Pennsylvania and Delaware District of the Communist Party of the United States of America, entered the premises known as 6217 Chelwynde Avenue, Philadelphia, Pennsylvania.

25. On or about September 24, 1952, Joseph Kuzma, also known as Joe Kuzma, and Sam Gobeloff, also known as Joseph Roberts, defendants herein, did attend and participate in a meeting held at 6217 Chelwynde Avenue, Philadelphia, Pennsylvania.

26. On or about September 5, 1952, Benjamin Weiss, also known as Ben Weiss, and Thomas Nabried, defendants herein, did attend and participate in a Communist Party rally held at Rockland Palace, 155th Street and 8th Avenue, New York, N.Y.

27. On or about September 26, 1952, Benjamin Weiss, also known as Ben Weiss; Thomas Nabried; and Sherman Marion Labovitz,

TEXT AND ANALYSIS OF SMITH ACT AND INDICTMENTS 249

also known as Sherman Labovitz, defendants herein, did attend and participate in a forum held at 1416 North Broad Street, Philadelphia, Pennsylvania.

28. On or about April 11, 1953, Benjamin Weiss, also known as Ben Weiss; Thomas Nabried; and David Dubensky, also known as David Davis, defendents herein, did attend and participate in a meeting held at Chinese Castle Restaurant, 939 Race Street, Philadelphia, Pennsylvania.

In violation of Section 3 of the Smith Act, 54 Stat. 671, 18 U.S.C. Section 11 (1946 ed.), and 18 U.S.C. Section 371 (1948 ed.).

Signed by Calvin H. Thomas, Foreman; Joseph G. Hildenberger, U.S. Attorney. Dated August 18, 1953.

In order that the reader may see more clearly the nature of the overt acts charged against the defendants in the indictment, a breakdown of the data follows, indicating the actions listed by the prosecution against each of the accused. (The Court's sentence, as handed down at the end of the trial, is added in each case.)

Dubensky: Attended and participated in two Communist Party conventions, one Communist Party conference, two Communist Party meetings, two Communist Party rallies, and one Communist Party fund-raising affair at a picnic ground. (Sentence: Three years.)

Gobeloff: Attended and participated in one Communist Party class, two Communist Party meetings, and one Communist Party convention. Entered a building as a Communist Party functionary. (Sentence: Three years.)

Katz: Attended and participated in four Communist Party meetings and one Communist Party conference. Prepared and circulated a letter and plan for recruiting Communist Party members. (Sentence: Two years.)

Klonsky: Attended and participated in three Communist Party meetings, one Communist Party convention, and one Communist Party conference. Circulated a letter and directives to Communist Party clubs in Pennsylvania and Delaware. Prepared and gave out a Communist Party press release. (Sentence: Two years.)

Kuzma: Attended and participated in one Communist Party convention, one Communist Party conference, and one Communist Party meeting. Issued instructions for raising Communist Party funds. Used a safe deposit box in a Philadelphia bank in handling Communist Party funds. (Sentence: Three years.)

Labovitz: Attended and participated in five Communist Party meetings, two Communist Party conferences, one Communist Party convention, one Communist Party class, one Communist Party fundraising affair at a picnic ground, and one forum. Prepared and circulated a letter and plan for recruiting Communist Party members. (Sentence: Two years.)

Lowenfels: Attended and participated in four Communist Party meetings, one Communist Party convention, and one Communist Party conference (Sentence: Two years.)

Nabried: Attended and participated in six Communist party meetings, one Communist Party convention, two Communist Party conferences, one Communist Party rally, and one forum. (Sentence: Three years.)

Weiss: Attended and participated in six Communist Party meetings, two Communist Party conventions, two Communist Party conferences, one Communist Party rally, and a forum. (Sentence: Two years.)

It should be emphasized that during all the time covered by the various actions listed above the Communist Party was an entirely legal organization.

## INDICTMENT, CLEVELAND SMITH ACT TRIAL, 1956

In the United States District Court for the Northern District of Ohio, Eastern Division: United States of America *vs.* Joseph Brandt, *et al.,* No. 21076 Criminal, U.S.C., Title 18, Sec. 10 (1946 ed.); U.S.C., Title 18, Sec. 2385 (1948 ed.); U.S.C., Title 18, Sec. 11 (1946 ed.); U.S.C., Title 18, Sec. 371 (1948 ed.)—Conspiracy to advocate the overthrow of the Government by force and violence.

### INDICTMENT

The Grand Jury charges:

(1) That from on or about April 1, 1945, and continuously thereafter up to and including the date of the filing of this indictment, in the Eastern Division of the Northern District of Ohio, and elsewhere, Joseph Brandt, also known as Joe Bruestein; Israel Kwatt, also known as George Watt; Martin Chancey, also known as Morris Chansky; Anthony Krchmarek, also known as Anthony Kacmarek; Robert Alfred Campbell, also known as Bob Campbell; Joseph

Michael Dougher, also known as Joseph Michael Walsh; Elvadore Claude Greenfield, also known as Claude Munson; Frieda Zucker Katz, also known as Frieda Zucker; David Katz; Frank Hashmall, also known as Frank Parker; and Lucille Bethencourt, also known as Lucille Carrasquero, the defendants herein, unlawfully, willfully, and knowingly did conspire with each other and with William Z. Foster, Eugene Dennis, John B. Williamson, Jacob Stachel, Robert G. Thompson, Benjamin J. Davis, Jr., Henry Winston, John Gates, Irving Potash, Gilbert Green, Carl Winter, Gus Hall, Elizabeth Gurley Flynn, Betty Gannett, Pettis Perry, Philip Frankfeld, and Arnold Johnson, co-conspirators but not defendants herein, and with divers other persons to the Grand Jury unknown, to commit offenses against the United States prohibited by Section 2 of the Smith Act (54 Stat. 671), U.S.C., Title 18, Section 10 (1946 ed.), and U.S.C., Title 18, Sec. 2385 (1948 ed.), in violation of U.S.C., Title 18, Section 11 (1946 ed.), being Section 3 of the said Smith Act while said section of said act remained effective, and thereafter in violation of U.S.C., Title 18, Section 371 (1948 ed.), by (1) unlawfully, wilfully, and knowingly advocating and teaching the duty and necessity of overthrowing and destroying the Government of the United States by force and violence, with the intent of causing the aforesaid overthrow and destruction of the Government of the United States by force and violence as speedily as circumstances would permit; and by (2) unlawfully, wilfully, and knowingly organizing, and helping to organize, as the Communist Party of the United States of America a society, group, and assembly of persons who teach and advocate the overthrow and destruction of the Government of the United States by force and violence, with the intent of causing the aforesaid overthrow and destruction of the Government of the United States by force and violence as speedily as circumstances would permit;

(2) It was a part of said conspiracy that the said defendants and their co-conspirators would become members, officers, and functionaries of said Communist Party, knowing the purposes of said Communist Party, and in such capacities would assume leadership in said Communist Party, and responsibility for carrying out its policies and activities to and including the date of the filing of this indictment;

(3) It was further a part of said conspiracy that said defendants and co-conspirators would cause to be organized groups, clubs, sections, and district, state, city, and national units of said Communist

Party in the States of Ohio, New York, Pennsylvania, and elsewhere, and would recruit, and encourage recruitment of, members to said Communist Party, concentrating on recruiting persons employed in key basic industries and plants;

(4) It was further a part of said conspiracy that said defendants and co-conspirators would publish and circulate, and cause to be published and circulated, books, articles, magazines, and newspapers teaching and advocating the duty and necessity of overthrowing and destroying the Government of the United States by force and violence as speedily as circumstances would permit;

(5) It was further a part of said conspiracy that said defendants and co-conspirators would write, and cause to be written, articles and directives in the publications of the Communist Party of the United States of America, including, but not limited to, *Political Affairs, Daily Worker, The Worker,* and the Ohio edition of *The Worker,* teaching and advocating the necessity of overthrowing and destroying the Government of the United States by force and violence as speedily as circumstances would permit;

(6) It was further a part of said conspiracy that said defendants and co-conspirators would conduct, and cause to be conducted, schools and classes in which recruits and members of said Communist Party would be indoctrinated in the principles of Marxism-Leninism and in which would be taught and advocated the duty and necessity of overthrowing and destroying the Government of the United States by force and violence as speedily as circumstances would permit;

(7) It was further a part of said conspiracy that said defendants and co-conspirators would agree upon, and carry into effect, detailed plans for the vital parts of the Communist Party of the United States of America to go underground, in the event of emergency, and from said underground position to continue in all respects the conspiracy described in paragraph (1) of this indictment;

(8) It was further a part of said conspiracy that said defendants and co-conspirators would use false names and false documents in order to conceal their identities and activities as members and functionaries of said Communist Party;

(9) It was further a part of said conspiracy that said defendants and co-conspirators would do other and further things to conceal the existence and operations of said conspiracy.

In pursuance and furtherance of said conspiracy and to effect the objects thereof, the defendants and co-conspirators did commit, in the Eastern Division of the Northern District of Ohio, and elsewhere, the following overt acts, among others:

## OVERT ACTS

1. During the period extending from November 28, 1948, to December 5, 1948, inclusive, Joseph Brandt, also known as Joe Bruestein; Martin Chancey, also known as Morris Chansky; and Anthony Krchmarek, also known as Anthony Kacmarek, defendants herein, did attend and participate as instructors on the subject of Marxism-Leninism in a Communist Party School held at the Slovenian Home, 31st and Pearl Street, Lorain, Ohio.
2. On or about October 17, 1950, Frank Hashmall, also known as Frank Parker, a defendant herein, did attend and participate in a Communist Party meeting held at 2547 Alaska Avenue, Cincinnati, Ohio.
3. From on or about November 20, 1950, to February 3, 1951, in Cleveland, Ohio, Martin Chancey, also known as Morris Chansky, a defendant herein, to conceal his true identity and to carry out the plans of the underground apparatus of the Communist Party of the United States of America, did use the false name and alias of Frank Williams.
4. In or about the month of December, 1950, at New York, New York, Israel Kwatt, also known as George Watt, a defendant herein, did prepare and cause to be issued and circulated in a preconvention bulletin of the Communist Party of the United States of America, an article entitled "A Cadre Policy Linked to Industrial Concentration."
5. On or about December 10, 1950, Israel Kwatt, also known as George Watt, a defendant herein, did attend and participate in a convention of the Eastern Pennsylvania and Delaware District of the Communist Party of the United States of America, held at April Farms, RD #2, Coopersburg, Pennsylvania.
6. On or about December 16, 1950, David Katz and Elvadore Claude Greenfield, also known as Claude Munson, defendants herein, did attend and participate in a Communist Party meeting held at 14101 Kinsman Road, Cleveland, Ohio.
7. On or about December 17, 1950, Joseph Brandt, also known as Joe Bruestein; Robert Alfred Campbell, also known as Bob Campbell; Joseph Michael Dougher, also known as Joseph Michael Walsh;

Elvadore Claude Greenfield, also known as Claude Munson; and Frank Hashmall, also known as Frank Parker, defendants herein, did attend and participate in the Ohio State Communist Party Convention held at the East Side Hungarian Hall, 11123 Buckeye Road, Cleveland, Ohio.

8. During the period extending from December 22, 1950, to December 24, 1950, inclusive, Israel Kwatt, also known as George Watt, a defendant herein, did attend and participate in the New York State Communist Party convention held at Stuyvesant Casino, New York, N.Y.

9. During the period extending from December 28, 1950, to December 31, 1950, inclusive, Joseph Brandt, also known as Joe Bruestein, and Israel Kwatt, also known as George Watt, defendants herein, did attend and participate in the Fifteenth National Convention of the Communist Party of the United States of America held in New York, N.Y.

10. On or about January 14, 1951, Joseph Michael Dougher, also known as Joseph Michael Walsh, a defendant herein, did attend and participate in a Communist Party class on the subject of "State and Revolution" held at 3815 Canton Avenue, Lorain, Ohio.

11. On or about January 20, 1951, Joseph Brandt, also known as Joe Bruestein, and Frank Hashmall, also known as Frank Parker, defendants herein, did attend and participate in a Communist Party meeting held at 315 Lincoln Street, Dayton, Ohio.

12. On or about January 21, 1951, Joseph Brandt, also known as Joe Bruestein, and Frank Hashmall, also known as Frank Parker, defendants herein, did attend and participate in a Communist Party meeting held at 3595 Wilson Avenue, Cincinnati, Ohio.

13. On or about January 21, 1951, Joseph Michael Dougher, also known as Joseph Michael Walsh, and Lucille Bethencourt, also known as Lucille Carrasquero, defendants herein, did attend and participate in a Communist Party class held at 3815 Canton Avenue, Lorain, Ohio.

14. On or about January 28, 1951, Frieda Zucker Katz, also known as Frieda Zucker, a defendant herein, did attend and participate in a Communist Party meeting held at Paradise Hall, 2226 East 55th Street, Cleveland, Ohio.

15. From on or about February 3, 1951, to February 24, 1951, in Cleveland, Ohio, Martin Chancey, also known as Morris Chansky, a defendant herein, to conceal his identity and to carry out the plans of

TEXT AND ANALYSIS OF SMITH ACT AND INDICTMENTS 255

the underground apparatus of the Communist Party of the United States of America, did use the false name and alias of Frank Waters.

16. On or about February 13, 1951, Lucille Bethencourt, also known as Lucille Carrasquero, a defendant herein, did attend and participate in a Communist Party meeting held at the Croatian Hall, 6314 St. Clair Avenue, Cleveland, Ohio.

17. On or about March 24, 1951, Joseph Brandt, also known as Joe Bruestein; Robert Alfred Campbell, also known as Bob Campbell; David Katz; and Martin Chancey, also known as Morris Chansky, defendants herein, did attend and participate in a Communist Party meeting held at the Croatian Hall, 6314 St. Clair Avenue, Cleveland, Ohio.

18. On or about April 1, 1951, Joseph Michael Dougher, also known as Joseph Michael Walsh, and Lucille Bethencourt, also known as Lucille Carrasquero, defendants herein, did attend and participate in a Communist Party class held at 341 W. 23rd Street, Lorain, Ohio.

19. On or about April 8, 1951, Joseph Michael Dougher, also known as Joseph Michael Walsh, and Lucille Bethencourt, also known as Lucille Carrasquero, defendants herein, did attend and participate in a Communist Party class held at 341 W. 23rd Street, Lorain, Ohio.

20. On or about June 24, 1951, Joseph Brandt, also known as Joe Bruestein; Robert Alfred Campbell, also known as Bob Campbell; Frieda Zucker Katz, also known as Frieda Zucker; Elvadore Claude Greenfield, also known as Claude Munson; David Katz; and Frank Hashmall, also known as Frank Parker, defendants herein, did attend and participate in a Communist Party meeting held at the East Side Hungarian Hall, 11123 Buckeye Road, Cleveland, Ohio.

21. On or about February 17, 1952, Elvadore Claude Greenfield, also known as Claude Munson, a defendant herein, did attend and participate in a meeting held at the Croatian Hall, 6314 St. Clair Avenue, Cleveland, Ohio.

22. On or about April 25, 1952, Elvadore Claude Greenfield, also known as Claude Munson, a defendant herein, did attend and participate, as a representative of the Ohio State Communist Party, in a meeting held at 1205 Superior Avenue, Cleveland, Ohio.

23. On or about September 20, 1952, Anthony Krchmarek, also known as Anthony Kacmarek, a defendant herein, did attend and

participate in a meeting held at the Bohemian Hall in Milwaukee, Wisconsin.

24. On or about October 11, 1952, Anthony Krchmarek, also known as Anthony Kacmarek, a defendant herein, did attend and participate in a meeting held at the Bohemian National Hall, 4941 Broadway, Cleveland, Ohio.

25. On or about October 27, 1952, Elvadore Claude Greenfield, also known as Claude Munson, a defendant herein, did attend and participate, as a representative of the Ohio State Communist Party, in a meeting held at 14101 Kinsman Road, Cleveland, Ohio.

26. During the period extending from on or about December 7, 1952, to April 13, 1953, in Pittsburgh, Pennsylvania, Martin Chancey, also known as Morris Chansky, a defendant herein, to conceal his identity and to carry out the plans of the underground apparatus of the Communist Party of the United States of America, did use the false names and aliases of William Schultz and George R. Miller.

27. During the period extending from on or about April 13, 1953, to August 3, 1953, in Pittsburgh, Pennsylvania, Martin Chancey, also known as Morris Chansky, a defendant herein, to conceal his identity and to carry out the plans of the underground apparatus of the Com munist Party of the United States of America, did use the fake name and alias of Joe Kramer.

28. From on or about July 20, 1953, to October 14, 1953, in Pittsburgh, Pennsylvania, Israel Kwatt, also known as George Watt, a defendant herein, to conceal his identity and to further the plans of the underground apparatus of the Communist Party of the United States of America, did use the false name and alias of Charles Vogel.

In violation of Section 3 of the Smith Act, 54 Stat. 671, 18 U.S.C. Section 11 (1946 ed.), and 18 U.S.C. Section 371 (1948 ed.). Dated November 9, 1953.

Following is a breakdown of the overt acts charged against each of the accused in the foregoing indictment, together with the verdict, and, in those instances where the defendant was declared guilty, the Judge's sentence. Of the eleven defendants, one was acquitted by directed verdict of the Judge in the course of the trial, on the ground of insufficient evidence adduced against him; four were acquitted by the final verdict of the jury; and six were held guilty by the jury.

Brandt: Attended a Communist Party school, and participated as instructor in Marxism-Leninism. Attended and participated in

# TEXT AND ANALYSIS OF SMITH ACT AND INDICTMENTS 257

Ohio State Communist Party Convention. Attended and participated in a National Convention of the Communist Party, U.S.A. Attended and participated in four Communist Party meetings. (Verdict: Guilty. Sentence: Five years.)

Kwatt: Prepared and published an article in a Communist Party bulletin. Attended and participated in a District Convention of the Communist Party. Attended and participated in a State Convention of the Communist Party. Attended and participated in a National Convention of the Communist Party. Used a false name. (Verdict: Guilty. Sentence: Five years.)

Chancey: Attended a Communist Party school, and participated as instructor in Marxism-Leninism. Attended and participated in a Communist Party meeting. On different occasions, used four false names. (Verdict: Guilty. Sentence: Five years.)

Krchmarek: Attended a Communist Party school, and participated as instructor in Marxism-Leninism. Attended a meeting at the Bohemian Hall, Milwaukee. Attended a meeting at the Bohemian National Hall, Cleveland. (Strangely enough, the indictment does not specify what organization was meeting on either of the two lastmentioned occasions. Nor is anything specific alleged to have hap pened at either of the meetings.) (Verdict: Guilty. Sentence: Five years.)

Campbell: Attended and participated in Ohio State Communist Party Convention. Attended and participated in two Communist Party meetings. (Verdict: Not guilty.)

Dougher: Attended and participated in Ohio State Communist Party Convention. Attended and participated in four Communist Party classes. (Verdict: Not guilty.)

Greenfield: Attended and participated in two Communist Party meetings. Attended and participated in a meeting at the Croatian Hall, Cleveland. (The indictment does not specify the nature of this meeting, nor the organization or group which met.) Attended and participated in Ohio State Communist Party Convention. Attended and participated in two meetings as a representative of the Ohio State Communist Party. (Verdict: Not guilty.)

Frieda Zucker Katz: Attended and participated in two Communist Party meetings. (Verdict: Not guilty.)

David Katz: Attended and participated in two Communist Party meetings. (Verdict: Directed acquittal by Judge, on motion of Defendant's Counsel made at close of Plaintiff's case. The ground on which the motion was granted was: "The Government has presented no evidence that there was any knowledge on the part of the defendant David Katz of the existence of any such conspiracy, or any intent to form or join it." The conspiracy referred to is, of course, that mentioned in the indictment.)

Hashmall: Attended and participated in four Communist Party meetings. Attended and participated in Ohio State Communist Party Convention. (Verdict: Guilty. Sentence: Five years.)

Bethencourt: Attended and participated in three Communist Party classes. Attended and participated in a Communist Party meeting. (Verdict: Guilty. Sentence: Three and a half years.)

In the actual wording of these Smith Act indictments, which are similar to those in all Smith Act "conspiracy" cases to date, the reader has an opportunity to observe how wide of the mark is the popular impression that those brought to trial under this law are charged with attempting to overthrow the government by force and violence. To be sure, they are charged with being in a conspiracy, *but not a conspiracy to overthrow the government by force and violence.* The conspiracy they are charged with is a conspiracy to teach and advocate a doctrine of forcible and violent overthrow of the government

Anyone who reflects upon the matter will appreciate that there is a vast difference between a conspiracy to overthrow and a conspiracy to teach a doctrine of overthrow. If you wish to claim that someone is involved in a conspiracy to overthrow a government by force and violence you must produce evidence showing some kind of preparation for or planning of acts of force and violence. (The public generally is probably under the impression that the defendants in the Smith Act cases were charged with, and convicted of, that sort of thing, whereas the indictment itself does not even allege anything of that nature.) If, on the other hand, you wish to claim that someone is involved only in a "conspiracy" (hardly a secret one in this instance) to teach and advocate some kind of a doctrine of revolutionary force and violence, you need not produce any evidence of preparations or plans for acts of force and violence. You need only produce evidence of actions like helping to plan for, organize, and carry out the functions of schools, clubs, meetings, conferences, conventions, publications, and the like.

Insofar as Communists are concerned, such "evidence" can, of course, be produced with the greatest of ease, and could have been multiplied a hundredfold beyond what was cited in the indictment, since none of the defendants has ever denied being an active member or leader, as the case may be, of the Communist Party. Where any given defendant is charged with attending a meeting, conference, or rally, sending out a letter, soliciting support, raising funds, and the like (the type of "overt act" on which the indictment is based) a hundred similar acts could easily have been added in the case of each of the accused. Such actions are nothing but the normal and daily routine of active members or leaders of a political movement; and most of this routine is open and public.

The question therefore cannot help but be raised: What is the importance or significance of such "evidence"? What does it prove, beyond the fact that the defendants were active Communists, something which needed no proof whatever, since the leading personalities of the Communist Party have not only not denied being Communists but have been at some pains to publicize their status and beliefs as Communists?

The reader will bear in mind that if there had been any evidence of attempt to overthrow, or conspiracy to overthrow the government, the "overt acts" would almost certainly have been *intrinsically criminal* in character: *illegally* using or secreting weapons; attempting seizure, or making plans for seizure, of government buildings; stealing, or making plans for stealing, government documents, and the like. Such acts are clearly proof of criminal intent. But there is not a single overt act cited in the indictments under discussion which was criminal in itself. Consequently, such acts in themselves could never add up to a crime.

The entire attempt to prove criminal guilt goes back to something *connected* with all these acts. What is that? It is the doctrines the defendants wish to teach, and do teach. As we have seen before, it all goes back to the content of the teachings, and nothing but the content of the teachings. In other words, Communists are accused of a crime because of what they teach. Take away the content of the teachings and there is not even the accusation of a crime left.

In this regard the situation is exactly as if two men were charged with conspiring to teach and advocate that certain persons be killed. The prosecution, upon being asked to present its evidence to back up this serious charge, says that the evidence is in a number of letters written by the accused to their friends.

However, to charge persons with being in a serious criminal conspiracy seems farfetched and implausible unless something significant in the way of overt acts can be cited, something that would suggest a clear and present danger. Now suppose the prosecution presents the following sort of overt acts: The two defendants went to a stationery store. They purchased paper and envelopes. They went to the post office. They purchased stamps. They posted letters. They met with each other. They talked. They conferred. One would have no alternative but to say to the prosecution: These overt acts prove nothing significant. The defendants readily admit that they posted letters and did everything that is involved in posting letters, such as purchasing paper, envelopes, stamps. They readily admit that they often met and talked. The entire case, therefore, rests on what is in the letters and on nothing else.

Further suppose that when the letters are examined in great detail it is seen that the defendants are not teaching and advocating that the persons in question be killed now. Moreover, the defendants have known these persons some thirty-five years and have never taught or advocated that they should be killed at any time during that entire period. What is being taught and advocated is that these persons (or any persons) should be killed under certain circumstances: when they are trying to commit murder and cannot be restrained from doing so in any other way. In other words, the contents of their letters disclose not an unjustifiable doctrine of indiscriminate violence but a justifiable doctrine of self-defense.

Such a situation would be exactly analogous to the trials and proceedings based on the Smith Act and similar legislation. The overt acts show nothing criminal. The entire case rests on the content of the doctrines and teachings. These teachings, when examined as a whole and in detail, disclose not a doctrine of indiscriminate force and violence but a doctrine of forcible and violent revolution under certain circumstances: when the government in question is unwilling and unable to carry out the wishes of the people, and there is majority support for the revolutionary step.

This doctrine of forcible and violent revolution must be presumed to be justifiable, since the basic preconditions it lays down for the right of revolution are the same as those set forth in our Declaration of Independence, on which our claim to sovereignty separate from that of Great Britain is based. If for any reason such a doctrine of revolution is not justifiable, then there would be nothing in logic to prevent every school board in the land, and a great many teachers, from being indicted under the Smith Act. They could then be charged with most of the same kind of "overt acts" as those charged against the defendants: They attended meetings and conferences, organized classes and courses of instruction, solicited support, wrote letters, raised funds, sent out press releases, and the like, for the purpose of teaching and advocating, among other things, the principles set forth in the Declaration of Independence, which principles justify force and violence.

Make one final supposition, that someone argues in the way that many actually do: "I admit that Communist *teachings* on the right of revolutionary force and violence, as expounded in their books, present the same basic preconditions for the use of force and violence as the Declaration of Independence. But I don't believe Communists will be guided by their doctrines and teachings. I don't believe they are sincere about their doctrines and teachings. I believe they are dangerous characters on grounds other than what can be found in their doctrines and teachings."

This line of argument would necessarily lead to two conclusions:

1. All Smith Act prosecutions of the kind we have been dealing with should be abandoned or nullified, since these prosecutions depend on the very teachings and doctrines in question. If these are ruled out, nothing remains as a basis for criminal accusation.

2. If there is any other case against Communists, based on some other type of evidence, let it be brought forward and tried. If there is not sufficient evidence to sustain any other case against them, let that fact be recognized and acted upon. This is the minimum requirement of justice.

Thus the question that remains logically, legally, and morally basic to all the Smith Act prosecutions (and to much else in our national life) is this: How is it possible to penalize Communists for teaching that there is a right to use force and violence under certain revolutionary circumstances while at the same time we ourselves must teach and accept the Declaration of Independence, which affirms the right of revolutionary force and violence under the same circumstances? Every American who takes his history and principles seriously will recognize the urgent importance of that question.

# Index

Adams, John, on right of revolution, 234
Aesopian language, 218
Alien Registration Act, 240
*American Communications Association v. Douds*, 233
Aristotle, 57

Barrot, Odilon, 136
Blanquism, 26, 85, 86
Blumberg, Dr. Albert E., 216 ff., 222
bourgeoisie, definition of, 37

*Capital*, Marx's, 27
capitalism, 142 ff.; and democracy, 142
Carr, Edward Hallett, 26
Chafee, Zechariah, 240 ff.
Chiang Kai-shek, 228
civil liberties, problems of in U.S., 15 ff.
Clay, Henry, on right of revolution, 234
*Communist, The*, 129, 217
Court of Appeals, U.S., 43, 187, 191, 193

Danger, clear and present, 43, 46, 49
Declaration of Independence, 28 ff.; and Marxism-Leninism, 28, 29 ff., 33, 46, 72, 96–97, 148, 183, 223 ff., 234, 260, 261
democracy, bourgeois, 141; and capitalism, 142; and socialism, 142
Dennis, Eugene, case, 43, 51, 136, 137, 144
dialectics, 111
dictatorship, Marxist meaning of, 68 ff., 188 ff.; nazi and fascist meaning of, 70; of proletariat, 68 ff.
Douglas, Mr. Justice, 230

Encirclement, capitalist and socialist, 122
Engels, Friedrich, 24, 25; *Communist Manifesto*, 87; on peaceful transition, 26 ff.
exceptionalism, doctrine of, 62, 67, 120 ff.
exploitation, definition of, 88

Fallacy, converse accident, 33; denying the consequent, 148
fascism, 141–142; in Italy, 21

Field, Jean, case, 17
First Amendment to U.S. Constitution, 183, 196, 230
Foster, William Z., 24, 108, 109, 112, 122, 129, 135, 143, 182; *From Bryan to Stalin*, 169; *History of the Communist Party of the United States*, 132 ff.; *Socialism the Road to Peace, Prosperity and Freedom*, 143, 156, 216; *Twenty-Three Questions*, 137, 156; *Twilight of World Capitalism*, 135
Frankfurter, Mr. Justice, 231
freedom of speech, 194

Germany, Nazi, 21
Grant, U. S., on right of revolution, 235

Hand, Judge Learned, 144 ff., 230, 231
Hegel, Georg W. F., 111
*History of the Communist Party of the Soviet Union*, 107, 168
Hitler, Adolf, 70; *Mein Kampf*, 185 ff.
Holmes, Mr. Justice, 196

Internal Security Act of 1950, 187
Italy, Fascist, 21

Jackson, Mr. Justice, 51, 233 ff.
Jefferson, Thomas, 25, 28, 50, 51, 55, 145, 148, 190, 220, 234; on French Revolution, 56; on Shays' Rebellion, 55
Jerome, V. J., 129

Kerensky, Alexander, 236

Lenin, V. I., 24; *The April Conference*, 86; on Blanquism, 26; *Can the Bolsheviks Retain State Power?*, 88, 155; on democracy, 185; *A Dual Power*, 26; *Elections to the Constituent Assembly and the Dictatorship of the Proletariat*, 38; *Imperialism the Highest Stage of Capitalism*, 218; *'Left-Wing' Communism, an Infantile Disorder*, 62, 87, 164; *A Letter to the Comrades*, 85; on majority and minority revolutions, 26;

263

Marxism and Insurrection, 77; *Paris Commune*, 68; *Proletarian Revolution and Renegade Kautsky*, 67; on Russia and Western Europe, 63; *State and Revolution*, 27, 64, 71, 156, 185; *The War and the Second International?*, 39, 63, 72, 151, 158, 159; *What Is To Be Done?*, 87
Lincoln, Abraham, 51, 55, 235
Locke, John, 25, 51, 55, 220; *Two Treatises of Civil Government*, 49 ff.

Majority, in Marxist-Leninist concept of revolution, 25 ff., 36 ff., 74 ff., 150 ff.; determination of, 71–72, 88 ff., 209 ff.
Marx, Karl, 24, 25; *Capital*, 27; *Civil War in France*, 67; *Communist Manifesto*, 87; on peaceful transition, 27 ff.
Maryland Declaration of Rights, on right of revolution, 235
materialism, historical, 25; dialectical, 131
McCarran Act, 182, 187, 191, 197 ff.
McCarthyism, 204
method, dialectical, 111, 112

National Labor Relations Board, 233
Nazi Germany, 21, 161, 162
*New York Herald Tribune*, 137
*New York Times*, 43, 145, 199, 202

Paris Commune, Lenin on, 65
peaceful transition, 27 ff., 60 ff.
Pennsylvania Declaration of Rights, on right of revolution, 234
Plato, 57
*Political Affairs*, 136, 140, 217
Pope Pius XII, 199 ff.
*Program of the Communist International*, 123, 125
proletariat, definition of, 37
putschism, 26, 43, 55, 141, 182, 227

Revolution, French, 41, 90; American, 41, 54, 90, 211; British, 54; Chinese, 228; Jefferson on, 56; meanings of, 70–71; Russian, 41

revolutionary situation, 39 ff., 54 ff., 67; and peaceful transition, 60; subjective conditions of, 159 ff.
right of revolution: American statements on, 233 ff.; Marxism-Leninism on, 25; and self-defense, 31, 32, 146 ff.
Russell, Bertrand, 215–216
Russia and Western Europe, Lenin on, 63
Russia, Soviet, 22

Shays' Rebellion, Jefferson on, 55
Smith Act, 109 ff.; convictions under, 16, 109; *membership clause* of, 206, 239 ff.
Smith, Representative Howard W., 223 ff., 229
*Soviet Philosophy*, 22, 69, 132
Stalin, Josef, 24; *Foundations of Leninism*, 53, 59, 78, 87, 119, 122, 164, 173; *Problems of Leninism*, 36, 57, 74, 83, 84, 117, 126
state, Marxist-Leninist theory of, 190–191; *withering away* of, 188
Stekloff, G. M., 27
*Strategy and Tactics*, 63
Subversive Activities Control Board, 187
Supreme Court, U.S.; opinion in Schneiderman case, 137, 138, 157, 230–231
Supreme Court, U.S., opinion in Dennis case, 43, 51, 138

*Theory and Practice of the Communist Party*, 141
Thoreau, Henry David, on right of revolution, 235
Tsar Nicholas II, 228

UNESCO, 16, 17, 22, 69, 223, 225
U.S. Court of Appeals, 43, 187, 191, 193

Vinson, Chief Justice, 43, 46, 51, 138
Vyshinsky, Andrei, *The Law of the Soviet State*, 176

*Western Political Quarterly*, 229
Wormuth, Francis, 229 ff.

# APPENDIX

## LAW, LOGIC AND REVOLUTION: THE SMITH ACT DECISIONS*

JOHN SOMERVILLE
*City University of New York*

THE RELATION of the Smith Act cases, and of the Smith Act itself, to the tradition of American democracy is a key question for us and for people all over the world. It is a question which involves more than the field of law. Its content significantly concerns fields like social philosophy, political science, history, and, one becomes increasingly convinced, basic logic. So perhaps a philosopher with a responsibility for logic need not apologize for trying to deal with certain aspects of it, in the light of concrete observation and participation as a non-Communist expert witness in several of the cases.

What now seems in special need of examination is the reasoning embodied in the series of opinions which have come from the United States Supreme Court and Courts of Appeals beginning with the decision handed down in June 1957 by the Supreme Court in the *Yates'* case. The Smith Act[2] being a law directed against advocacy or teaching of violent revolution, at least in the sections of it applied in the prosecutions of Communists, these recent opinions are centrally concerned with speech and teaching about forcible revolution?

The *Yates* decision ended one whole phase in the handling of Smith Act cases, a phase strangely out of keeping with the American tradition, and inaugurated a new approach. This approach, while closer to the constitutional demands of our tradition, will undoubtedly have to go further to meet them squarely. However, very few people of the bar or bench anticipated the change that came in 1957, when the Supreme Court for the first time reversed convictions obtained against Communists under the Smith Act.

Perhaps the general stunned reaction in the lower courts to the *Yates* decision when it was handed down was best expressed by Judge Chambers when he wrote the opinion for the Court of Appeals reversing eleven Smith Act convictions in *Fujimoto*[4] and *Huff*[5] He then stated: "One may as well recognize that the *Yates* decision leaves the Smith Act, as to any further prosecution under it, a virtual shambles...." The decisive reasoning in *Yates* turns on the drawing of a certain distinction, which is in no way an unusual one. What is unusual, and seemed so unexpected in the circumstances, was the novel emphasis and application given to that distinction in Smith Act cases. The distinction itself is simply one between language which is calculated to incite action (whether that action be present of future) and language which may express belief, but which is not calculated to incite action, either present or future.[6]

---

* Reprinted from the Western Political Quarterly, 14:4 Dec. 1961, pp 839-849.

From a logical viewpoint, it is not at all surprising that the Supreme Court finally came around to insisting on the drawing of that kind of line in relation to prosecutions under a sedition law. What seems surprising from the standpoint of logic is, first, that the Court, having drawn and emphasized that line, still attempts to justify the *Dennis*[7] opinion; and second, that the Court still tries to avoid the heart of the teaching-of-revolution problem, that is, the pre-conditions under which violent revolution is to be engaged in, if ever. In the long run, the second failure, if it persists, will have a more serious effect than the first, since it touches more closely to that which is decisive of the constitutional issue.

The way the majority of the Supreme Court was disposed to approach the first of these matters in the *Yates* opinion is expressed in the following terms:

> In failing to distinguish between advocacy of forcible over-throw as an abstract doctrine and advocacy of action to that end, the District Court appears to have been led astray by the holding in *Dennis* that advocacy of violent action to be taken at some future time was enough. It seems to have considered that, since "inciting" speech is usually thought of as something calculated to induce immediate action, and since *Dennis* held advocacy of action for future overthrow sufficient, this meant that advocacy, irrespective of its tendency to generate action is punishable, provided only that it is uttered with a specific intent to accomplish overthrow. In other words, the District Court apparently thought that *Dennis* obliterated the traditional dividing line between advocacy of abstract doctrine and advocacy of action.
>
> This misconceives the situation confronting the Court in *Dennis* and what was held there. Although the jury's verdict, interpreted in the light of the trial court's instructions, did not justify the conclusion that the defendants' advocacy was directed at, or created any danger of immediate overthrow, it did establish that the advocacy was aimed at building up a seditious group and maintaining it in readiness for action at a propitious time[8]

In other words, the majority of the Supreme Court on this occasion took the position that neither *Dennis* nor *Yates* established that the Communist defendants' teaching or other utterances constituted incitement to any present violent overthrow of government, and that *Yates* did not even establish any incitement to future violent overthrow. But the majority opinion holds that in *Dennis* the jury's verdict, interpreted in the light of the trial court's instructions, did establish some kind of incitement to future violent overthrow.

However, anyone familiar with the procedures in the Smith Act trials, and especially with the whole type of evidence presented as a foundation for all of them, cannot help but feel that there are insuperable logical obstacles to the attempt to separate the evidence in *Yates* from the evidence in *Dennis*.[9] There is no difference in principle. The Smith Act prosecutions of Communists were not instances of disparate groups of persons who just happened to be indicted under one law, but who had found their way to court by variegated paths of activity, and against whom different types of evidence were presented. This might be the case, let us say, with various unconnected groups of persons accused of bank robbing. But the situation in these trials was not that. The main and decisive corpus of evidence presented against each group of Communist defendants went back to the same source, that is, what was to be found in the published teachings of Marxism-Leninism.

It is not too much to say that there was practically nothing of significance, that is, nothing concerning force and violence, which was established about any single defendant, or any group of them, which could not easily be established about any Communist or group of Communists. There was singularly little even charged about advocacy of force or violence which was personal or specific in relation to particular defendants. The principal evidence presented by the prosecution in every trial was in the form of standard writings of Communist authorities, chiefly Marx, Lenin, and Stalin. The conspiracies alleged all went back to the same leaders. The whole effort was obviously to convict the Communists by what was common to them all, not by what was peculiar to any. The conclusion is well-nigh inescapable that they are either all guilty together or all not guilty together.

The issues so far discussed are obviously important. But there are involved issues of even greater importance, which, because of their logical content, must be recognized as decisive in the constitutional sense. Here we confront what was characterized at the outset as a persistent failure on the part of the federal courts. While the majority opinion in *Yates* was a great step ahead, both from the standpoint of logic, and of the American constitutional tradition of civil liberties, the failure in question manifests itself in that opinion, and in subsequent ones patterned after it in the Court of Appeals, as well as in the earlier opinions. A concrete and typical instance of this failure can be seen in part of the language quoted above from *Yates:* "In failing to distinguish between advocacy of forcible overthrow as an abstract doctrine and advocacy of action to that end, the District Court appears to have been led astray by the holding in *Dennis* that advocacy of violent action to be taken at some future time was enough."

That is, it had been maintained in *Dennis,* and is here implicitly accepted in *Yates* that advocacy (in inciting language) of violent action at some future time, even though the time be indefinite, is properly punishable under the Smith Act, and that the Smith Act, in making it punishable, does not fall afoul of the First Amendment. Thus the 'Majority opinion is here taking the view that there can be genuine incitement to an action which is conceived of only as a possibility of an indefinite future, an action which, in the "incitement" itself is stated to be one that might never take place.

It need hardly be argued at length that this is not a logically defensible view. Punishable "incitement to action" no doubt involves *more* than the envisagement of some definite time period in which the action is to take place, but *at least* it involves that. Teachings which have not incited the feared crime over a span of forty years can hardly be argued punishable on the ground that they incite to criminal action.

However indefensible, let it be granted for argument's sake that incitement, properly so called, could occur even in relation to action at an indefinite future time. Perhaps the simplest and most concrete way to see the nature of the root logical fallacy still involved is to consider the following fact. Any believer in the Declaration of Independence must be prepared to assert (and as one such, the present writer here and now does assert): "I advocate, in the strongest possible terms, in the most inciting language at my command, that any time in the future any government becomes a tyranny, violent action should be taken against it if it will not peacefully cease to be a tyranny." Such a statement, if seriously accepted and believed, incites to future violent action in just the way the Communist teaching does. If such teaching is constitutionally protected, the conclusion is logically inescapable that the Communist teaching on violent action is also constitutionally protected, since in this instance they are the same teaching; and since we take it for granted that no person can be denied the equal protection of the laws.

It is the implications of this situation which are ignored by the majority of the Supreme Court in the *Yates* opinion as much as in the *Dennis* opinion. *Yates* argues as if the only question to be asked in deciding whether or not the advocacy of forcible action is properly and constitutionally punishable should be: Is the language of the advocacy or teaching actually calculated to incite action? If so, the teaching is punishable; if not, it is not punishable. The necessary presupposition of such an approach is that any conceivable violent or forcible action against government must be held to be properly punishable; and that is the whole trouble with this approach. It leaves out of account the whole question of the conditions under which such action might be called for.

Obviously, it is a matter of cardinal importance to inquire into the specific pre-conditions attached to the use of force in any particular revolutionary teaching which is dealt with. There is all the more reason this should be done in these cases, since in each of them the evidence accepted by the courts, and especially that evidence which was mainly relied upon by the prosecution—the published writings of Communist authorities on the subject of violent revolution—is explicit and repetitive concerning these conditions.

Anyone who looks into the exceptionally voluminous record of the evidence accepted in the Smith Act trials, or who has otherwise examined the teachings of leading Communist authors, cannot help but be aware of the fact that explicit pre-conditions of violent revolution occupy a central place in those teachings. One simply does not find an unconditional advocacy of violent revolution in these writings any more than in the Declaration of Independence or among Jeffersonian democrats. In fact, one finds just about the same pre-conditions to violent revolution laid down in the Communist writings as are laid down in the Declaration. This should be in no way surprising, since it is a well-known historical fact that the revolutionary thought of the nineteenth century, of which Marxism is a part, utilized and carried on the eighteenth-century tradition. In this matter, there is a direct line of influence from figures like Jefferson, Paine, and Franklin to figures like Marx, Engels, and Lenin.

There are, of course, many vital disagreements as between these two groups of social thinkers. But there are some agreements, and one of the agreements is on the basic pre-conditions which justify violent revolution. The Declaration uses eighteenth-century language, but its meaning is very clear. Among the "self-evident" truths is that whenever any government becomes destructive of certain ends (life, liberty, pursuit of happiness) it is the "right" of the people to alter or "abolish" it. Also, when the people suffer under "a long train of abuses and usurpations" and become convinced that the government is a despotic one, "it is their right, it is their duty, to throw off such government...."

What are the pre-conditions found in the Communist teachings? After a thorough search, the present writer summarized them as follows in the book, *The Communist Trials and the American Tradition*. He found "emphasized again and again that revolution by force was justified only when two conditions were simultaneously present: (a) when the existing government was unwilling or unable to carry out the will of the majority in vital matters, and (b) where so drastic a step as forcible revolution had the support of the majority and represented the will of the majority." "These two conditions amount to saying that revolution is justified only where the government represents some kind of a tyranny which will not carry out the will of the people peacefully, and where the majority are ready to support revolutionary action against such a government."[10]

An idea of the centrality of such pre-conditions in the Marxist-Leninist teachings about revolution may be gained from the fact that in the first third alone of the text just cited, more than fifteen passages are quoted from the record of the District Court in *United States* v. *Kuzma*[11] in which the necessary pre-conditions of violent revolution are emphasized in the classics of Marxism-Leninism. This is the kind of conditional teaching about revolution found in the Communist works originally brought into court by the prosecution in all of the Smith Act trials as the principal evidence against the defendants.

However, there is practically no reflection of this situation in the ruling opinions handed down in the Supreme Court and the Court of Appeals. Reading these opinions, one would gain the impression that the Communist teachings accepted in evidence said nothing of any importance about any necessary preconditions of the revolutionary situation. One would conclude, contrary to the historical evidence of a century of the most explicit and vehement polemics, that Communists were *putschists* of the purest water. One would never be led to suspect what is just about the truth: that from the early days of Marx and Engels on down, Communist authorities have been united in rejecting and refuting as dangerous heresies various views flatly ascribed to them in these judicial opinions.

What is in a sense even stranger, in the light of American history and American political philosophy, is the fact that one would also gain the impression that it is to be taken for granted that there could be no justifiable violent revolution in the future, that any advocacy of future forcible revolution could claim the protection of the First Amendment only on the ground that it was not taught in any way calculated to result in action. One would be tempted to conclude that the federal courts had forgotten that the protection of the First Amend, ment must be granted to the teaching of the right of revolution as expressed in the Declaration of Independence not on the ground that such teaching be carried on in a way that will incite to no future action, but precisely on the ground that future action will be necessary if there is a future tyranny.[12]

It is plain enough in all logic: either there are or there are not conditions under which violent revolution is justified. Everyone admits there are.[13] Therefore future violent revolution cannot be treated as criminal activity *per se*, and laws which so treat it must certainly be subject to constitutional review. Therefore, if someone is teaching, in a way calculated to lead to action, that future violent revolution is justified under certain conditions, it cannot automatically be concluded that he is properly punishable. Yet the federal courts seem to be drawing precisely that conclusion. If someone is brought to trial on the ground that he is teaching, in a way calculated to lead to action, that some future revolution would be justified under certain conditions, it obviously calls for analysis and evaluation of the conditions. Yet the federal courts never seem disposed to do that. What is done in the prevailing approach may be seen from the following instances.

The appellate court's opinion reversing conviction of five Smith Act defendants in *United States* v. *Silverman*,[14] as failing to meet the new standard set by *Yates*, nevertheless says:

> ... it is reasonable to find that the bulk of the Party membership was in agreement on 'the desirability of the Party some day leading a violent insurrection against the Federal Government. From the members' continuous membership despite persecution the jury could further infer their willingness personally to engage in such a *putsch* should the opportunity arise and the signal be given.[15]

First of all, in the light of the record, as well as that of the most elementary common sense, it would of course have to be admitted that the "bulk of the Party membership" believed it more *desirable* to come to power without risking their lives in violent insurrection than by so risking them. Even were they the most hardened criminal types, this would still be so. It seems likely the Court would readily agree with this. What the bulk of the party membership was in agreement upon, then, was that a violent insurrection would be appropriate under certain conditions, and should be undertaken if those conditions were some day to come about. The heart of the matter is, clearly: what are these conditions? The Court's opinion gives them no recognition save to say, "should the opportunity arise and the signal be given." But is there an explicit and repeated teaching among the membership and leadership as to what this "opportunity" consists in, when it shall have arrived, and when the "signal" shall be given? There is, but the Court, incredibly, does not relate it to the matter here being decided. The Court proceeds as if it did not exist.

This strange procedure, wherein that part of the teaching which is of primary relevance to the issue is ignored, may account for the rather surprising pattern of reasoning expressed in this opinion (in very candid language) at the point where the question is treated as to what could be inferred from "the members' continuous membership despite persecution." The only conclusion admitted is that they must have been personally willing to engage in criminal violence. But is it not equally, or indeed, even more likely, that if masses of people continue, "despite persecution," to be members of an organization whose teachings they continue to print and publicly disseminate, they do so because they feel they are not committed to anything criminal? To persist with a publicly printed program despite the fact that they are persecuted for holding to this very program, as publicly printed, suggests not the psychology of criminals, but of persons with an unusually developed sense of moral righteousness. Now if one wishes to contend that even if such persons possessed such a sense, it was nevertheless so distorted and wrong as to be in fact criminal, one must of course carefully examine their teachings to ascertain the pre-conditions, if any, which they attached to any possible use of force or violence. That is what the courts have not been disposed to do.

In *United States* v. *Bary*,[16] which, on appeal, resulted in reversal of conviction and remanding for new trial as to all seven Smith Act appellants August 23, 1957, the opinion handed down asserts in like manner: "There was evidence of a conspiracy to make statements and utterances reasonably intended and calculated to promote and encourage incitement to concrete action in an effort to overthrow the Government by force and violence as speedily as circumstances would permit...."[17]

Here again a whole segment of teachings is brushed aside, and advocates of the teachings judged as if that whole segment did not exist. Upon reflection, one might well be staggered by the irony of this situation. How does the Court know the accused have any teachings at all about revolution? Chiefly, if not exclusively, from published writings of authorities in their movement, which were submitted in evidence by the prosecution. On what basis does the prosecution claim that there is anything at all dangerous about the teachings of the accused? Chiefly, if not exclusively, from the same published writings which it submitted and which were accepted in evidence by the Court. In these circumstances it is obviously mandatory for the Court to take into account all relevant aspects of the teachings. There would be no way, either in logic or in morality, to justify a procedure wherein only those parts of the teachings which sounded damaging to the accused were taken into account while all other aspects of the teachings were disregarded as the insincere window dressing of clever rascals. If rascals want to be clever about their beliefs, do they put anything at all in print concerning violent revolution? For more than a century adherents of this movement have been publishing their teachings in what now must amount to hundreds of millions of copies, in practically every language which has a written form the world over. And it is these published teachings which are used to accuse them of being secret conspirators to do something allegedly criminal which is set forth in the teachings! It is impossible to believe, on any known calculus of human probability, that even stupid rascals, let alone clever ones, would ever take such pains to give themselves away.

At another point in the same opinion it is stated: "Given certain objective and subjective conditions, the ultimate aims and objectives of the Communist Party were the destruction of imperialism and its governments through force and violence, the establishment of the dictatorship of the proletariat, and the establishment of socialism."[18] Here at least is an abstract nod of acknowledgment that the Communist teachings include pre-conditions to any call for force and violence. But that is as far as it goes. The Court does not enumerate, summarize, analyze or evaluate the "certain objective and subjective conditions." It would seem as if, in the Court's mind, they have no bearing on the main issues. This is very like a Court saying of an individual: "Given certain objective and subjective conditions, the ultimate aim and object of this person was to use violence against his neighbor," assuming, without further inquiry, that he would necessarily be guilty of crime if he did use violence. But we need to look into the conditions. "Given certain objective and subjective conditions" it is of course our right and duty to use violence against a neighbor.

A concurring opinion in the same case concludes "that the evidence establishes the formation and continuation of the conspiracy as charged ... that they (the defendants) advocated affirmative steps to be taken in preparation for and looking to an ultimate attempt to overthrow the Government by force and violence at a propitious time; and that such evidence was sufficient to establish the conspiracy to advocate the overthrow of the Government of the United States by force and violence."[19]

Once more we meet with the assertion that Communists teach the propriety of overthrowing the Government by force and violence "at a propitious time." But the analysis goes no further, as if the Communists did not also teach what time is propitious. Can we determine what makes a time "propitious" in the eyes of Communists? We can, by reference to their teachings. But can we credit their teachings? If we cannot credit their teachings, how would we be able to say that they want to destroy imperialism, set up the dictatorship of the proletariat, establish socialism, and other like matters which we find in the judicial opinions? We cannot have our cake and eat it.

On June 5, 1961, the U.S. Supreme Court, in a 5-4 decision, upheld the conviction of Junius Irving Scales under the so-called "membership clause" of the Smith Act, which clause penalizes membership in an organization advocating violent overthrow. The majority opinion (though the majority here dwindled to a margin of one vote) continued to show the same logical gap, that is, the ignoring of the pre-conditions of forcible revolution found in Communist teachings. Delivered by Mr. Justice Harlan, this opinion in at least six places repeats the well-worn formula, "as speedily as circumstances will permit," or some synonymous variant, without once taking due account of the specific conditions laid down in the party's doctrine concerning those circumstances which permit the use of force. The closest approximation to a recognition of those conditions that can be found in the majority opinion occurs where the content of material studied in a party class on Marxism-Leninism is referred to. The opinion puts it "that the time for the proletarian revolution would come when the objective conditions of political or economic crisis coincided with the 'subjective condition' of a Communist Party which was large enough, and with enough 'influence' among the working classes 'to give the necessary leadership to lead to the seizure of power.'"[20]

Here the attempt, clearly inadequate, is made to summarize the "objective conditions" under the loose and vague expression, "political or economic crisis," as if the doctrine were that any such crisis would do. No acknowledgment is given to the fact that such a crisis must include the existence of a tyrannical government unwilling to carry out peaceably the will of the majority, and majority support for revolutionary measures against it. Yet there is abundant explanation of these vitally important pre-conditions in the evidence given at this trial, as at every Smith Act trial.

Tucked away in a footnote in *Silverman*[21] is a statement which, without apparent intent, puts what is decisive of the constitutional issue in remarkably concrete and pertinent fashion: "The district judge in his charge to the jury took the position that it could not convict for advocating force against some possible future government of the United States which 'denied the right of the majority of the people to remove it from power by the peaceful democratic means provided under our present constitution.'" One may note in passing that this formula was expressed antecedently to the Supreme Court decision in the *Yates* case, and that if it had been consistently applied, its effect could have been even more powerful than that of *Yates*.

The reason is plain: the Communists' teachings on force fall squarely within this formula. That is, as *Yates* points out, it is clear enough that the Communists are not advocating force against the present government of the United States. Their beliefs about force apply, at most, to some possible future government. Any possible future government? Hardly, since the future might have the same kind of government, with basically the same surrounding conditions as at present. What kind of future government, then? The conclusion is inescapable, in the light of repeated emphases in the Communist teachings, that it must be a government which would, among other things, fit the standard laid down by the district judge just quoted, that is, a government which would deny peaceful implementation of the basic majority rights.

Consider, for example, the famous passage written in 1872 in which Marx cited England and the United States as countries "in which the workers may hope to secure their ends by peaceful means,"[22] indicating that, so long as this was the case, no violent revolution would be necessary. ("The workers," of course, meant the majority.) Later on Lenin and Stalin maintained that while Marx was right for his day, conditions had changed, so that in their day the prevailing governments in those countries could not be expected to accede peacefully to the will of the majority if the majority will were for socialism. (It is important to note that they never maintained that the majority will *was* for socialism in those countries, that they accepted the fact that it was not, and that therefore there was no revolutionary situation.) In his turn, William Z. Foster, leader of the Communist Party of the United States during the period covered by the Smith Act indictments under discussion, maintained that conditions had once more changed on a world scale, especially in regard to the existence of socialist governments, and that a peaceful transition to socialism was again quite possible in the United States if the majority should want socialism. Foster continued to hold, as Lenin, Stalin and Marx had held, that even if peaceful transition were impossible, no forcible measures should be undertaken unless there was majority support for such measures. In other words, the only future government that would be overthrown by force would be one which refused to implement the majority will, that is, one which, in effect, "denied the right of the majority of the people to remove it from power by the peaceful democratic means provided under our present constitution." There is nothing in the teachings in question which violate this standard.

However, more important than the fact that the Communist teachings would fit the district judge's standard of what is non-convictable, is the fact that the Supreme Court continues, even in *Yates,* to ignore the constitutional implications pointed up by this situation. For, as we have seen, there is no recognition in *Yates,* any more than in *Dennis,* that there is a root incompatibility between the Smith Act and the Declaration of Independence, or more precisely, between the Smith Act and the First Amendment, if the First Amendment protects serious advocacy of the principle expressed in the Declaration. Since it unquestionably does, there can be little doubt that the Smith Act will eventually be declared unconstitutional. *Yates* is but a half-way house.

Another conceivable path is to interpret the Smith Act as a law which does not penalize all inciting teaching of the propriety of future violent revolution, but leaves open a certain area of exceptions, as the author of the Smith Act himself seems inclined to do. In that case, the exceptions will have to be clarified. If one of these exceptions is a tyrannical government, there will certainly never be another doctrinal trial under the Smith Act. For where can the doctrine be found which teaches revolution against a non-tyrannical government?

[1] 354 U.S. 298.

[2] 18 U.S.C. 2385.

[3] The heart of this part of the law is expressed in the following language, from section 2: "Whoever knowingly or willfully advocates, abets, advises or teaches the duty, necessity, desirability or propriety of overthrowing or destroying the government of the United States or the government of any State, Territory, District or Possession thereof, or the government of any political subdivision therein, by force or violence ..." is subject to criminal penalty. This sort of provision was what moved the late Professor Zechariah Chafee, Jr., to write about the Smith Act with such indignation, one might almost say, incredulity. Cf. his *Free Speech in the United States* (Cambridge: Harvard University Press, 1941), p. 463; "No proof was offered of any evil which had to be remedied by the unprecedented provision of section 2. The plain reason for it is, that the persons and organizations who have been hankering for such a measure during the last two decades took advantage of the passion against immigrants to write into an anti-alien statute the first federal peace-time restriction on speaking and writing by American citizens since the ill-fated Sedition Act of 1798." (The Smith Act was passed June 28, 1940, as a measure providing for registration of aliens.)

[4] 251 F. 2d 342.

[5] *Ibid.*

[6] There was also involved in Yates the distinction between a broad and narrow construction of the term "organize," but the central role has been played by the incitement problem.

[7] 341 U.S. 494.

[8] 354 U.S. 320-21.

[9] We have in view here principally the "conspiracy" trials, which involved the great majority of defendants. However, the few "membership" cases, though different in some respects, turned basically on the same kind of evidence as the "conspiracy" cases, which were the main ones. In these the charge was not conspiracy to overthrow the government, but conspiracy to teach such overthrow.

[10] Pp. 25, 26 (New York: Cameron, 1956).

[11] Criminal Action 17418, Philadelphia, July 21, 1954.

[12] The "clear and present danger" issue in these trials may here be seen in its full logical perspective. That is, not only is it something of a mystery how there could be a clear and *present* danger of violence which is admittedly a possibility only at some indefinite *future* time. It is even more of a mystery how violent overthrow of future tyranny could be regarded as a *danger.* Overthrow of tyranny can hardly be classed as a substantive evil.

[13] Including the author of the Smith Act. Cf. in Somerville, op. cit., p. 219, text of correspondence with Representative Smith. "I have your letter of May 14, in which you ask whether I in any way intended by the provision of the Smith Act to repudiate the principle stated in the Declaration of Independence of the right of the people to overthrow a tyrannical government. Personally I had no such intention, nor was it considered, as far as I know, in the debates in the House."

[14] 248 F. 2d 671.

[15] *Ibid.,* p. 685.

[16] 248 F. 2d 201.

[17] *Ibid.*, p. 214.
[18] *Ibid.*, p. 209.
[19] *Ibid.*, p. 217.
[20] No. 1, October Term, 1960, 32.
[21] *Op. cit.*, p. 680, footnote 4.
[22] G. M. Stekloff, *History of the First International* (New York: International Publishers, 1928), p. 240.

www.ingramcontent.com/pod-product-compliance
Lightning Source LLC
Chambersburg PA
CBHW032035150426
43194CB00006B/286